CONTESTING THE FORESHORE

CONTESTING THE FORESHORE

Tourism, Society, and Politics on the Coast

Edited by Jeremy Boissevain *and Tom Selwyn*

MARE Publication Series No. 2

Centre for Maritime Research

AMSTERDAM UNIVERSITY PRESS

The publication of this book is made possible by a grant from the University of Amsterdam (Centraal Onderzoeksfonds).

Cover illustration: Spinola Bay, Malta (by courtesy of the Malta Tourism Authority)
Cover design: Sabine Mannel/NAP, Amsterdam
Lay out: JAPES, Amsterdam

ISBN 90 5356 694 5
NUR 741

Series Foreword

The coastal environment has become one of the new frontiers and fastest growing areas of the world's tourism industry. Coastal tourism is having many ecological, economic, societal, and cultural consequences, which, while providing new opportunities for economic prosperity, are challenging for coastal communities. Old occupations, such as fishing, are making way for jobs in hotels and restaurants. Coastal resorts are making ever-increasing claims on resources and land, and power relations are shifting. In view of these developments, it is curious that this part of the tourism sector has attracted very little attention from the social sciences. Important questions regarding the nature of changes that are occurring and the interactions, which are taking place with other coastal peoples and activities, have thereby remained underexplored.

This is the second volume of the *MARE Publication Series*, an initiative of the Centre for Maritime Research (MARE) that was established by the University of Amsterdam and Wageningen University in 2001. MARE's aim is to provide a platform for the development and exchange of scientific knowledge on the use of marine and coastal resources. In addition to the publication series, MARE organizes conferences and workshops and publishes a journal called *Maritime Studies* (*MAST*).

We, the editors, aim to create a series that addresses topics of current relevance to the relationship between people and the sea. Our intention is to ensure the highest academic standards through the involvement of specialists in the field and through the instrument of peer review.

This volume, put together by Jeremy Boissevain and Tom Selwyn, meets the series' intent admirably. First of all, as mentioned above, coastal tourism is a phenomenon of global importance. Secondly, the editors have succeeded in gathering contributions from a range of social science disciplines. This is in line with MARE's mandate of furthering interactions between academics in various branches of learning.

We acknowledge once more the competent guidance of Amsterdam University Press. Linda Emmelkamp and Iris Monnereau, our editorial managers, have again done an excellent job.

Svein Jentoft (University of Tromsø, Norway;
e-mail: sveinje@nfh.uit.no)

Maarten Bavinck (University of Amsterdam, the Netherlands;
e-mail: mbavinck@marecentre.nl)

Contents

Acknowledgments

This collection of essays has emerged from some of the presentations made during the workshop on '*Aquatourism and multiple-use conflicts*' held during the 'People and the Sea' Conference marking the inauguration of the Centre for Maritime Research (MARE), in Amsterdam, September 2001. We are grateful to all those who participated in the discussions. Other contributions were solicited during the course of editing. Our thanks also go to the authors for cheerfully rewriting their contributions, to the members of the MARE team – Maarten Bavinck, Linda Emmelkamp-Boutachekourt, Iris Monnereau and Derek Johnson – for their help, patience and, in particular, the sterling editorial support they gave us, to Ann Holleman for her help, and to Carmel Fsadni and the University of Malta for office space at critical moments. Finally, we would like to thank our respective families for accepting our lapses while we were entangled in editorial tasks.

Jeremy Boissevain
University of Amsterdam, The Netherlands
email: boissevain@pscw.uva.nl

Tom Selwyn
London Metropolitan University, Great Britain
email: t.selwyn@londonmet.ac.uk

I

Introduction

Tom Selwyn and Jeremy Boissevain

Aims and Approaches

This volume of essays is concerned with questions of place and space on coasts and is rooted in the ethnographic study of coastal villages, towns, resorts and marine parks, together with the land, sea, and natural resources that surround them. Although the larger part of the collection consists of work on the European coastline, the book is intended to have implications for geographical areas elsewhere in the world. The primary focus is upon coastal settlements and the contexts under which these evolve. These contexts are routinely underpinned by conflict between different interest groups contesting the ownership and control of the foreshore and its resources. We shall turn to the structural nature of this contestation at the conclusion of this Introduction.

Each chapter examines particular sites framed by structures, processes and relations, each having dimensions which are at once economic, environmental, political, social, and symbolic. The aim of this Introduction is to identify and draw out these dimensions. In approaching the ethnographic data in this way, our intention is to point to threads of argument binding the chapters together into a coherent whole.

Tourism and its development play significant roles in many coastal economies and societies, and the essays in the book reflect this. However, as implied above, we are concerned not so much with tourism itself but with the complex sets of relations within which the organisation and development of tourism are located together with other aqua-cultural and coastal practices.

Structures, Processes and Relations

Place and Imagination: Land and Landscape

In saying that the essays in this collection are infused by a primary concern with place, it is worth emphasising the dual nature of this term. It mirrors the distinction between terms that are in some respects comparable, namely land and landscape. Whilst the former normally applies to the tangible and physical, the latter applies pre-eminently to *ideas* about the land as these are manifested in images, myths, values and other products of the human imagination. The duality of the term place is similar. On the one hand, there is the physical realm of land and the natural and built objects associated with it. On the other, there is the realm of the imagined, ideological, and interpretative. Parts of this duality are to be found in such varied forms as pastoral paintings and poetry, tourist brochures, post-cards, and the discourses of estate agents, politicians, and environmentalists. Other parts are found in the metaphorical associations carried by the buildings and other features of built environments. Yet further aspects are found in what may sometimes appear as the more prosaic (but in fact routinely complex) everyday ideas that attach themselves to all inhabited spaces.

Our book is thus concerned with places in both their material and imaginative aspects, recognising the obvious fact that the relationship between them is dialectical (before a stretch of land becomes a natural park, for example, it needs imagining as such). We also take as axiomatic that the *shaping* of places results from structures, processes and relationships which themselves have both material and ideological dimensions. We will return to this discussion in the conclusion.

In the remainder of this Introduction we will examine the subject of place and space from the five distinct, yet fundamentally interdependent, points of view mentioned above, namely the economic, environmental, political, social and, finally, symbolic. For the sake of analytical and organisational clarity we will proceed by using a small selection of particular chapters to help tease out what seem to us to be the salient features of each of these spheres, making comparative observations about other chapters where appropriate.

Economy: Modes of Coastal Production and Consumption

All the papers in this volume are concerned with modes of coastal production and consumption. Although, not surprisingly, the emphasis is mostly on fishing, tourism and aquaculture, consideration is also given to those aspects of inland agriculture, as well as other economic activities, which are relevant to an understanding of the coast. A persistent and comprehensive point of interest throughout is the extent to which capitalist modes of production are spreading and deepening in areas previously organised by various, more traditional modes of economic and social exchange. Another pre-occupation in some papers involves the role played by kinship in coastal economies, as these are transformed by tourism, aquaculture and the extension of markets. Interestingly, processes of capitalist economic development turn out to be more complex and uneven than might have been assumed.

Bianchi and Talavera trace the emergence of the contemporary service economy in the village of Playa de Mogán, Gran Canaria, from the agricultural and fishing economy of the 19th century. They identify significant transformations to the island and Mogán economy over the subsequent 120 years or so, pointing out how these are articulated within wider regional and global developments. The authors identify the shifting interrelationships between agricultural, fishing and tourism sectors as these react to the changing formation and mode of capital penetration in the island. As far as Canary Island tourism is concerned, they show how the early tourism of the 19th century was linked to export agriculture associated with British capital and merchant shipping. At that time, and up until just before the Second World War, wealthy British visitors were attracted to the luxurious island hotels for their perceived 'health giving' potential and the exoticism of the landscape within which they were set. Following the war a broader constituency of northern European tourists appeared on the islands to stay in self-catering accommodation. Resort development – the 'urban tourism' with which we are familiar from other Southern European coastlines at that time – exploded from the 1960s onwards in the Canaries, and this reached Mogán in the early 1980s. Fundamental changes in the village from the 1980s onwards consisted, *inter alia*, of immigration into the resort of foreign residents and entrepreneurs and the speculative development of the urban tourist infrastructure, in some cases driven by Spanish and international consortia of investors. The capital of these consortia was not infrequently underwritten by public funds managed by public authorities. For Bianchi and Talavera this is the point at which what they nicely term an 'infrastructure of pleasure' emerges, which both 'reflects the new spatial and symbolic arrangements of capital through which new sources of value are created in the tourist economy' and which consists of 'urban spaces (with) consumption at the centre'.

Pascual's essay, also from the Canary Islands, picks up several of the above themes. Of particular interest is the way in which people in the fishing communities he describes are actively entrepreneurial in their engagement with the emerging tourist economy of the littoral but much more cautious in their approach to aquaculture. Pascual ascribes several reasons to these differing responses, at the heart of which are the relationships between kinship, capital, inheritance and new technology. Thus, kinship links play significant roles in the transmission of both capital and skills from one generation to another in artisanal fishing and tourism. Aquaculture, on the other hand, demands higher amounts of capital (which in turn involves the difficult business of obtaining capital grants from European Union funds and elsewhere), longer lead times for gaining profit, and greater risk. Moreover, the technical, biological, and economic knowledge required to manage aquacultural enterprises is beyond the capability of artisanal fisherman, who are poorly educated for the most part. Pascual claims, however, that links between artisanal fishing and aquaculture *could* be stimulated – and even thought desirable by the *cofradias* and their members as well as the general public – provided the right kind of economic and social context was engineered by thoughtful policy interventions guided by close ethnographic observation. Pascual suggests, for example, that taking sons and daughters of fishing families into a two-year vocational training programme with promises that they could become involved (even as future owners) in aquacultural enterprises would diminish existing prejudices about this sector. Such a claim is of considerable significance for this book, positioned as it is at the interface of social science and policy-making in fragile coastal environments.

There are four immediate lessons to be learnt from the Canary Islands chapters. First, they both demonstrate the need precisely to chart *local* configurations of economic and social transformation as these develop within wider global contexts. Second, and continuing on from this, they show how understanding coastal tourism also involves paying close attention to the evolving relationships between agriculture, fishing and aquaculture within the wider economy. Third, they highlight the uneven nature of capitalist development on the coast. Despite the substantial inroads of foreign capital, there are still important economic roles played by small family enterprises that remain partially outside the overall capitalist economy. Fourth, and linked to all of the above, they effectively warn us against making overly simple generalisations about the nature of capitalist development.

In various ways these two chapters point us towards themes picked up in other chapters: to discussions, for example, about the environment and natural parks, about social change, kinship and gender, and to issues concerning the 'symbolic economy' examined in Izola by Rogelja and in the Mediterranean region more generally by Selwyn.

Having looked at two chapters concerned with the charting of economic development, we may now move towards considering the environment. Following a brief general overview we will look at five chapters concerned with this sphere.

Environment: Natural Resources and Cultural Constructions

Our essays follow Kousis's broad definition of coastal 'environment' (see below). Consideration is given to matters ranging from the management of maritime resources – including the implications of the decline of, and changes to, fish stocks – to questions concerned with the development of the natural and built environment of the foreshore itself. The kinds of issues that arise include the environmental implications of patterns of ownership and control of fishing, tourism and other coastal industries. Then there are matters relating to environmental regulations and controls – and the extent to which, and by whom, these are implemented, and the actual impact they have on the environment and the quality of life of the inhabitants. There is the particular issue of setting aside parts of the coast to be designated as national, natural or marine parks. Such parks enable development to be regulated and managed in line with the needs of the environment and its people rather than the needs of shareholders and other private interests. This leads, finally, to the ubiquitous interest in the way that land and sea on and near coasts are sites of economic and political contestation between private and public interests. The chapters by Kousis herself, by Frangoudes and Alban, by Alban and

Boncoeur, by Clifton, and by Boissevain are particularly concerned with these themes. All five chapters start from reflections about maritime resources and the dangers posed to them by over-use. It is worth pointing out that such concerns are also, of course, widely manifested beyond the covers of our book – in the growing public anxiety about the effects of climate change on natural species, for example. This merely clarifies what we know already, namely that our present discussion about coasts is part of a much wider debate about the politics of environmental management in the contemporary world as a whole.[1]

The nub of the issue, as it finds expression in each of the chapters, turns on the relation between the natural resources of the sea and the human interest groups on the coast with which these are associated.

Frangoudes and Alban look at three areas of coast – in Greece, Spain and France – which have experienced pressure on such maritime resources as fish and the Mediterranean seal (in the Greek case), and the marine ecosystem generally, including life on the seabed. One of their arguments is that pressure on particular maritime resources cannot be met successfully by 'single issue' campaigning groups alone. Management of coastal environments and resources needs coalitions made up of the plurality of users – as well as the various levels of government from the most local to the global. This is, of course, easier to say than to implement in the real world, and on the face of it, the exacting organisational and managerial demands posed by environments under physical strain would seem well met by the special arrangements of a marine or natural park. However, the value of their chapter lies in the precision of the comparisons they make between three parks in three countries. This makes it abundantly clear that the designation of an area as a park does not, *in itself,* lead to any guarantee that environmental problems will be solved. What a park needs is the sensitive bringing together of scientific expertise, political will, and involvement by those living and working there. In many ways the idea of a maritime park is a utopian idea resting on the assumption that it is indeed humanly possible to organise economic and social life for the benefit of people and the natural environment.

Kousis opens with a diagnosis of environmental problems in the Mediterranean region, asserting boldly that 'the most serious problems facing marine and coastal resources in regions around the globe are environmental ones'. She refers to the environmental consequences of pressures on natural maritime resources, some kinds of tourism development, chemically based agriculture, oil extraction, waste disposal, and the huge amount of shipping. We will pick up the political implications of her approach to the environment shortly.

Alban and Boncoeur consider the challenge of stimulating a high diversity of small-scale activities in response to the pressure on fish stocks. In the process of some very detailed observations about different kinds of fish, the spots on the coasts at which they are found, and the relation between social structures and techniques of fishing, they consider the feasibilities and practicalities of a marine national park in the area they study. They argue that the creation of such a park would go some way towards addressing the complex legal and economic difficulties associated with the transformation from fishing to multi-activity.

Clifton's chapter, too, considers marine protected areas (MPAs). He offers us a comparative study of two MPAs in Indonesia and identifies the significant differences between them. From our point of view the significance of the chapter is that it clearly identifies policies in one place which make the impacts of eco-tourism a benign influence for those living and working there, whilst policies in the other allow the impacts to be contrastingly malign.

Boissevain's chapter fits into the wider corpus of his recent work on the urban development of the Maltese foreshore. His three cases trace how local and foreign interest combined to exploit Malta's foreshore resources. The first involved a proposal to extend the Hilton Hotel. This would deprive local residents of leisure space along the coast, damage the ecologically important nearby sea grass meadows, pollute popular swimming beaches and destroy a historical fortification. The second was a plan to construct a leisure complex on Munxar point near Marsascala. The project would deprive the inhabitants of several inland villages and towns of the only coastal recreational area to which they had ready access. The third case analyzes a project to catch, pen and fatten young tuna for lucrative export to Japan. NGOs, local fishermen and members of the public protested that the enterprise would deplete the breeding stock of the tuna on which the Maltese fishing community depended, endanger a unique colony of rare sea birds, burn out large areas of the sea bed, and pollute swimming areas important to both locals and tourists.

All three projects were designed to maximize profits for entrepreneurs by satisfying the demands of foreign consumers at the expense of local residents. All would contribute to the ongoing destruction of the overcrowded country's dwindling natural environment and leisure space, thus negatively affecting the quality of life of local inhabitants. Grassroots action groups and NGOs formed a loose coalition to resist this threat. In spite of their vigorous campaigns, the Hilton developers and the aquaculture entrepreneurs defeated their efforts. On the other hand, a defensive coalition resoundingly vanquished the Munxar scheme just four months after it was formally launched.

Boissevain's dissection of the reasons for the variable success of the environmental networks has lessons for coastal environmental movements within and beyond the Mediterranean. The absolute necessity for a strong planning regime capable of combining the capacity to incorporate scientific data effectively whilst preserving rigorous independence is stressed. So too is damage caused by 'the density of the personal networks linking politicians and entrepreneurs' as this 'ensures that their appropriation of the environment will continue (even if) at a somewhat more moderate pace.' In the end, however, Boissevain concludes that the environmental movement's efficiency continues to grow, despite losing some battles, and that, whilst it has placed the environment firmly on the political agenda, it has also strengthened civil society and, most encouragingly, is 'challenging the traditional clientistic system of decision-making'.

Politics: Public Policy and Private Interest

Political questions pre-occupy all the papers, although in a wide variety of ways. As we have seen, many are concerned in one way or another with coastal environments, including the political responses to environmental threats. Another of the more general themes is the politics of coastal development. Discussions here focus on conflicts over land use, the extent to which property and other developments are regulated by local public authorities, the relative power of private institutions, such as banks and development companies, and public institutions, such as municipalities and park authorities. Then there are the issues concerning the roles of the non-governmental sector and of international agencies such as the European Union. If we look at three of the chapters we used in the previous section, namely those by Kousis, by Frangoudes and Alban, and by Boissevain, in addition to the chapter by Van der Duim and Lengkeek, we will see how they develop these themes.

Continuing on, from her observation that 'in their drive for profitable capital accumulation, powerful economic actors often manage to attain direct or indirect control over natural resources [which] leads to ecological disorganisation', Kousis argues that the identification and analysis of organised resistance to such control is amongst the more important tasks of social scientific studies of coasts. She thus directs her attention to local protests over the use and exploitation of coastal and marine resources, taking examples from Greece, Spain and Portugal. Surprising as it may seem, there are, she maintains, few studies of this kind. Interestingly, her own studies allow her to conclude that the lion's share of environmental protests by local communities are related in the first place to questions of waste, manufacturing, energy installations, and the lack of sound environmental policy and implementation. Although tourism development is certainly one activity which attracts routine protest, as Boissevain's chapter demonstrates, it ranks below these other issues in importance.

Kousis then looks at protests against a waste-water treatment plant in Corfu, a tourist development in Catalonia, and a fossil fuel plant in Portugal. Against considerable odds in each case, each particular protest achieved its immediate short-term aims. Nevertheless, she concludes her paper with the cautionary remark that in the cases examined such short-term success did little to alter the long-term underlying structures of environmental stewardship in the areas in which they were set. 'Such evidence', she says, 'points to the vital importance of addressing deeper issues involving the politics of sustainable development and the sustainability of production, rather than that of consumption.' Anyone who has been involved in a substantial single-issue protest movement will know exactly what Kousis is saying here. Successful confrontation with established and well resourced public and/or private sector institutions and alliances necessarily requires huge amounts of individual and collective effort. Yet single-issue successes are often overshadowed, sometimes at the very point of 'victory', by the thought that in the end nothing much has really changed. The story told by Boissevain[2] of the invasive 'development' of a precious part of the Maltese foreshore by the Hilton Hotel is a good case in point. During a long and difficult struggle, a coalition of environmentalist pressure groups won considerable backing to prevent the Hilton building a leisure complex (hotel, business tower, apartment block and marina) on this part of the coast. Although the Planning Authority's own technical staff and a considerable segment of the public opposed the project, a combination of political and private forces ensured that the development went ahead.

Reflections on single-issue contestations thus inevitably lead to wider debate about the nature of democratic processes themselves. This is a challenge taken up in some detail by Frangoudes and Alban. In their comparative analyses of three different marine parks, they build on the three part foundation of Kousis's chapter – her careful comparative ethnographic charting of the protest movements, her argument that such work is a vital part not only of coastal studies but also of analyses of environmental politics, and her assertion that successful single-issue protests are not in the end a substitute for the achievement of fully sustainable development policies. They take a detailed look at the extent to which each of the parks they study has achieved a political structure based on such policies (interrogating the meaning and substance of the term sustainable development at all points along the way).

What then do we learn about democracy on the coast from their study? Quite a lot emerges if we look at each of the parks in turn.

The National Marine Park of Northern Sporades in Greece provides us with a classic case of a non-governmental organisation, the Hellenic Association for the Study and Protection of the Mediterranean Seal (MOM), taking the leading role in the determination of the political structures of a protected coastal area. MOM was extremely successful in raising European funds, achieving the backing of the 'great and the good' of the European environmental movement, and winning the confidence of the central government for their idea of creating a marine park around the island of Alonnisos. MOM managed to drive its own aims and objectives through the patently weak and partial government structures. But the fishermen became increasingly disenchanted by progressively more restrictive regulations about where and when to fish. Parts of the tourism industry were thought to suffer. Although some favoured MOM's operations, the authors report that 'management of the park by the environmentalists ... is challenged by everybody interviewed. The organisation is looking after its own interests and leaving other groups' interests by the wayside. The fact that the organisation monopolises power within the park lends weight to this feeling'. Moreover, and remarkably, some fishermen expressed the view that even the seals themselves had been better off before the park.

The second case, that of the Cap de Creus Natural Park in Catalonia, Spain, offers a considerable contrast to the Alonnisos case. From early on in the process of creating the park, a management committee was formed which, on the face of it, encompassed all the users of the coastal area in question, including the fishing community. However, members of the fishing organisations (*cofradías*) in and around the park came, in a relatively short time, to acquire progressively more ambivalent attitudes to the restrictive orders placed by the park authorities on fishing. Their own experience indicated that a reserve which promised to benefit fish stocks actually benefited parts of the tourist industry more. The real winners of the park's operation were divers in search of the park's 'very rich seabed'.

Their third case is a study of the creation of a National Park in the *Mer d'Iroise*, Brittany, France. What the authors find striking about this case is the sheer length of time it is (still) taking to set the park up. The idea of a national park first surfaced in the 1980, but it wasn't until 2001 that the French prime minister ordered a study of the implications of a park in the area. The important feature of this study was its aim to 'reconcile the protection of the environment with the development of human activities'. The park was thus not imagined as just a wildlife sanctuary but as a space in which a dynamic mixture of activities, objectives and interest groups could co-exist. The authors paint a portrait of a process taking shape in which a relatively benign and 'listening' central government, an international agency (UNESCO), the Regional Committee of Brittany, a number of different associations and councils of fishermen, a diverse range of fishing communities themselves, scientists and other members of the ecological lobby, slowly experiment with ideas about the feasibility and desirability of the park. In the end, despite some radical opposition, the impression is of a lengthy, complex, and ultimately democratic process which will eventually lead to a successful marine park.

For Frangoudes and Alban, one of the main lessons for our understanding of the democratic process is that it takes time. Another is its sheer complexity. There is no single-issue 'quick fix'. There is no way the 'environment' can be hived off (either in the real world or in the imagination) and separated from its foundations in the needs of both the natural species and resources which inhabit it or the human economic activities that take place within it. The idea of an environmental lobby made up of the great and the good saving the natural world – perhaps through recruiting the good offices of an institution such as the EC – is ultimately inadequate: there really is no alternative to active involvement in general political processes at the local, regional, national, continental and global levels. If the cases of the Northern Sporades and the *Mer d'Iroise* point us towards examples, respectively, of relative failure and success of democratic processes (with *Cap de Creus* somewhere in the middle), then that is interesting too.

Finally, the chapter by Van der Duim and Lengkeek confirms the central importance of a local government system which should be at once strong, transparent, scientifically astute, sensitive to real and/or imagined local concerns, and committed to the provision of social spaces constructed by the guiding principle of 'liveability'. This has to be done in a context in which agriculture is declining and tourism increasing. The position taken by Van der Duim and Lengkeek, and shared by most of the chapters in this book, is that it is not tourism *itself*, in any intrinsic way, which poses the danger to adopting a politics based on the primacy of 'liveability', but the *commoditisation of space* which typically accompanies tourism. The question then becomes: in a world suffused by the mythologies and rhetoric of 'free trade' and deregulation, is a 'politics of liveability' actually possible? Many of the authors in this volume do indeed seem to think it is. Furthermore, they also offer extremely practical prescriptions for achieving such a goal. Is it *really* too difficult, we might then ask, to adopt Van der Duim's and Lengkeek's recommendation that the local authority in Texel Island should strive to 'recognise the problem' (of discontent with tourism-related development) 'and create trust' (amongst the population of the island)? Or that the municipality should take a leading role in the regulation of tourism development? The alternative is, as they put it, that 'the combination of closed policy networks and local interest groups that distrust the policy-making practices blocks adequate planning for the future and innovative approaches to the issues of tourism growth on an island with limited space and resources'. It is now time to turn to coastal society.

Society: Class and Kin

The shape and structure of coastal society form a theme which occupies, to varying degrees of emphasis, several of the authors. The saliency of kinship, gender, class, status and ethnicity in social organisation are topics explored in varying ways and to varying degrees. In this context, as in others, questions of space and spatial structures play a considerable part in discussions. Indeed, as already noted, the relation between the spatial and the social constitutes one of the principal themes underlying the volume as a whole.

The chapter more pre-occupied than others with class and kin-ship at the level of village society is Ireland's examination of the Cornish parish of Sennan. Ireland traces social transformations that have followed the gradual inflow of visitors and tourists into Sennan Cove since before the Second World War.

Since at least the eighteenth century (and by implication earlier), the main social division in Sennan parish has been between the coastal community living in Sennan Cove and the agriculturalists liv-ing inland. The 'Covers' and 'Overhillers' are status groups whose membership is based predominantly on kinship underwritten by such factors as the different demands of labour and skill transmis-sion by fishermen and agriculturalists, the propensity of the latter to be more entrepreneurial and geographically mobile, and the Overhillers' view of the Covers as slightly uncouth.

Having established the historical centrality of kinship related sta-tus in Sennan society, Ireland's chapter is devoted to tracing the so-cial transformations in the parish flowing from the introduction of visitors and tourists since before the Second World War.

This story begins with upper-middle class visitors coming to the seaside from the 1920s onwards and renting out houses from the in-digenous Sennan population. Sennan women not only worked for the visitors but often 'went out' (of houses let to visitors) 'to sleep'. A relationship developed between the locals and these visitors which was deferential, the former regarding the latter as 'gentry'. After the war, with the advent of holidays for all, other types of visitors came to Sennan. Initially, these visitors, who tended to be more ordinary working-class people, lived in the same houses as the locals on a bed-and-breakfast basis. Later an increasing number of self-catering units were set up to cater for the swelling numbers of visitors.

Over the years some of both types of visitor (the 'better class of vis-itor' and the 'Emmets' or 'Andy Caps', as locals termed them) came to live, or take second homes, in the village. Ireland reports that while the 'Emmets' (a term of mild abuse) were looked down upon in Sennan partly because they were thought routinely to 'take the Micky' out of Cornish culture, the descendents of the 'upper crust' visitors began to assume prominent positions in village society, tak-ing over the running of the Ladies Lifeboat Guild and organising an annual 'Cornish Fayre' at which 'local resident' (an appellation at-tached to incomers) women dressed up in what they claimed to be 'traditional Cornish costume'. Ireland points us towards not only the lack of historical authenticity of this 'Fayre' but also to an occasion at which seating arrangements at a Lifeboat concert resulted in the humiliation of a respected Sennan couple. The structural significance of this was that it illuminated the underlying and actually increasing, but normally hidden, social distance between the incoming residents and the local population.

Ireland contrasts the activities of the Lifeboat Ladies with those of the Covers on the occasions of the 'Mullet Seine'. This is an annual activity involving the fishing of high value mullet fish. He shows that membership in the mullet fishing group is based strictly on ties of local kinship and local investment in this fishing venture. Incoming residents, as well as people from other towns and villages on the coast, are kept away.

The Sennan case is one in which the social and cultural transformation of a village follows the change to its economic base. As tourism entered an economy formerly based on fishing and agriculture, a predominantly kin- and status-based social structure yielded to a class-based one with a flavouring of caste-like characteristics. Underlying points of conflict and antagonism (alternating with flashes of solidarity) were occasionally visible – in relations between the indigenous population of Sennan and, on the one hand, the 'Upper Crust' incomers and, on the other, the 'Emmets', as well as between the 'Upper Crust' and the 'Emmets' themselves. Additionally, the historical sense of difference and mild antagonism between Covers and Overhillers continued even if at a more subterranean level than previously – although it is also clear that, in this relationship too, a sense of solidarity occasionally surfaced in the face of potential incoming residents.

We might learn general lessons from the Sennan case stemming from the continuing importance of symbolised kinship (most dramatically in the Mullet Seine arrangements), the central role of women (and the terms and conditions of women's work), and the emergence of the sense of 'insiders' and 'outsiders' stimulated by the continuing arrival to the area of visitors (who routinely become second-home owners).

A final thought. 'Social' questions play more or less significant roles in the chapters by Bianchi and Talavera, Boissevain, Clifton, Selwyn, and Van der Duim and Lengkeek – and form backdrops to most of the others. Nevertheless, with the exception of Ireland's chapter they do not occupy centre stage. Perhaps one area for future coastal research is thus precisely the kind of detailed ethnographic examination of social structures, processes and relationships on the coast ex-

emplified by Ireland's chapter. We surely do need a social anthropology of coastal societies which, in turn, takes the kind of environmental, political, economic, and symbolic issues we are concerned
with here into *its* centre. Nadel-Klein's (2003) examination of a Scot-
tish fishing community and the translation of its history to an imagined 'heritage' is an example of such a new and promising genre.

The Symbolic: Myths and Mirrors

Nataša Rogelja's chapter is an ethnography of coastal fishing and
tourism in Izola, Slovenia. She looks, in particular, at the excursions
taken by tourists with local fishermen in fishing boats. Her reading
of the formation of tourist-related perceptions, imagery and myth,
and the relation of these to the environmental and economic realities
of life in Izola, is an exemplary study of the relationship between local conditions and global cultural processes. She starts from the presupposition that the ethnography of local tourism and of localities
bidding for tourist attention shows the role of larger processes that
define economic and cultural realities.[3] In this view the two aspects of
place referred to above come to the fore clearly. On the one hand,
there is the Izola of fluctuating numbers of fish and fishermen, of
boats with ordinary nets and dragnets, of changing political borders
and wider political and policy movements and arrangements ema-
nating from the changing relationship between Slovenia and the EU,
and of its summer visitors. On the other hand, there are the myths
and fantasies about the place generated by the postcards, brochures,
guidebooks and other, less tangible, sources of tourist-related images and ideas. The Slovenian coast (including Izola and Piran) is, in
short, both place and 'market-place' in which the pragmatic realities
of making a living from coastal resources (fish and tourists amongst
these) intersect with the fantasies and mythologies of potential tourists. Izola trades in sea and fantasy. Those who live and work there
are involved in harvesting the fruits of both.

It is worth saying, as a significant aside, that (in our view) the
realm of tourist-related fantasies, myths and images does have a certain degree of autonomy and that it is perfectly possible to look at and
analyse this realm in terms which are universal, culturally non-spe-
cific and *sui generis*. For example, Rogelja tells us that tourists come to
Izola because they perceive it as a healthy, relaxing place in which
some 'authentic' activities (such as net fishing) take place. The same

is probably true for all the coastal sites to which tourists go within and beyond the covers of our book. Tourist 'motivations' (somehow a curiously unsatisfactory word to describe complex cognitive, intellectual and emotional processes involving, at the very least, various kinds of desire and quests for knowledge – not least about the nature of self and other) for heading to our coastal locations are said to be based on the search for health, relaxation and authenticity. Together with a myriad of other terms, these are clearly in the mainstream of global cultural pre-occupations. It is thus useful and legitimate, to emphasise the point, to study this global cultural landscape in its own right.

But this is not what Rogelja does. Rather, taking the interest in such topics as health, sociability, relaxation and the authentic as elements of the raw material of global cultural concern, she explores the way in which the people of Izola take an active part in the fashioning of these into the quite specific forms in which they then find expression on the Slovenian coast. Showing how local brochures and other tourist-related promotional material stress 'Mediterraneaness', the sea itself, and the aura of 'good old times', Rogelja argues that these are associated in turn with Slovenia's present political trajectory into the Mediterranean and out of the Balkans, with freedom and health and with a 'just traditional society'. We may readily see in these themes local expressions of universal pre-occupations.

Moving from representations to the sea itself, she then describes how, as tourist workers, Izola fishermen use local conditions and cultural resonances to engage and entertain their visitors. She describes, for example, how tourists are taken by boat to look at the international 'border' between Slovenia and Croatia (which, being located in the water, is, of course, invisible). She also reports that boat excursions are taken mostly by Slovenian organised groups: schools, work collectivities and professional associations. She suggests that here we have a case not so much of the 'centre-periphery' relations beloved of many traditional tourist studies but more of 'periphery-periphery' relations. At any rate, what she establishes beyond doubt is that visitors and fishermen in Izola are effectively engaging in conversations about changing identities and solidarities, the place of Slovenia in the world, and the changing nature of 'work' and 'play'.

Rogelja's essay makes an original contribution to the field of study of tourist representations in that it achieves what few others manage, namely to observe and describe a case of tourist imagery being forged out of the relationship between tourists and tourist workers. In this sense she avoids the trap of 'seeing people' (in her case the fishers of Izola) 'as the passive recipients of external influences' and demonstrates how they are 'not only aware of the external images based on themselves, but are also trying to co-operate actively with them and make them part of their daily activities'. This is a particularly clear example of what Polanyi[4] termed the 'embedding' of the market into social relations. We return to this idea, and to Polanyi, in the conclusion below. There are, of course, a host of questions which the Izola material poses. To what extent, we might ask, is this an example in which the relationship between tourist and local is unusually egalitarian? How much of that derives from Slovenia's Yugoslav and socialist past? And what lessons might be learnt from this ethnography, set as it is in what used to be called the 'second world', about the relationships between 'hosts' and 'guests' in both the 'third world' and the 'first world'?

Towards Conclusions:
Coasts as Sites of Invasion and Defence

Up to this point, our intention has been to outline some of the findings of our chapters, indicating ways in which each extends our understanding of coasts and those who live and work on them. The purpose now is to move beyond the individual chapters and draw threads together in order to suggest how the volume as a whole makes a contribution not only to our understanding of coasts in general, but also to the shaping of the interdisciplinary project of coastal studies itself.

Our vantage point throughout has been the analytical space in which the physical realities and symbolic representations of the coast meet. It is here that the two aspects of place, the physical and the symbolic, come together. This is where interests in the land (that is, material interests in the land and its resources) and ideas about the land come face to face. It is from here that we can see most clearly the dynamic and transformative relations and interrelations between economy, environment, politics, and society.

One underlying pre-occupation of the volume as a whole is the extent of penetration of capitalism and the market system in the coastal locations we have studied. Another is the extent to which such penetration has been and is being resisted. We consider these questions in turn.

It is clear from studies by several authors that market principles have extended their reach into most corners of the coastal spaces our essays have described. Some of the politico-economic and socio-spatial consequences of this are considered in Selwyn's general summary of the penetration of the market in Mediterranean coasts. The bare outline of his argument is that shifts of economic gravity to coasts, associated to a considerable extent with tourism, have been accompanied by deepening extensions of purely capitalist relations of production and consumption in both rural and urban coastal areas. The kinds of evidence adduced to support this view include the type of unfettered tourism development known since the 1960s as *balearisation*, the use of coastal political institutions for their own ends by developers,[5] and inward migration to coastal resorts which creates a sense of 'insiders' and 'outsiders',[6] the rise in the employment of women and youth in tourist-related contexts (with all the implications for kinship structures and practices these have), and the promotion of coasts by media, which increasingly de-couples the physical realities of coasts from the fantasies about them embraced by the tourism and second-home industries. All of this is very familiar and seems effectively to frame and define the subject of coastal studies in terms of charting the environmental, political and social consequences of the spread of capitalism and the market on coasts.

But our essays also suggest that the process of the onward march of coastal capitalism is neither quite as simple nor as all encompassing as it might appear. If we take the small family bed-and-breakfast and restaurant enterprises which still, in some respects, remain outside the overall capitalist economy of the Canary Islands, or the underlying kinship and spatial solidarities in Sennan Cove exemplified by the Mullet Seine, or the success of the fishermen of Izola and Piran not only in using but also shaping the fantasies of tourists for their own ends, we gain a sense that there are swathes of economic, social and symbolic life that are not yet subject to pure market principles and thus still under some sort of social control. Furthermore, the entry of localised, but often globally connected, environmental movements into political and institutional processes, speaks of a more generalised resistance to the 'disorganising' (to use Kousis's effective term) depredations of coastal capitalism. Let us look at these more closely.

It is worth saying, firstly, that all the authors in this volume confirm that environmental issues have become increasingly central to the politics of coasts and islands, particularly island states such as Malta.

Secondly, the environmentalist opposition to the marketisation of coasts illustrates the essentially long-term perspectives upon which such opposition is founded. There is a contrast here with the values of the market, which are essentially and necessarily short-term. This is an issue taken up by Frangoudes and Alban, who argue convincingly that long-term perspectives are essential not only for the smooth running of national parks but for the democratic process itself, a view clearly shared by Boissevain.

Thirdly, following the issue of the political foundations of national parks, it becomes clear that collectivities such as fishing associations, unions, environmental NGOs, scientific research units, planning teams and academic networks, when working together, can and, as described in several chapters, do exercise considerable power over the coastal zones in which they live and work.

Fourthly, moving to the issue of consumption, we may take note of Rogelja's reports of tourists nurturing fantasies which include senses of collective enjoyment shared with tourist workers, the imagined 'justice' of traditional social relations, and what may credibly be seen as the metaphorical expression of the long-term and 'authentic'[7] relationship between fishermen and the sea, namely 'traditional' looking fishing nets (rather than the drag nets of the excursion boats). Attitudes such as these seem considerably removed from the kinds of approaches to consumption represented in the pages of the more glitzy market-oriented tourism promotional literature.

What are we to make of all this? What are we to do with ideas and practices which seem out of step with the onward march of market forces? Let us step back a pace.

Concerned with describing the historical evolution of the global market system, Polanyi (1944) tells us that land is an element of nature inextricably interwoven with man's institutions. To isolate it and form a market out of it was perhaps the weirdest of all undertakings of our ancestors (op. cit.:178) and that labour and land are no other than the human beings themselves of which every society consists and the natural surroundings in which it exists. To include them in the market mechanism means to subordinate the substance of society itself to the laws of the market (op. cit.:71) and, furthermore, that to allow the market mechanism to be the sole director of the fate of human beings and their natural environment .. would result in the demolition of society (op. cit.:73).

Polanyi helps us focus on the possible meanings of some of the phenomena discussed in the chapters. Thus, we can see in the best examples of the environmental movements on the world's coasts the development of a language which not only defines relationships between the natural and social environment and evokes his (Polanyi's) own observations rather than those of the apostles of the market, but which increasingly underpins several of the more notable contributions to coastal studies. Michaud (1976), for example, has followed Polanyi in putting forward his 'political manifesto for the coast', arguing that this is needed because of the priceless resources of the coast and the threats to them from, for example, tourism, development, and privatisation.

Taking up the challenge, and closely following Michaud's arguments, Gubbay (1990) proposed that the dangers were so serious and imminent that the entire British coast should be subject to a special political and economic regime. A decade later Haslett's (2000) *Coastal Systems* described in detail the different kinds of coastal systems in Britain and the main management issues and responses to the threats faced by them. He describes the British 'Heritage Coast Scheme', which aims to conserve the quality of the scenery (and) to foster leisure activities based on the natural scenery rather than man-made features.

Other volumes, rather like the present one, have taken up particular issues in coastal zone management. Wong's (1993) edited collection of scholarly papers looking at the relation between tourism and the environment is, perhaps, closest to the present volume.

Polanyi's intellectual influence is clearly present in the above body of work, as it is in our own chapters. Amongst the latter we would point in particular to the essays on maritime parks, as these deal with forms of regulatory policies which are supposed to take the management of the environment out of the hands of the market. At their best, park regimes have proved capable of devising and implementing democratic and environmentally sound policies, enlisting the support and involvement of those living and working in the designated areas as they proceed. Of course, alongside the examples of good practice, there is also evidence of the continuing vulnerability of coastal environments and their inhabitants not only from unfettered capitalist development but also from weak systems of governance, as Frangoudes and Alban and Clifton show in their accounts of the Sporades and Wakatobi National Marine Parks. Nevertheless, the growing success, locally and globally, of environmental movements, of which the spreading influence of parks is one aspect, provides evidence of stiffening resistance to the take-over of coasts by market forces.

In moving towards a conclusion, we may allow ourselves a brief, and broad, reflection on the nature of coasts. As places on the edges of inhabited territories, coasts are readily associated with invasion and defence. This is an association that runs deep in many cultures (see, for example, Williams (1797) for an intriguing eighteenth-century English example of an essay written on the subject). Mediterranean coasts alone have been subject to periodic military invasion by big powers and pirates for thousands of years – an historical feature ingrained in the topography of the islands of the region, the fortress capitals of which are typically placed inland, well away from coasts. Further north there is a country whose south coast enjoys almost mythic status as a site of past invasions, one of which, in 1066, gave birth to the modern state itself.

The juxtaposition in this latter case between invasion and birth points us towards other aspects of ambivalence in the meanings attached to coasts, such as their simultaneous association with order and disorder. Coasts are linked, for example, to smugglers and smuggling and, in tabloid tropes, with refugees and 'illegal' immigrants. Sometimes, as in the case of the tragic drowning in February 2004 in England's Morecombe Bay of 20 or more Chinese cockle fishers, apparently controlled by Mafia-type companies, the coast appears (and was described precisely in these terms by the local Member of Parliament) as a literally uncontrollable place beyond the law where high gangsterism is to be found together with extreme human exploitation, misery, and death. On the other hand, of course, coasts are traditionally linked to family outings, holidays and the re-enforcement of 'family values' in the bracing sea air. Furthermore, in northern Europe at any rate, coasts are closely linked to the beginnings of mass industrial tourism during summer closures of factories designed to raise the productivity of workers. In these cases we can see the role of coasts in the re-enforcement of work ethics, class values, family values and national values.

In many senses, therefore, coasts are deeply ambivalent landscapes. And those who protect them, coast guards (along with lifeboat crews), occupy symbolically highly charged spaces between danger seaward and safety landward. In this regard it is tempting to emphasise the etymological continuity of meaning between the word coast and the word from which it is partly derived, namely the Old French *coste* (modern French *côte*) – rib. Whilst the latter protects the internal organs of the upper body, including the heart and lungs, the former appears as a protective shield for the heart and soul of the nation itself.

There is one further preliminary point before coming to the issue which is central to this book. This is that coasts are not only places to be defended but points from which relations with other nations are made through trade and diplomacy. In this context another theme which underlies all the chapters here is that the *terms of trade* between states and regions are felt directly by those living and working on coasts – whether these are fishermen anxious about foreign fishing fleets poaching their fish stocks or local tourism authorities concerned at the appropriateness and fairness (or lack of it) of the terms under which the tourism industry operates in their domain.

These concerns have been with us for many years. A letter from Walter Raleigh and others (Burroughs and Raleigh 1701) to a member of the British Parliament over 300 years ago makes the point eloquently. The letter concerns the Dutch fishing fleets taking too much fish from English seas, but is written in terms that combine this anxiety with comments about the differences between the Dutch and English national character. The authors write that

> The Hollanders and other nations gain their wealth, power and strength by fishing on the coasts and seas of Great Britain (how advantageous it would be to our own nation if that trade were well-established in England)... but they (the Hollanders) are not to be quarrelled with, but rather commended for their industry; and we be justly reproach'd, for our sloth and negligence, in not partaking of such a blessing, which providence has thrown at our very doors.

All of the above leads directly to our own central concern, namely the 'invasion' of the market and market principles into the life and work of the coastal sites examined here and the ways in which to defend against such an invasion. In our view what makes coastal development particularly interesting is that the struggle between market forces and the forces of regulation on coasts is not merely about the nature and quality of the government of the economic, social, political and environmental structures and processes our chapters examine, but also the fact that these questions are so manifestly and intimately interwoven with basic questions about social order, organisation, local identity, national character and international relations.

What then, finally, is at the root of the contestation on the foreshore of which the title of this volume speaks? Our essays point us towards differing interests at work on the coasts – between competing private interests, private and public interests and, at a more general level, the cross-cutting interests of fishing, tourism, conservation and development. They also point to differing ideas and values – between, for example, the use value placed on maritime resources by fishing communities and the exchange value placed on coastal landscapes by those concerned with tourism and the market in images and myths of coast and sea.

Furthermore, one theme running through the book as a whole is that of the inherent contradictions between short-term and long-term economic, political and environmental dispositions towards the coast. As a way of encompassing all of the above, we might like to conclude by bringing back together the two aspects of place, the material and the ideological, with which we started out this Introduction. If we approach it in this way, we see that at the heart of the struggle on the foreshore is the contest to find a language capable, firstly, of accurately defining the long-term interests of coasts and their populations and, secondly, of mobilising local, regional and global political support for those interests. If those politically engaged on the ground in finding, and effectively using, that language are in the front line of this contest, the emerging discipline of coastal studies, to which our own volume is a contribution, is clearly in close attendance.

Notes

1. At the time this Introduction was being written, Thomas's (2004) article in the journal *Nature* was receiving worldwide media coverage. The article predicted that a million natural species could die out unless immediate measures were taken to halt the damage presently being done to the environment. It was produced at a time of continuing anxiety and anger about the failure of the US to ratify the Kyoto environmental accords.
2. In addition to Boissevain's chapter in this volume, see Boissevain and Theuma (1998).
3. This is a quotation by Rogelja from Pálsson and Durrenberger (1996).
4. Polanyi (1944).
5. Two particularly clear cases of this are discussed in Boissevain and Theuma op. cit. and Waldren's (1998) 'The Road to Ruin: The politics of development in the Balearic islands', both in Abram and Waldren (Eds.) op. cit. (Also discussed in Selwyn's chapter).
6. Waldren (1996).
7. The use of 'authentic' here corresponds with Selwyn's discussion in his Introduction to Selwyn,T. (Ed) (1996). The three shades of meaning he identifies – those which relate to senses of 'authentic' self and of 'authentic' society as well as the 'authenticity' associated with scientific truth – seem present in the way Rogelja uses the term for the Izola material.

Bibliography

Abrams, S. and J. Waldren (Eds.)
1998   *Anthropological Perspectives on Local Development.* London: Routledge.

Boissevain, J. and N. Theuma
1998   Contested Space: Planners, Tourists, Developers and Environmentalists in Malta. In: S. Abram and J. Waldren (Eds.), *Anthropological Perspectives on Local Development.* London: Routledge.

Burroughs, J. and W. Raleigh (Eds.)
1701   *A Letter to an Honourable Member of the House of Commons.* London: Company of the Royal Fishery.

Gubbay, S.
1990   *A Future for the Coast?* Ross-on-Wye: Marine Conservation Society.

Haslett, S.K.
2000   *Coastal Systems.* London: Routledge.

Michaud, J-L.
1976   *Manifeste Pour le Littoral.* Paris: Berger-Levrault.

Nadel-Klein, J.
2003   *Fishing For Heritage.* Oxford: Berg.

Pálsson, G. and E.P. Durrenberger (Eds.)
1996   *Images of Contemporary Iceland: Everyday Lives and Global Context.* Iowa: University Press.

Polanyi, K.
1944   *The Great Transformation.* Boston: Beacon Press.

Selwyn, T. (Ed.)
1996   *The Tourist Image.* Chichester: Wiley.

Thomas, C.D. (Eds.)
2004   Extinction Risk from Climate Change. *Nature* 427:6970.

Waldren, J.
1996   *Insiders and Outsiders:Paradise and Reality in Mallorca.* Oxford: Berghahn.
1998   The Road to Ruin: The Politics of Development in the Balearic Islands. In: S. Abram and J. Waldren (Eds.), *Anthropological Perspectives on Local Development.* London: Routledge.

Williams, N.
1797   *An Essay on Invasions and Defence of the Coasts.* London: Owen, Piccadilly and Newberry.

Wong, P.P. (Ed.)
1993   *Tourism vs Environment: The Case for Coastal Areas.* Dordrecht: Kluwer Academic Publishers.

2

Privatising the Mediterranean Coastline

Tom Selwyn

Introduction

Mediterranean Coastal Space

This chapter[1] is concerned with social space and geographic space and their transformations on Mediterranean coasts. The aim is to make certain generalisations about the impact of advancing capitalist relations and coastal development in the region. The chapter uses the development and organisation of tourism to illuminate the general processes it seeks to identify. These have to do with the privatisation of the coastline and some of its associated social, cultural and environmental consequences.

Balearisation and Beyond

Let us begin, then, by making some generalizations about the role of tourism in Mediterranean regional development. All are familiar. First of all, tourism development has played a significant role in the extension and deepening of capitalist relations of production on the coast, being one of the main engines which transformed semi-feudal coastal economies into thoroughgoing capitalist ones. Second, this transformation was accompanied by the decline in influence of traditional landowners (both local and absentee) and the rise in influence of a combination of development companies, banks, and foreign tour operators. Third, there were at least two accompanying demographic consequences: the movement of indigenous populations to the coasts, and migration to coastal resorts by hotel staff and other workers for the expanding tourist industry. Fourth, the ownership and control of space are presently, and often bitterly, contested. On the one hand, there are the forces of speculative development, favouring a *laissez-faire* approach to building. On the other hand, there are the forces associated with some public authorities attempting to contain private speculation within a framework of public interest. Fifth, one of the main questions for Mediterranean coastal development in the decades to come will be concerned with the way in which this contest is played out.

The development of coasts, often achieved through rapid, unplanned building with all its associated social, environmental and political consequences, came to be known, in relation to the Balearic Islands of the early 1960s, as *balearisation*. Similar processes have become familiar in many other parts of the Mediterranean. Sivri (1997), for example, reports depopulation of some of the inland settlements of Thasos in the face of coastal development, and also draws attention to the better known cases of such development in islands such as Mykonos and Rhodes. Coastal development has gone hand in hand with the marginalisation and underdevelopment of interiors, particularly island interiors.

The ingredients of *balearisation* and its associated consequences, then, included the disruption of local agricultural economies. The extent and nature of this disruption needs to be the subject of prolonged, detailed, local research. Sivri (op. cit.) reports, for example, that some inland villages and towns in Thasos avoided the depopulation experienced by many. Some have retained a mixed economy, including both tourism and agriculture. Such examples notwithstanding, however, it seems more or less safe to make the generalisation that the *polyculture*, mixed agriculture, characteristic of the historical Mediterranean has, to a considerable extent, been replaced by the monocrop of coastal tourism. This has had environmental consequences, of course, such as the falling into disrepair of many inland agricultural terraces. At the same time, particularly in islands, the populations of inland towns and villages has declined – a fact that is particularly noticeable in the case of young men and women. This process, in turn, has led to various types of changes in family organization.

At the local level, municipal and other planning authorities have found it consistently hard to assert or retain local control over tourist developments. It needs to be said, though, that whilst many coastal developments may be controlled from the outside by outsiders – by multinational tour operators and their associated financial institutions, for example – there are often significant local players on the inside. These include returning immigrants with capital, such as those described by Kenna (1993) for the Greek island of Anafi. The issue is thus not so much one of insiders versus outsiders (a red herring of an argument much favoured by some sustainable tourism lobbies in northern Europe) but rather of the extent to which tourism development is subject to democratic control. These processes may be illustrated by taking a small number of indicative examples from Mallorca and Malta.

Transformations of Coast and Interior: A Case from Mallorca

Rapid tourist development of the coast of Mallorca in the 1960s was accompanied by the abandonment of much of the agricultural land in the island's centre. This caused Picornell and others (1997) to observe that space on the coast, which was once economically marginal to the island, has now become of central importance to its economy. At the same time, the once most economically significant space covering much of the interior has become economically marginal since it has not traditionally been included in the development plans of the tourist industry. Other research in Mallorca (Selwyn 1997; Waldren 1996) has broadened the ethnographic base from which further generalizations may be made about the nature of coastal development and the forces unleashed by it.

To begin with, the case of Calvia District located on the southwest coast of Mallorca may be considered. The district has come to possess one of densest stretches of tourism development in Europe and includes such well-known tourist resorts as Magaluf and Santa Ponça. The district underwent radical transformation from a semi-feudal agricultural economy to one based on tourism in the space of a very few years. The first boom in tourist building on the Calvian coast happened in the early 1960s. It took place as a result of the confluence of three local and global trends: the growth of mass tourism following post-war austerity in northern Europe; the *laissez-faire* economic policies of the Franco era; and the complete absence of local government and local planning policies. Together, these factors provided the context for a free-for-all building bonanza. The boom lasted for about 15 years and consisted mainly of hotel building. The Middle-East War and subsequent oil crisis ended this period, and for about 10 years building was largely confined to the construction of apartments. A second boom of hotel building began in the mid-1980s and coincided with the simultaneous growth of effective local planning. At the same time a new regional level of government came into existence. More recently, in the last years of the 1990s, hotel building has slowed, while apartment building has continued.

Local and regional authorities have put much effort into checking the growth of building development and continuing the long process of salvaging the coast from the effects of the speculative builders of the 1960s. In many respects this has met with considerable success. The effectiveness of Calvia Municipality itself as a planning authority has been recognized throughout the Mediterranean. Nevertheless, there are some observers who are far from complacent, noting that speculative building and the forces fuelling it have only temporarily retreated from the island. Furthermore, despite being one of the most powerful in Spain, Calvia Municipality has found it difficult, and is continuing to find it so, to assure that such building is contained within what it considers reasonable bounds. At any rate the coast of Calvia is one of many locations in the Mediterranean where the struggle between speculative private development and publicly organized and controlled development, shaped by concern for the social and economic well-being of those who live and work in the district, will take place in the decades to come.

It is important to reflect at this stage about what existed *before* the building boom of the 1960s. Elderly residents speak of general poverty, lack of public facilities, persistent emigration (notably to France, Cuba, and elsewhere in Latin America) and seem to be in no doubt that mass tourism has brought previously unknown levels of wealth to Calvia. However, it would not be accurate to paint an unremittingly gloomy picture of the life and times of the district before the coming of tourism. Photographic evidence from the municipal archives spanning the past 100 years (Amengual 1990) shows clear evidence of enterprise, style, and good living. There are photographs of musical bands and dancers in Calvia village at the turn of the century, of family picnics and celebrations on the Santa Ponça headland, of the festivities of St. Jaume, of women enjoying the La Granja café – well known for its ice cream and tapas – in 1945, of the village football team in 1949, and so on. Furthermore, Calvia's valleys are reminders that the district contained areas of considerable abundance. There is good, fertile land suitable for vegetable and fruit production, and there is plenty of evidence of former orchards and market gardens. Further up the valley slopes there are dry stone walls supporting terraces on which dry farming (carob, almond, fig, olive) was practised. These areas of agricultural production were, for the most part, managed as part of large estates, some of which were extremely wealthy.

It is even worth positioning the history of, say, the past few hundred years, in a longer-term context. Describing the estate (*possessiò*) of Valldurgent, named possibly after the French *Val d'Argent* (i.e., valley of silver), Andreu (1987:27) remarks that it would be easy to imagine that before the conquest in 1229 by the Catalan King Jaume Ist over the then Muslim population of the island, the land produced all kinds of fruit and vegetables and was generally an abundant producer.

The purpose of this small historical reflection is not to deny that Calvia is a great deal wealthier now than it was historically. That would, of course, be unrealistic. Equally unrealistic, however, would be to make claims about the benefits of contemporary tourist development, which rest upon assumptions of Mallorca having been nothing but a poverty stricken backwater or economic *tabula rasa*. As in other parts of the region, coastal development in Mallorca has been accomplished at the cost of substantial underdevelopment of the agricultural interior.

In more recent times, Calvia's coastal development has caused substantial demographic changes. Not only was there the pronounced population drift to the coast from the centre of the island that has already been noted, but Calvia District has the highest population of mainland Spanish workers of any municipality on the island.

The Significance of the Tourism Offer

There are a number of issues having to do with the tourism offer in Calvia that have far-reaching economic, environmental, demographic and political implications for the district. It is probable that these have resonances in other destinations in the Mediterranean region. One of the concerns that municipal planners in Calvia have is that the district should maintain an appropriate balance between hotel and self-catering apartment accommodation. Their argument is that a shift towards the latter would have a number of overlapping consequences. Firstly, it is likely that building self-catering apartments would be accompanied by the creation of additional golf courses in the district. Clearly, this would have environmental impacts not only on the landscape itself but also on the already hard-pressed water supply. Secondly, such a move would result in a reduction in the demand for labour in the hotel industry and thus cause unemployment. Such unemployment might cause some 'return' migration,[2] which might, in turn, have significant political consequences.[3] Put very broadly, as note three explains, demographic changes resulting from transformations in tourism might result in the movement away from the politics of environmental intervention and regulation towards more *laissez-faire* policies.

The Struggle between Public and Private Interests

While local and specific details of party affiliations, party policies, voting patterns, and so on clearly vary across localities in the region, the *general* significance of the Calvia case for the coastal Mediterranean lies in the different policy and planning dispositions and capacities held and enacted at the local level by local authorities. As has already been said, this is a landscape where the forces of speculative building and controlled development are increasingly in fierce competition with one another. Since the mid-1950s, development in Calvia itself has taken place within the framework of the municipality's *General Plan*, an extremely detailed document describing the environmental and urban consequences deriving from the municipality's economic dependence on tourism and composed by teams of planners, architects and landscape designers. It outlines the strategies and legal frameworks to be followed by developers. The central aim of the *Plan* is the rational organization of space, including tourist space. Furthermore, it is self-consciously informed by a *regional* perspective on Mediterranean tourism, being based on the forecast that an island such as Mallorca will not be able to compete with such new destinations as Turkey for the cheap holiday market. The implication is that the island's hotels and other tourist structures need to be upgraded in order to attract higher spending tourists.

Calvia's *General Plan* is illustrative of a dominant principle of the Council itself, namely its belief in strategic local intervention backed up at regional, national and European levels. This principle is found in many of the Council's policy initiatives. These include the declaration of a large area of the District as a natural park and an ongoing program involving the opening-up of the interior of the District to tourists by re-opening ancient paths used in the past by peasant farmers, wood-cutters, charcoal burners, shepherds, and others. It is precisely these kinds of actions, as well as the presuppositions which guide them, which have brought the Council into conflict with a number of local landowners and developers who are pressing for controls on public access to land in favour of more exclusively private access.

In Calvia itself, therefore, the 1960s era of unplanned and haphazard development gave way in the 1980s and early 1990s to regulated development planned in such a way as to make private development seem contained within a public planning framework.

The question remains. For how much longer can private speculative building development be contained by public policies? Anecdotal (but quite typical and certainly indicative) evidence helps us move towards an answer.

Part of the business of a development company in Calvia District consists of the building of tourist-related residential developments that, increasingly, have consisted of estates of luxury apartments for sale to foreign residents. Along with the apartments themselves, there is the associated infrastructure to make such developments attractive to potential buyers, golf courses being a particularly popular offering. Closely linked to both of these is the other main part of the company's business, namely the building of public roads, which are not only for use by the general public but also part of the infrastructure of the company's own developments. When complete, the roads are sold to Calvia municipality. This is where the weak link appears. Because in the early days of its existence the municipality borrowed large sums of money, it presently pays an extremely high fraction of its budget on interest payments, a fact which periodically makes it late in paying for its roads. This puts the municipality in something of a vulnerable position, opening the way for arrangements to be made between it and the development company. These may take a number of forms. Granting permission to build golf courses might be one. It was recently argued in Calvia, for example, that there are substantial economic benefits to the municipality to be obtained from the hosting of international golf tournaments. Dilution of legislation governing natural parks (in which building development is forbidden) might be another. Allowing road building to serve further private developments might be a third.

Disputed Landscapes: Cases from Mallorca and Malta

Before making some generalizations about the shape and character of tourist development in the Mediterranean littoral, we may consider the implications that the general forces and processes taking place on the coast have for areas in the interior. This may effectively be done ethnographically using one example from Mallorca and two from Malta.

Waldren (1996) points towards the ever-increasing power of the private construction sector on Mallorca in general, and particularly in its interior, by showing how road building programs adopted by the regional government of the Balearics have been pushed through at enormous expense. Such projects, like the hotly disputed widening of the coast road between Deià and Sóller, for example, are frequently carried out in the face of local opposition and informed environmentalist criticism. According to estimates of the Mallorcan Green Party and the islands' well-respected *Grup Balear d'ornitoleg* (GOB), road development projects in the single year of 1997 destroyed 700 hectares of forest, agricultural terrain, and protected natural spaces. Waldren points out that these developments are at odds with the Mallorcan Tourist Board's rhetoric about the desirability of forms of sustainable tourism based on existing traditional local agricultural economies. As she says, the very direction of these projects is in complete contradiction to the new types of tourism the Tourism Board wants to attract. At the heart of the matter, Waldren argues, is the fact that development in the island is generally driven by private interests articulated through municipalities and the island's parliament (which) take precedence over collective and/or environmental objectives.

In his chapter in the present volume, as well as in Boissevain and Theuma (1998), Boissevain sharpens the focus of this pattern of power relations in his discussion of the Hilton and Cottonera cases from Malta. In the first of these, permission was granted by Malta's planning authority for the development of a US$122M project involving the construction of a new Hilton hotel, together with a development of 250 luxury apartments, yacht marina, and business centre. Apart from the general dislocation and inconvenience to local residents and businesses, the project destroyed a unique part of the island's historical fortifications built in 1530 by the Knights of St. John and led to pollution of nearby sea grass meadows and beaches. Environmental groups vigorously opposed the project. Indeed, the project involved high profile legal and political engagement, since the public was very largely opposed to the development.

In the second case, a United States-led development corporation was on the point of receiving permission to take over the front of one of the famous three cities opposite Valletta across the Grand Harbour. This particular idea became the focus of a political trial of strength between the then ruling Labour party which, with its majority of one, was publicly selling the project on the grounds of it bringing inward investment and providing employment opportunities to a part of Malta marked by poverty and unemployment, and the opposition Nationalist Party who took the opportunity to oppose the plan. Following a rejection by the former Prime Minister Dom Mintoff of his party's whip on this issue, the government itself fell and in the ensuing election lost its majority to the Nationalists. Boissevain concludes with the wry observation that the Nationalists certainly are committed to the implementation of many of the other ambitious up-scale tourist projects which the Labour Party had adopted. In his view the confrontations over Malta's landscape are set to continue.

This notion of the landscape being subject to confrontation and disputation is an accurate one that finds echoes throughout the Mediterranean littoral. In Malta's own case, for example, the number of tourists visiting the island's ancient capital, Mdina (upwards of 750,000 annually) has for some time been thought by residents (who number 220) to be excessive (Boissevain 1997). But, or so it seemed to them, there was little that they could actually do about controlling numbers. Malta lacked any system of local government, and there appeared few other effective avenues through which to take appropriate action. Recently, however, local municipal government has been introduced throughout the island. One of the first actions taken by the newly constituted municipality of Mdina was to limit visitor numbers. Clearly, however, it will be a while before the long-term effectiveness of Mdina Council in asserting control over the spaces of its town in the face of the island's tourist industry can accurately be assessed.

Summary

These ethnographic sketches allow us to make several working assumptions as follows. One of the consequences of the tourism-related development in many parts of the Mediterranean littoral in the second half of the 20th century has been the relocation of the centres of economic activity from inland agricultural settlements to coastal tourist resorts. Semi-feudal, remittance-aided agricultural modes of production, in some parts of the region dominated by large estates, has given way to more thoroughgoing capitalist modes of production based to a considerable extent on tourism. One important aspect of these transformations has involved land on the coast. Formally, this had little agricultural use value. With tourism development, however, it rapidly acquired development value. Some of the owners of coastal lands (typically younger sons or daughters of families whose elder siblings owned land in the interior) became rich. The majority, lacking capital to develop the lands themselves, sold them to developers. In the early days, coastal development was essentially opportunistic and unplanned. As the tourism industry grew, the centres of economic gravity expanded to include tour operators, many of them foreign. Economic power on the coast increasingly came to be located in combinations of development companies / banks and (often foreign) tour operators – although the extent to which individual members of previously dominant families have retained power in the new economic climate must be a matter for ethno-financial investigation. The mode of tourism-related development on the coasts has had wide-reaching effects in inland areas. With few exceptions (where elements of traditional agricultural economies have managed to co-exist with tourism), inland areas have also been incorporated, even if only through their own underdevelopment, in tourist-dominated island economies. In the process, development decisions are often taken in locations that are out of reach of those who live and work in the sites of actual tourism development. In general, the forces of private speculative development are a good deal stronger than those of combinations of local municipalities, non-governmental organizations, and public movements. For example, it is clear from the point of view (and involvement) of those living or working near the sites, or those who simply care about them, that the development of the Deià/Sóller road and the Malta Hilton have passed out of any form of democratic control. However, there *are* times when alliances between environmental groups, local government authorities, and tour operators anxious about the sustainability of their product can come together in opposition to the development companies. This is what happened briefly in Mallorca in the mid- to late 1990s. As far as the ownership and control of space is concerned, it is these unfolding structures of alliances and the sites of struggle in which they operate that provide the most interesting set of questions for students of tourism and tourism development, and readers of this book.

CHAPTER TWO

So far, this chapter has considered aspects of the political economy of tourism development in the coastal Mediterranean. The next stage is to consider some of the social, cultural and environmental consequences.

Coast, Culture and Nature

Culture and Space: The Principal of Socio-Spatial Counterpoint

The term culture itself is, of course, complex and catch-all. It covers just about everything in all areas of life and is thus found as often in spheres of economic and political practice as in religious, artistic or culinary ones. Thus, when we speak of culture in the Mediterranean, as indeed anywhere else, we need to think in terms of such categories as family life and values, economic and productive practices, religious, artistic and architectural practices, and so on. The term refers to the way people live in a general and inclusive sense, together with the accompanying symbolic paraphernalia.

The particular interest here is with the *cultural uses of space*. In what follows, therefore, there is a concern with the social spaces occupied by families, communities and individuals and the physical spaces in which these are located. One way to approach these questions is to consider some of the consequences of changing kinship structures.

The relationship between the generations, to take one aspect of family life, has clearly been affected by the movement away from the centrality of agriculture and pastoralism in inland areas to participation in coastal tourism-based economies. Thus, Black (1990) has written of the emancipatory effect of tourism in Malta for young women, many of whom have moved away from patriarchal and matriarchal structures by finding economic roles in the tourist-dominated economy of the island, making them less dependent on parents and the Catholic Church. Eber and Aziz (1997) have described how Bedouin children, particularly girls, work the beaches of the Sinai selling friendship bracelets to tourists on the coasts, again re-defining their role *vis-a-vis* their parents, particularly their mothers. Evidence from Corfu suggests that there is a radical loosening of the authoritative proximity of generations following the leaving by young men of villages in the interior to pursue business opportunities on the coast. This generational dislocation has been one of the contributory causes behind the spread of HIV/Aids as well as several well-publicized outbreaks of violence on the island.[4]

Examples such as these suggest a pattern not so much of family breakdown but of growing autonomy and individualism within kinship structures. Furthermore, there is less overlap between the spaces inhabited by the family and the spaces in which moral decisions are taken. Formerly, with a core of members of extended families inhabiting contiguous space, there was an overlap between kinship and spatial boundaries, providing a recognizable spatial arena in which moral sanctions were exercised. Increasingly, with the growing autonomy of family members in tourist-dominated economies, moral sanctions are becoming more of a matter for individual consideration.

The development of coastal tourist economies seem generally to have involved the dispersal of family members into heterogeneous spaces within and beyond coasts. The same applies to larger communal structures, such as some of the quarters of historic cities. Schembri and Borg (1997), for example, describe the exodus of the working class population of the Three Cities in Malta, a pattern repeated in some of the historic cities in Turkey, Greece and elsewhere (Orbasli 1997). Typically what has accompanied this exodus has been the *inflow* of middle-class investors from the metropolis into second homes. Investors from Rome are most visible in the case of the Three Cities, whilst wealthy Athenians are investing in the settlements and towns of Greek islands (Sivri 1997; Chelidoni 1997).

As this movement of population has taken place and the basis of the economy of such towns and settlements has been determined to a greater extent by the tourism and second home economy, the character of coastal towns has undergone a spatial transformation which may be introduced as follows.

One of the most remarkable features of the *historic* Mediterranean urban landscape has been a distinctive structure of spatial order and economy. This is based upon the capacity to construct spaces – public, semi-public, private – in which different individual persons, families, groups of families, and communities may live closely together, simultaneously maintaining senses of difference and coherence, separateness and communality. This may be achieved, as in the *Casbah* in Algiers or in the historic Old City of Jerusalem, through subtle combinations of the use of courtyards, which are more or less closed to the streets, openings to roof terraces, organization into communal *quarters,* and so on. In the case of Valletta and the Three Cities (as in some quarters in the Old City of Marrakesh or the Ottoman parts of Nicosia), it is partly achieved by the use of balconies jutting out into the street from the upper floors of houses. This gives residents (particularly women) opportunities to move at ease between the realm of the semi-public and the private. Such spatial economy and order at the level of the house finds expression at the level of the whole town in such features as historic grid systems, as in Valletta and parts of the towns of the Canaries. It is also expressed in the tendency of historic Mediterranean cities, in general, to have mixed economic use linked to residential patterns. This has placed people of different economic and social standings in close proximity to one another. For example, as Amyuni (1998) has pointed out, in several Mediterranean cities craftsmen and working-class families have traditionally lived in the lower floors of buildings whose upper stories are inhabited by the wealthy.

I would like to suggest that we see in such features as these examples of the historic Mediterranean's capacity to structure social and cultural life in its cities according to principles of *socio-spatial counterpoint.*

Similar processes are at work in the Mediterranean countryside. The *polyculture* and mixed usages of historic Mediterranean agricultural land mirrors the kind of processes noted above for urban settlements. On the large canvas, the relationship between the desert and the coast (in the south of the region) or the mountains and the coast in the north also provides us with examples of socio-spatial counterpoint. In the 14th century, Ibn Khaldun argued that the society and history of the Arab Mediterranean was structured by the relationship between the desert and the city. Pastoralists, herdsmen, and shepherds resided in the desert. In the city there were labourers, craftsmen, moneylenders, scholars, priests, soldiers, and the court. Agriculturists were in between. But as the middle-classes move into town and country, as coasts become separated from interiors (by roads and tourist development), and as whole categories of occupation (from pastoralist to most types of craftsperson) disappear, and the overall basis of coastal economies change, spaces become increasingly individuated, decorative and cut off from the field of relations in which they were embedded.

In sum then, the historical landscape of the Mediterranean, both urban and agricultural, was one in which boundaries of space and family tended to coincide. It was also a landscape in which considerable value was placed both on public space and on the routine ability to enter the spaces of others. Indeed, elaborate codes of hospitality and politeness were available to guide strangers through the spaces of others (Selwyn 2000a). Moreover, categories of people who later came to be regarded as marginal – pastoralists, those involved in transhumant shepherding, or Romas, for example – found convenient and available spaces for themselves either inside or outside the city. Towns and villages could cope with the periodicity that was a feature of their lives.

It was also a social landscape marked by *patronage* of several kinds. There was the type of patronage of the poor by the rich and powerful made famous by such classics of Mediterranean anthropology as Campbell (1964) and Gellner (1969). There was patronage of the arts and sciences in the historical Mediterranean by cities, courts, and prominent families. There was the patronage of local churches and mosques by rich members of congregations, and the patronage by smaller towns and village of festivals of patron saints and/or holy figures.

Some of these features and relationships are changing under the influence of economic shifts to contemporary tourist-dominated free market economies. The historic spatial economy, and what I have termed socio-spatial counterpoint, is breaking down. The landscape generally is in the process of being *privatised,* and access to spaces in both town and country is increasingly restricted. At the same time, and partly as a result, pastoralism and transhumance are disappearing, and Bedouin, shepherds and Romas are being more routinely marginalized. Allied to such movements, systems of patronage are also breaking down (except perhaps in cases of competitive religious or nationalist movements and/or in cases of foreign patrons supporting some kinds of buildings and activities to curry favour in scrambles for political influence).

The new cultural landscape of the Mediterranean is one shaped by the increasing emancipation of the individual from such overarching social structures as family, communal city quarter, estate, constituency of patron, and so on. One implication of this is that properties and spaces in both town and country are also shedding remaining links with larger communal spaces. The Archduke Lluis Salvador and a well-known Hollywood film star share the distinction of being the owners (the former in the nineteenth century, the latter in the twentieth) of the same Mallorcan *possessió*. However, while the estate in the nineteenth century was accessible to Mallorcan residents – hunters, fishers, collectors of wild fruits, walkers – the twentieth-century estate is surrounded by fences. As a result, it has become a significant political issue in Mallorcan politics – not only for itself but for what it represents, namely the removal of space from the public domain. At the same time, in the centre of Palma City, now a heavily commercial area full of privately owned bars and restaurants for tourists, the presence of Romas using urban spaces previously able to accommodate them has also become a political issue. There is mounting pressure by the bar and restaurant owners to remove what are sometimes described as the unsightly living conditions of such citizens. The issue takes different forms, but the question everywhere is the same: as space is being privatised, how are communal rights (including those held by different constituencies and categories of people working and living in them) to those spaces to be exercised and maintained?

Cultural Appropriation

Apart from the above processes, all of which are consequences of tourism-related development and the kind of politico-economic changes it brings in its wake, tourism also takes part more directly in cultural formations. Of the many possible examples, here are three. The first is the appropriation of cultural sites and practices by national and international authorities in the name of tourism and tourist-related conservation practices. The second consists of one of the ingredients of such appropriation, namely what has been called façadism (Orbasli 2000). The third has to do with a phenomenon that appears to be at odds with the spatial privatisation identified above, but which is in fact closely tied to it, namely the nationalization of cultural spaces.

Odermatt (1996) has described how the Sardinian bronze/iron age monuments, the *nuraghi*, are presently the focus of a dispute between the Italian authorities and local residents. Whilst the former claim that they are of major importance to world heritage and thus need protection (including fencing off), the latter use the area where the monuments stand as a meeting place in the evening. They argue that since the site is located in their village, it is they who should take responsibility for its management and protection.

This case is just one illustration of a particular kind of cultural appropriation. In the name of protection and/or conservation, historical sites are removed from everyday access. Nowhere are the complexities of this process better described (albeit in a different geographical context) than in Bender's *Stonehenge* (1998).

The making of national or natural parks is another example of the appropriation by state authorities of sites that are often used for everyday purposes by communities living near those sites. Crain's (1996) work on the Andalusian Donana National Park is an excellent case in point. This park, one of Europe's largest game reserves, was identified by the European Union and ecologically aware local and national planners, together with those predominantly wealthy locals who stood to gain out of increased ecotourism, as a good site for international protective status. Appropriate measures were taken, including the donation by the European Commission to the government of Spain to make the park into a European heritage site. Environmentally friendly tourism by bird- and animal-loving northern Europeans was encouraged. The only snag was that, for centuries, the area was a hunting ground for the predominantly working-class inhabitants of nearby villages.

The issue of hunting raises several questions that are not as easy to answer as might at first be supposed. Who has the right to hunt? Who has the obligation to conserve? What processes of decision-making are available to resolve contradictory and conflicting demands on the land and its produce? Who owns the space on which hunting takes place? Who should own it? And so on.

These are precisely the issues in relation to historical monuments and even whole towns (such as Mdina) that have been taken over, to a greater or lesser extent, by tourists and tourist authorities. Once again the question concerns *the control and organization of space, including sites of national and international scientific significance.*

Façadism, Internet-ism, Museumization, Experience-ification

Processes stimulated by the tourist industry which Boissevain and Theuma (1998) describe as the movement from utilitarian space to 'Heritage' take several forms.

There is, first of all, the urban façadism (i.e., the emphasis on conserving the façades of buildings) much debated by architects concerned with historic towns. This preservation at any price approach to the historic cities on the tourist trail is one emphasizing external appearance above all else and is, suggests Orbasli (2000), a fear-laden response to spoiling a desired image. As she goes on to explain, such an approach is ultimately the enemy of urban conservation, since towns and cities need constantly to be renewing themselves to remain alive. However, it is legitimate to ask when considering the three UNESCO World Heritage Sites on Mediterranean islands, namely Valletta, Rhodes Old Town, and Paphos, how such renewal can be achieved? And who is going to achieve this renewal? One may also wonder about the extent to which the authorities (whether from the tourist sector or UNESCO itself) are, indeed, concerned with image more that the gritty day-to-day life of one of these cities.

Then there are the various forms of what one might term internet-ism: the offering on the internet of properties and sites for sale which are described effusively in terms of their cultural, natural and historic value. Internet-ese builds on the kinds of language (of tourist/real estate brochures) described and analysed by Dann (1996) and others. In one of the *Sardinia* websites, for example, the viewer reads that:

> Villa Ebner ... sleeps 8 ... a holiday villa of 6000 sq. meters of Mediterranean bush, pinewood and eucalyptus wood ... located close to Port Pino ... an area which boasts a wide range of typically Mediterranean natural habitats, most of which are very much unspoilt ... Inland there is a rich archaeological heritage which includes settlements of the first inhabitants of the island, the Nuraghe, the typical Sardinian houses dating back to the Bronze Age.

Nested in a box on the bottom left-hand side of the website, at once discrete and reassuring, is the additional information that ... *Restaurants and Pizzerias are in Porto Pino, 2 km from the property. Supermarket, pharmacy, bank, Post Office are in Santa Anna Annesi village. There is a golf club at 50km.* Such language is, as noted, familiar from sales brochures of Mediterranean properties elsewhere, such as the 1993 brochure offering a luxury apartment in Calvia: *Los Pampanos offers reminiscences of the old Mediterranean wrapped in subtropical gardens, created from materials of the finest quality, bringing forth a dream of architectural excellence combined with comfort.* Once again there was a golf course as part of the package for the buyer of a *Los Pampanos* apartment, the whole complex being built and supplied by the development company whose other function was the building of roads over much of the island. Apart from these connections, the other point of significance is that *Los Pampanos* is framed by an appeal to a private domain in which the Mallorcan landscape serves as a back-drop. These two cases suggest that we have arrived in a dreamlike world of sensual experiences of an essentially private kind.

The emphasis on *experience* follows seamlessly from the villas *Ebner* and *Los Pampanos*. In Valletta tourists are invited (by varieties of strategically placed advertisements, including those offered in the in-flight glossy magazine distributed by Air Malta) to visit the perma-nently running show called the Malta Experience. This is a multime-dia presentation of the best-known pieces of Maltese history, its foun-dation by the Knights, the siege of the island by the Turks, the heroism of the island and its people in the Second World War, and so on. Mdina has an equivalent, Mdina Experience, which is advertised by a sign at the entrance to the Old City. As Orbasli (2000) observes, tour-ists seeing the Mdina sign for the first time are liable to be confused – for unless there is the knowledge of the associated multi-media and film show, does the unsuspecting visitor not assume that the walled town itself is the experience? In other words, the tourist is taken a step away from experiencing the site itself in order to sample an off-site ex-perience of the site. Furthermore, the Experience feels as if it were an *authoritative* experience, a super guidebook, the real McCoy.

Such experience-ification is not far removed from the sort of museumization described, amongst others, by Boissevain (1997). He estimated that Mdina could earn around $2 million annually by redefining itself as a museum – its citizens, becoming objects as it were, losing the right to be treated as subjects and citizens in the pro-cess.

Nationalisation of Tourist Space

Tourism is related to nationalism in several ways. One of these is the overlapping nature of promotional and nationalist rhetoric. Akay (1997), for example, has shown that northern Cyprus is promoted in nationalistic terms. Turkish Cypriot tourism authorities, he argues, have been engaged in recasting the Cypriot historical and cultural mosaic in terms of a Turkishness which is counter-posed to the Greekness of the south. Sites with Greek associations have been de-fined in terms of them being Byzantine or Roman. Villages with Greek names have been given Turkish names that now appear on tourist maps. At the same time, the Greek Cypriot tourist authorities present the south of the island as if the foundation of Cypriot history was co-terminus with the first traces of the Greek population in Cyprus. Akay effectively demonstrates that while the heritage of North Cyprus (as the territory typically appears in English language guidebooks) is presented as Turkish, this process cannot be disconnected from the comparable processes engaged in over the years by Greek Cypriots in Hellenizing the whole island of Cyprus. He further observes that because guidebooks subtract politics from culture (in the sense that the impression is given to the naive tourist that the north is *culturally* Turkish and the south *culturally* Greek), they take part in the process of the 'ethnic-isation' of both territories, and in doing so add political legitimisation to the entities of the Turkish Republic of North Cyprus, on the one hand, and the state of Cyprus on the other.

The notion of cultural mosaics being manipulated by rival nationalist movements is one that resonates elsewhere in the Mediterranean. I have reported above and elsewhere (Selwyn 1997), for example, that some observers in Mallorca trace links between Mallorcan/Catalan nationalism and the political economy of tourism in the island. These observers point to a correlation between economic downturns and the rise of anti-Spanish and pro-Mallorcan nationalist expressions. Such an association is to be expected in a context in which many workers in the hotel industry on the island come from the mainland. I also suggested that one of the reasons why Mallorcan and Spanish nationalisms have not, unlike Greek and Turkish nationalisms in Cyprus, resulted until now in hot conflict in Mallorca is that government (particularly local government) on that island has been powerful enough to have regulated the provision of services (health, education, and so on) and employment to both indigenous Mallorcan and immigrant Spanish workers in the tourist industry to safeguard the well-being of both communities. Calvia Municipality achieved this in the early days of its existence by borrowing significant sums of money to build schools, homes for the elderly, sports-centres, and other facilities. This is the reason why presently the municipality is still in debt (see above). It may plausibly be speculated that if tourism and other development policies that were to be adopted failed to meet the employment needs of the present population of the island, and if there were to be a sustained period of unemployment, then expressions of nationalist sentiments would be likely to increase. In the case of Mallorca such unemployment could easily be imagined were the ratio of self-catering apartments to hotels (the former being much less labour intensive than the latter) to increase.

It would be tempting, following these two examples, to link strong nationalist sentiments to weak civil institutions, and *vice versa,* and there is probably something to be said for such a link. But there are clearly also other factors, not least those coming from external forces.

Tourism studies and studies of nationalism overlap in several ways. Three topics of interest are touched upon here. The first arises from the apparently contradictory fact that while regional tourism demands a certain degree of co-operation between nations (nowhere more true than in the Mediterranean region), it also promotes (in both practical and symbolic senses) competition between nationalisms. Thus, tourism in Mallorca needs workers from mainland Spain in the same way that tourism in Israel historically needed workers from Palestine. Indeed, in the latter case, Israeli and Palestinian tourism are (or were) clearly locked into mutual interdependence. Nevertheless, in both Mallorcan/Spanish and Israeli/Palestinian tourism, rival nationalist agendas are promoted in the course of tourism promotion and practice. The second topic of interest concerns the capacity of public authorities to contain rival nationalisms through economic regulation and good management, largely by providing all sides with senses of well-being. The third, the political extension of the second, concerns the extent to which public authorities, including local municipalities, can so include and involve their populations, to use contemporary Third Way language, as to reduce the propensity for nationalist expressions.

Inscriptions on Coastal Mediterranean Landscapes

Coastal tourist and other developments are writing a script on the natural and built spaces of the Mediterranean region, the decoding of which involves looking three ways: backwards at features of the historic Mediterranean environment, sideways at how that environment is presently changing, and forwards at how it may become in the future.

The best way to introduce a discussion on the natural environment of the Mediterranean is to refer back to the extensive and now very well-known description and analysis of the region's environment by Grenon and Batisse in 1989. In their *Futures for the Mediterranean Basin: The Blue Plan* these authors identified six primary features of the Mediterranean environment.

The first consists of the environmental *diversity* of the region. This may be seen in the interplay among mountains (acting as a physical boundary between the region and what lies beyond), pastures on the mountain slopes, the forests with their chestnut groves and variety of other trees, the villages with their associated terrace farming, the shrublands (home to birds and other fauna), meadows leading to cultivated crop lands, lagoons and marshes, and the pines on the edge of the sea. The diversity found in these different terrains and niches may also be seen in another feature of the region's agriculture, namely the practice of what the French term *polyculture* – the growing of many different kinds of agricultural products next door to one another. The second feature is the close *interrelationship* between nature, on the one hand, and agriculture and other productive or extractive practices, on the other: everywhere in the Mediterranean basin, human activity has always been one agent of environmental and geological change and development. The third, which arises from the first two, consists of the *systematic* nature of the region's environment. Thus, for example, the ancient cycle of pastoral transhumance, whereby sheep, goats and other livestock would be shepherded down to the plains in the winter, where they would give birth in the spring before being taken back up to the mountain pastures in the summer, is illustrative of the fundamentally cyclical nature of the Mediterranean environment as a whole. Spaces and times of agricultural use and activity are followed by spaces and times of inactivity and renewal, the year itself is dominated by a water cycle fed and regulated by mountains that capture snow and rainfall, which they feed to the slopes and valleys. The fourth follows from this: the *relatively scarce resources* of the region mean that the systematic interrelationship between the various parts of the natural environment and between it and the cultural environment depend to a large extent on the sparing use of those resources. Indeed, as the *Plan* itself makes clear, the above underlies not only much of the region's agriculture, but also much of its culture. As Grenon and Batisse say, there is a common stock of attitudes and behaviour with deep cultural and religious roots. These are related to the realities and features of the environment. For example, agricultural methods made sparing use of the land, soil, and water. (For this reason) food consumption was always tinged with frugality (op. cit.: 12). The fifth point is that it is precisely the *blend* of natural and cultural heritage that is the true wealth of the Mediterranean basin (op. cit.: 4). The final point is that the very rapid *technological, economic, demographic, and social changes* in the region in the past half century – of which the growth of tourism and tourism-related development has played a substantial role – have placed the environment of the region under threat. (One French research report produced in the late 1980s, for example, estimated that 526 types of plant species were under threat of extinction, a fact which in turn had led to the radical reduction if not actual extinction of several animal species, the large forest mammals such as bears and lynxes, antelopes, and large birds of prey such as eagles and vultures.)

Using the *Blue Plan* as a starting point, what contribution may we begin to make to the understanding of the features and structures of the Mediterranean landscapes and environments?

We may start from observing that what we have called the coastal mode of (tourism-related) production has significantly changed the relationship between the people and the land. The radical decline of biodiversity, manifested as much in the decrease of the *polyculture* characteristic of the historical Mediterranean as in the use, abuse and neglect of the *garrigue*, is both cause and consequence of this changed relationship. Secondly, it is clear that the *systematic interrelationship* between nature and agriculture, symbolically marked most potently by the seasonal transhumance of sheep and shepherds in the north and goats and Bedouin in the south of the region, has been replaced by a different sort of seasonality. This is driven not by the needs and life-cycles of livestock but by the dispositions and demands of northern European tourists coming and going from the region in the summer months. One of the several implications of this kind of seasonality is the enormous demand for food and other resources in the high season. Thus, an area once characteristically 'tinged with frugality', to emphasise Grenon's and Batisse's nice phrase, has become an area subject to regular bouts of over demand and over use of resources, particularly water.

The processes of social relocation and dislocation described here have had their effect on the landscape and environment. One (of many) ways into this discussion is provided by Hordern and Purcell (2000:237). Speaking of Mediterranean terraces and irrigation, and following the spirit of Grenon and Batisse, they observe that '… terracing and irrigation are represented within the microregion as strategies of improvement in miniature, part of that symbiosis between production and the environment which is so characteristic of the Mediterranean'. This idea of 'improvements in miniature' relates closely to the way Horden and Purcell describe one of the special agricultural and environmental characteristics of small Mediterranean islands (op. cit.: 224-230). They refer to the '... tiny niches of high potential for intensification ... (being) ... long recognised as special features of the Mediterranean landscape'. But they qualify this generalisation by also observing that while some historical periods have, indeed, provided contexts for flexible micro-agricultural responses by islanders to regional market opportunities, other periods have been marked by the incorporation of islands into regional market systems dominated by mainland centres. In these latter contexts islands were often forced into mono-crop production. No wonder, they say, that the population of early modern Corsica begged the authorities in Genoa to 'spare them economic growth or improvement' (229). The relevance of this to our present theme is clear. The mono-crop of tourism has, in some senses, drawn islands into a kind of dependency on centres elsewhere. In the process the landscape itself, no longer shaped and constantly reshaped by small farmers and pastoralists, has become increasingly objectified and aestheticised in its transformation into a tourism product.

Conclusions

The marketisation of the Mediterranean coast, led in many localities by tourism development, has been accompanied by a series of social and cultural changes. Spatial and kinship boundaries are becoming disassociated from one another. The working class communities of the inner areas of historic towns and cities are giving way to incoming second homeowners. As this happens, a social economy embedded within a system of *spatial counterpoint* is giving way to a system based on the occupancy of privatised space by largely unrelated individuals. This, in turn, gives rise, in both urban and rural settings, to a kind of aestheticisation of the landscape that is increasingly unrelated to the uses to which it is put. The tourism industry itself (which, in this case, includes the various arms of the heritage and conservationist industries) thrives off such aestheticisation, paying increasing attention (partly under the influence of tour operators anxious about their cultural products) to the façades and appearances of historic buildings and other sites of cultural interest. Just as tourism stimulates nostalgia for the communal spaces of the past, so it also can take part in efforts to nationalise space. As for the natural world, the diversity and *polyculture* of the historic agricultural Mediterranean is giving way to the homogeneity of the mono-crop of tourism (one of the consequences being that terraces are being largely left to decay). Many of the historic interrelationships of agricultural practices and social relations are being broken up in the wake of the development of the coastal mode of tourist production. Resources, historically used frugally, are being exhausted. There has been talk in the last decade, for example, of replenishing water in north Cyprus by Turkish water transported to the island in balloons on their way to Israel.

Overall, we could say that the Mediterranean coast is undergoing a process of privatisation. If left unchallenged, it is a process that might lead to the 'de-Mediterraneanisation of the Mediterranean'.

Notes

1. Earlier versions of this chapter have appeared in Selwyn (2000b) and Selwyn (2001).
2. Such terms as 'return' migration need to be used with extreme caution. People whose parents migrated to Mallorca from mainland Spain in the late 1950s and early 1960s to take part in the expansion of tourism can hardly be described any longer as 'migrants'.
3. Two of the principal political parties in Calvia, the PSOE (*Partido Socialista Obrero Español*) and the PP (*Partido Popular*) have different power bases and also differing attitudes to regulation. Whilst the former, which generally attracts support from hotel workers (who have mainly Spanish mainland backgrounds), has always stood for interventionist policies in matters of property development, the latter favours a more *laissez-faire* approach. The PP would thus be less ready to take a hard line on landowners who closed off their property and be generally less in favour of extending the areas of natural parks.
4. I am indebted to students from the Tourism and Society course at the then University of North London for this piece of information gained by some from experiences as tour representatives on the island.
5. C. Fsadni and T. Selwyn (Eds.) (1997) may be obtained from Tourism Concern, London Metropolitan University, Stapleton House, 277-281 Holloway Road, London N7 8HN (info@tourismconcern.org.uk) or from the MED-CAMPUS office of the University of Malta (carmel.fsadni@ UM.EDU.MT).

References

Akay, K.
1997 Tourism and nationalist discourse: The case of North Cyprus. In: C. Fsadni and T. Selwyn (Eds.), *Sustainable Tourism in Mediterranean Islands and Small Cities.* Malta: MED-CAMPUS, University of Malta. Pp. 91-94.[5]

Amengual, J.
1990 *Cent Anys a Calvia.* Calvia: Ajuntament de Calvia.

Amyuni, M.
1998   *La Ville: Source d'inspiration.* Beirut: Franz Steiner.

Andreu, M.
1987   *The Landscape of Calvia.* Calvia: Ajuntament de Calvia.

Bender, B.
1998   *Stonehenge: Making Space.* Oxford: Berg.

Black, A.
1990   In the Eyes of the Beholder? The Cultural Effects of Tourism in Malta. *Problems of Tourism* 13: University of Warsaw:112-43.

Boissevain, J.
1996   *Coping with Tourists: European Reactions to Mass Tourism.* Oxford: Berghahn.
1997   Problems with Cultural Tourism in Malta. In: C. Fsadni and T. Selwyn (Eds.), *Sustainable Tourism in Mediterranean Islands and Small Cities.* Malta: MED-CAMPUS, Pp. 19-30.

Boissevain, J. and N. Theuma
1998   Contested Space: Planners, Tourists, Developers and Environmentalists in Malta. In: S. Abram and J. Waldren (Eds.), *Anthropological Perspectives on Local Development.* London: Routledge. Pp. 96-119.

Campbell, J.
1964   *Honour, Family and Patronage: A Study of Institutions and Moral Values in a Greek Mountain Community.* Oxford: Clarendon Press.

Chelidoni, K.
1997   Presentation of an Interventionist Policy: A Case Study of the Island Town of Kos. In: C. Fsadni and T. Selwyn (Eds.), *Sustainable Tourism in Mediterranean Islands and Small Cities.* Malta: MED-CAMPUS, University of Malta, Pp. 125-35.

Crain, M.
1996   Contested Territories: the Politics of Touristic Development at the Shrine of El Rocío in Southwestern Andalusia. The Danona National Park. In: J. Boissevain (Ed.), *Coping with Tourists.* Oxford: Berghahn. Pp. 27-56.

Dann, G.
1996   *The Language of Tourism: A Sociolinguistic Perspective.* Wallingford: CAB International.

Eber, S. and H. Aziz
1997   *Bedouin and Tourist Landscapes in Sinai.* Aix-en-Provence: Centre International de Recherches et d'Études Touristiques.

Fsadni, C. and T. Selwyn (Eds.)
1997   *Sustainable Tourism in Mediterranean Islands and Small Cities.* Malta: MED-CAMPUS, Pp. 19-30.

Gellner, E.
1969   *Saints of the Atlas.* London: Weidenfeld and Nicolson.

Grenon, M. and M. Batisse (Eds.)
1989   *Futures for the Mediterranean Basin: The Blue Plan.* Oxford: Oxford University Press.

Hordern, P. and N. Purcell
2000   *The Corrupting Sea: A Study of Mediterranean History.* Oxford: Blackwell.

Kenna, M.
1993   Return Migrants and Tourist Development: An Example from the Cyclades. *Journal of Modern Greek Studies* 11:75-81.

Odermatt, P.
1996   A Case of Neglect? The Politics of (re)presentation: A Sardenian Case. The Sardinian Nuraghi. In: J. Boissevain (Ed.), *Coping with Tourists: European Reactions to Mass Tourism.* Oxford: Berghahn. Pp. 84-112.

Orbasli, A.
1997   Historic Towns and Tourism in Turkey. In: C. Fsadni and T. Selwyn (Eds.), *Sustainable Tourism in Mediterranean Islands and Small Cities.* Malta: MED-CAMPUS, University of Malta. Pp. 36-46.
2000   *Tourists in Historic Towns: Urban Conservation and Heritage Management.* London and New York: E. and FN Spon.

Picornell, C., J. Benitez, and A. Ginard
1997   Tourism, Territory and Society in the Balearic Islands. In: C. Fsadni and T. Selwyn (Eds.), *Sustainable Tourism in Mediterranean Islands and Small Cities.* Malta: MED-CAMPUS, University of Malta. Pp. 30-36.

Schembri, J. and M. Borg
1997   Population Changes in the Walled Cities of Malta. In: C. Fsadni and T. Selwyn (Eds.), *Sustainable Tourism in Mediterranean Islands and Small Cities.* Malta: MED-CAMPUS, University of Malta. Pp. 114-24.

Selwyn, T. (Ed.)
1996   *The Tourist Image: Myth and Myth Making in Tourism.* Chichester: Wiley.

Selwyn, T.
1997   Tourism, Culture and Cultural Conflict. In: C. Fsadni and T. Selwyn (Eds.), *Sustainable Tourism in Mediterranean Islands and Small Cities.* Malta: MED-CAMPUS, University of Malta. Pp. 94-114.
2000a   The Anthropology of Hospitality. In: C. Lashley (Ed.), *In Search of Hospitality: Theoretical Problems and Debates.* Oxford: Butterworth Heinemann.
2000b   The De-Mediterraneanisation of the Mediterranean? *Current Issues in Tourism* 3(3):226-245.
2001   Sustainable Tourism in Mediterranean Islands. In: D. Ionnides, Y. Apostolopolous, and S. Somnes (Eds.), *Mediterranean Islands and Sustainable Tourism Development.* London and New York: Continuum International. Pp. 23-44.

Sivri, M.
1997   Tourism and Development Policies for Traditional Settlements: The Case of Thasos and Dimitsana. In: C. Fsadni and T. Selwyn (Eds.), *Sustainable Tourism in Mediterranean Islands and Small Cities.* Malta: MED-CAMPUS, University of Malta. Pp. 46-60.

Waldren, J.
1996   *Insiders and Outsiders: Paradise and Reality in Mallorca.* Oxford: Berghahn.

3

Littoral Fishermen, Aquaculture, and Tourism in the Canary Islands: Attitudes and Economic Strategies

José J. Pascual

Introduction[1]

The artisanal fisheries in the Canary Islands are surrounded by different economic activities that have an important effect on the fishery-dependent populations. Two of these are of special relevance: tourism and aquaculture. Tourism and related economic activities have been the economic motor of the archipelago since the 1970s. The coast of the islands has been colonised by apartments, hotels, tourist resorts, and harbours. This process first began in the north of islands like Gran Canaria and Tenerife, for example places like Puerto de la Cruz on Tenerife, and later concentrated in the south of the islands Gran Canaria and Tenerife. The construction of harbours was justified in some cases as a refuge for the artisanal fleet, but the harbour infrastructure has been increasingly monopolised by activities related to tourism. There has also been an expansion of aquaculture activities in the littoral zone of the islands, again particularly in the south west of Tenerife and on Gran Canaria. From a few farms some years ago, this sector has undergone a recent boom. Many applications for new enterprises were under consideration in 2002, and the impact on marine ecology, the tourist industry, and fishing has progressively increased. In this paper we analyse the role of fishing-dependent populations in the expansion of aquaculture in the archipelago, their problems of access to this economic activity, and the impact of tourism on both realms.

The Artisanal Fisheries of the Canary Islands

In the artisanal sector of the archipelago, nearly 2,000 fishermen are distributed along more than 1,500 km of coastline. The coastline of the islands is a combination of steep cliffs and open beaches, but in most places the coastal shelf is not extensive. The marine ecosystems which surround the archipelago are characterised by biodiversity and fragility, resulting from the scanty representation of each species, the complex interrelations between the species, human modification of the shoreline, and the influx of significant quantities of contaminants (Bacallado *et al.* 1989; Aguilera *et al.* 1994).

Within this broad framework, a large number of fishing ports are distributed along the coast of the archipelago. Most of the ports are small with only a few artisanal units carrying out extractive activities, frequently changing their fishing techniques, and marketing their products through informal channels (Pascual 1991; Macías *et al.* 1999, 2000).

All of this makes it almost impossible to define with any precision the level of fishing effort, the volume of catches or to even determine the exact size of the active fleet and the number of fishermen employed. Although this may change in the near future, due to the new decrees about the marketing of fish, we are in fact rather sceptical about the success of these measures.[2] The combination of activities in different economic sectors is one of the main problems in evaluating the relevance of the sector. In the households involved in artisanal fishing, women and young people work in alternative occupations in hotels and restaurants, commerce, and construction. This strategy of combining economic activities is not new. Since the 15th century, the littoral communities have survived by means of a complex matrix of interconnected labour in different sectors. The work onboard coastal vessels, agriculture, and fishing in the Saharan bank fleet were the alternatives until recently, and were frequently carried out by the fishermen themselves. Fishermen shifted activities in some periods of their life or simply from season to season, especially in winter, and this pattern continues even today.

For centuries the fishing carried out on the coasts of the islands was of little significance. The majority of the rural fishing communities on the islands were not established until the 1900s. Fishing neighbourhoods, which combined fish salting and commerce, occurred only in those coastal towns where a flourishing sea trade already existed. In several areas of the islands salting factories, which used tuna as the raw material and which were established between the late 1880s and early 1900s, formed the basis for some of the most important contemporary fishing communities. In general terms, fishing off the coasts of the islands up to the turn of the 20th century did not develop beyond seasonal fishing. This was due to the difficulties of fishing in the winter months, especially off the northern coasts of the islands, and to the difficulty of maintaining the existence of small autonomous fishing communities exclusively dependent on a resource of low abundance in a socio-economic context characterised by a low level of exchange (Cabrera and Díaz 1991).

In recent decades, an increase in population and urbanisation and a new market system with much better communications created a quantitative and qualitative transformation of the demand for fish products (Cabrera and Díaz 1991; Díaz 1993). The poorest sections of urban society, immigrants in search of new employment and with relatively low purchasing power, sought both low-priced fresh and salted fish. Moreover, the related service sectors, with a higher income level, and the privileged classes constituted a segment of important demand for the higher value white fish and crustaceans that are found along the islands' coastline and on the African seaboard. These factors increased exponentially the pressure on the limited fishing grounds that surround each island of the archipelago.

Table 3.1. Canary Islands area, coast length, and submarine platform (up to 50 m. depth)

Island	Area (km²)[1]	Coast Length (km²)[2]	Submarine platform (km²)[3]
Tenerife	2,034	398.18	315
Fuerteventura	1,660	325.91	695
Gran Canaria	1,560	236.64	324
Lanzarote	846	213.26	461
La Palma	708	155.75	152
La Gomera	370	117.65	216
El Hierro	269	106.50	93
Canarias	7,447	1,553.89	2,256

1   Source: Instituto Geográfico Nacional
2   Source: Consejería de Política Territorial y de Medio Ambiente
3   Source: García Cabrera 1970

Table 3.1 shows the variability of the coastal shelf of the different islands. For instance, Fuerteventura has a coastal shelf almost 700

percent larger than that of La Gomera. There are also large differences between other islands. These contrasts roughly reflect the
meagre possibilities of increasing the fishing effort on demersal species, especially where the coastal shelf is smaller. The productivity of
the waters surrounding the archipelago is also low in comparison
with areas like the neighbouring African coast. Almost 2,000 littoral
fishermen carry out their activities in these coastal areas. The
changes in consumer habits since the 1950s have combined with
new demand from the tourist and public service related sectors to
strengthen the exploitation of demersal resources and increase the
value of fresh fish caught in the littoral zone. Along with the establishment of canning and salting factories for processing the tuna
catch, this stimulated the growth of many small fishing nuclei on the
islands' coasts throughout the archipelago.

Many of these factories were set up in the *calmas* or 'calms' of the
islands, in the south west, where the seas are calmer because the
high land masses of the larger islands offer protection against the
dominant winds. This phenomenon has been known since the conquest of the islands:

> The height of the mountains opposes a barrier to the dominant
> winds that blow usually from N.W., all the southern coast of the
> islands enjoying this protection. The islanders use the name calms
> for the sea zone that bathes those coasts of the Canary Archipelago.
> The fishing schooners sometimes must be towed rowing this entire
> littoral, when the S.W. winds are not favourable to navigation (Webb
> and Berthelot 1836).

Several factors affected development in the Canary *calmas*. The year-
round good weather made it possible to fish pelagic tuna species almost continuously and also made the area an ideal place to live. The
construction of factories and the market demand for the fish that
they generated made feasible the permanent settlement of fishery-
dependent populations in the most arid and least inhabited areas of
Tenerife, Gran Canaria, and La Gomera. Earlier, the absence of dense
agriculture-dependent communities and the consequent impossibility of commerce had prevented settlement in these areas. An additional obstacle to further settlement had been the absence of communication and transport facilities, but with the construction of tourist
resorts, first in the south of Gran Canaria and later in the south of
Tenerife, better infrastructure was built. The weather, the large tracts

of available land, the improvements in communications and the availability of an adaptable workforce configured a potentially ideal destination for tourism development. Another factor contributing to the increase in tourist arrivals in the 1990s was the peaceful political climate of the islands in comparison with the instability of other areas. Thus, the Canary *calmas* initially encouraged the settlement of fishing companies, but later attracted the tourist industry with conditions that were even more favourable for its development.

Table 3.2. Influx of foreign tourists by island 1995-1999

	1995	1996	1997	1998	1999	2000	2001
CANARY ISLANDS	7,971,928	8,007,118	8,433,873	9,349,152	9,855,255	9,975,977	10,137,202
Lanzarote	1,348,700	1,381,195	1,466,570	1,662,427	1,719,949	1,750,507	1,791,722
Fuerteventura	912,087	911,201	958,975	1,131,983	1,272,648	1,305,874	1,341,319
Gran Canaria	2,592,007	2,602,220	2,733,978	2,987,098	3,136,262	3,109,066	3,058,759
Tenerife	3,012,568	2,993,084	3,157,343	3,440,551	3,591,020	3,675,206	3,811,990
La Gomera	-	-	-	-	-	-	-
La Palma	106,566	119,418	117,007	127,093	135,376	135,324	133,412
El Hierro	-	-	-	-	-	-	-

Source: Aeropuertos Españoles y Navegación Aérea (AENA).
Source: Instituto Canario de Estadística (ISTAC)

The expansion of tourism from the 1960s onwards has been almost continuous, with occasional crises related to energy or economic issues. From 1995 to 2001 the total number of tourists increased by more than two million (see Table 3.2). The official data describe a situation where the tourist sector in the islands plays the central role in the economy. As this expansion has taken place first and foremost in the littoral zone, the fishery-dependent populations and the activities that take place in these coastal areas have received the lion's share of the impact. Fishing and lately aquaculture are two of the activities that have experienced a continuous process of adaptation, due to the expansion of service industries.

Littoral communities suffered from many impacts of the tourist expansion. At the core of these impacts were the displacement of fishing families from the shore, the construction of tourist infrastructure, the impossibility of using many of the traditional beaches for fishing or even for preparing nets, the transfer of the workforce to new activities, and the destruction of fishing grounds near the shore due to the building of tourist resorts (Santana 1997:104-114). Normally, the possibilities of local people for directing patterns of transformation are rather limited, but they always devise strategies to cope with new circumstances and new policies and political actors. Fishing families have been involved in tourist activities in the Canary Islands for many years. However, the linkages with aquaculture have been sparse and difficult. In the following sections, we shall analyse the different obstacles to the development of aquaculture or service-related activities for fishing families.

Aquaculture in the Canary Islands

The first modern aquaculture experiment in the islands was promoted by ICONA, the Spanish Institute for Nature Conservation in the 1960s, with a trout farm in La Orotava (Tenerife) that is still in operation. A conference on aquaculture (CONCUMAR) in Lanzarote in 1980 generated the next stimulus to this activity, leading to the first experiments in marine aquaculture at sea and on land, and to government-supported research programs in the universities and research institutes of the archipelago (Macías *et al.* 1999a). The introduction of the first industries took place between 1986 and 1989, with six companies and investment plans of more than 2,000 million pesetas, distributed across 12 project installations. Only three of these survived, however, and they underwent many changes from the original forecasts (Macías *et al.* 1999a:5).

The aquaculture sector in the islands has expanded recently. Expansion in the industry began in 1998, when there were only four companies in operation. Now there are fourteen companies. The largest company, Alevines y Doradas S.A. (ADSA), is a member of a national level group, and the rest are small companies, some of them family-type operations. All the new projects are for in-sea installations with cages.

The largest units, with more potential productive capacity and linked employment, are in Gran Canaria. However, in Tenerife the total number of units is greater, and the expansion of the activity has been especially important there recently. There are presently around fifteen new projects (2002) awaiting government authorisation, and eleven of these are located in the same municipality of Tenerife, Adeje. Near this area there are already six production facilities, specifically in the Los Cristianos area.

Until recently, the volume of the sector in the islands made a hatchery in the archipelago non-viable, but with the recent expansion Tinamenor, one of the leaders in this business in Spain, is planning to build one in Gran Canaria. There are two main reasons for the expansion of aquaculture units in the islands, water temperature and European Union subsidies. The average year-round water temperature in the archipelago is higher than the temperatures in the Mediterranean or other Atlantic areas, and this can improve fish growth, reducing the period required until commercial size is reached and so reducing feeding costs. This advantage should be invalidated by the transportation costs to European markets, but the European Union has subsidised a part of those expenses through the POSEICAN program, a measure that has been crucial for current expansion.

Aquaculture has expanded rapidly in a context where the artisanal fisheries are declining, yet fishermen have not been involved in this development. In some cases the impulse behind this activity has been publicised as an alternative to fishing, but at present no capital and almost none of the workforce have been transferred from littoral fisheries to aquaculture. One way to illustrate the differences between these activities is to define the entrance barriers in aquaculture and artisanal fishing. This may help to explain why fishermen have not become involved in aquaculture but have, in some significant cases, made incursions into service-related activities.

The Entrance Barriers in Artisanal Fisheries

The first barrier is the required membership of a fishing family. In many places this fact is of crucial relevance for the social reproduction of this activity. Usually, apprenticeship of the necessary abilities and knowledge takes many years, and it is essential to work in the father's (or near relative's) boat. Recruitment of fishing crews always begins with sons or very close relatives, and only exceptionally are non-family members accepted. Formal education procedures have a limited impact; very few people engage in them, and many skills need to be learned by direct experience in a fishing boat. This learning process clashes with the workforce demands of the service industries, construction, and tourist sectors that are particularly attractive to young people, due to the advantages of fixed working hours and a salary. Also, the social prestige associated with being a good fisherman has changed. Working at sea is now frequently negatively valued due, for instance, to poor working conditions on board.

Access to boats and fishing equipment is also much easier for a fishing family member. Inheritance, which frequently occurs prior to the father's death, constitutes the easiest way to acquire this equipment. Even the cost of the boat when setting up a new productive unit may not represent an insurmountable barrier. The small boats still used in many areas of the islands, 5-9 meters in length, are relatively inexpensive, and in some communities there are even fishermen with special skills as carpenters who are able to build these boats. The second-hand market can also supply boats, even among different islands. The *cofradías* (local fishermen organizations) frequently act as a communication mechanism for the dissemination of boat offers and demands. The relevant obstacle may be the ship's entry into the fishing list, obligatory for professional fishing.[3] The growth limits to the fishing fleet in Spain, due to the European Union Multiannual Guidance Programs (MAGP), make the addition of new boats to this list difficult, and construction of new ships or their elongation is allowed only when submitting equivalent tonnage. This creates a 'papers' market, where boats can be bought only 'for their papers' with no interest by the fishermen in the boat itself. This constitutes a barrier for the expansion of the littoral fisheries in those places where young people wish to continue with the activity. However, perhaps the most relevant impact of these conditions is the limitation on the renovation and elongation of existing fishing boats. Where the presence of fishing harbours and expanding markets favour the activity, the need for better working facilities and security on board push for the ship's renovation or elongation. For years, modifications already carried out on ships were not legalised or documented, as this was perceived as superfluous, and a large percentage of the fleet now has problems related to the fact that the actual ships and their description on the documentation differ in many aspects.

Another obstacle is that of obtaining the necessary qualifications as skipper or sailor. The recent reform of the curriculum has increased the difficulties of obtaining those qualifications, as the course hours needed are too many. Previously, the *cofradías* could organise courses that in a few weeks and with limited difficulties could provide professional fishermen with these qualifications, but nowadays the courses to qualify as local fishing skipper (*patrón local de pesca*) require 250 course hours. This exceeds the capacities of *cofradías* and, frequently, the time availability of working fishermen.

Working without the necessary qualifications or registration in the social security system is usual in some harbours, but to maintain the boat registration in the register list of professional fishing boats, at least the skipper must be enrolled. In some areas, when the skipper is of retirement age, he must continue to work for several years while one of his sons obtains the qualifications as *patrón local de pesca*.

The Entrance Barriers in Aquaculture

Perhaps the most relevant barrier is the availability of financial capital. The amount required simply for the physical infrastructure and installation of a small unit (four cages with a diameter of 19 meters) can reach 270,000 euros, and this is only a small fraction of the total investment. The costs of setting up the company, studying the location, and obtaining the necessary permission (which includes a deposit) may also be considerable. But the main expenses involve buying young fish and feeding them until they reach commercial size. This may even triple the investment for physical infrastructure before profitability is reached, and payment to the workforce is another important outlay.

EU subsidies have been crucial for the development of aquaculture in the archipelago. Many of the pioneer projects were designed with these European financing supports in mind, but the delays in receiving the subsidies and the fact that these supports only covered a part – albeit a substantial part – of infrastructure costs and not operation expenses, led to the demise of several initiatives which had not taken into adequate account the relevance of these operational costs. As mentioned above, these costs can easily triple the infrastructure expenses and saving money in this area, especially in fry, feeding and workforce, may be difficult. Thus, subsidies cannot be seen as a crucial contribution to the viability of the aquaculture enterprise, but should be considered a financial support that may lead sooner to profitability. Also, the greatest expenses must be paid out before arrival of the supports. It can be fifteen months from the anchor of the cages to the first fish harvest, and investment during this period is continuous. Early income must also be reinvested in buying more fry, and in feeding other fish that are nearly commercial size and so cost more to feed. Three years after the initial installation, income may finally exceed payments, but the invested capital may by then be higher than a million euros.

Permission for the installation of aquaculture cages in the littoral zone of the islands is not easy to obtain. The process of finding an adequate location near a harbour to facilitate the daily feeding of the fish, the availability of maintenance labour, and the subsequent elaboration of a written project to be submitted to national and regional government authorities, are costly and time consuming. The delay in obtaining the necessary permissions may be lengthy, especially when there is local opposition to the installations.

Local fishermen may oppose the projects, but those most reluctant to endorse aquaculture may be tourism or building promoters. The visual and ecological impacts of aquaculture pens are the arguments most commonly used. The most vigorous opposition appears when many aquaculture facilities are concentrated in a limited zone, as in the Los Cristianos area (Pascual *et al.* 2001:203-220). However, in different contexts, low-profile enterprises may get the support of *cofradías*, fishing-related populations, and even the public, as in Tazacorte. The development of an *escuela taller* (a two-year vocational training program) with local young people, including the sons and daughters of fishermen, and the promise of being involved as workforce or even capital owners in future related companies have currently diminished prejudices against the activity in this area.

Besides capital availability, the biological, technological, and economic knowledge needed to manage aquaculture exploitation may constitute the second most relevant entrance barrier. The academic qualifications of fishing-related populations are very low, and a large percentage of littoral fishermen are almost illiterate. Yet literacy is now a prerequisite for the successful management of investments and expenses that are essential for profitability. Commercial experience and knowledge of distant markets are also essential. Basic business skills remain unattainable for many littoral fishermen. Information about the industry and the available institutional subsidies and support does not flow homogeneously, and frequently the fishermen's knowledge about these aspects is non-existent.

The Potential Advantages to Fishermen of Adopting Aquaculture

Daily work in aquaculture enterprises may be compatible with some fishing strategies, and incompatible with others. For instance, the use of passive techniques like the fish trap or gill net, or even fishing with line and bait may be carried out in one's spare time. Frequently, fishing activities take place in the morning, and the opportunities to tend cages when sailing to fishing beds or even when coming back from them is evident. Also, in the afternoon, time free from fishing responsibilities allows for concentration on aquaculture activities. These could be integrated with the daily work process and seasonal cycles, in an attempt to take advantage of the household workforce (Bailey *et al.* 1996:11). Daily work hours may be higher, but the larger productive units with several members and abundant workforce can probably assume this increase. Above all, if the concession is located near a harbour, transportation costs may be low, and compatibility with other activities in the sea higher. However, at present tending an aquaculture facility with a boat registered on the third list (professional fishing) is not allowed, although the surveillance may not be exhaustive. The qualification as skipper (*patrón local de pesca*) allows working in boats (fourth list, aquaculture boats) of less than twelve meters in length, and many of the skills related to navigation, fish manipulation, work with nets, et cetera, may be useful in an aquaculture facility, as can be the infrastructure in the harbours already controlled by fishing units. However, regardless of potential advantages such as time availability or skipper qualifications, fishermen still lack some skills and facilities necessary for developing aquaculture enterprises; they may have no knowledge of fish biology, aquaculture techniques or marketing, for instance.

Marketing strategies in the archipelago littoral fisheries are varied. For a long time women from fishing families sold fish in the city or in villages nearby. However, as demand increased, in many areas marketing became the domain of co-operatives, *cofradías*, middlemen, or even restaurants that acquire the catch of several boats. In some communities, fishermens' wives, sisters, or daughters still sell fish, yet their marketing strategies are ill adapted to the large volume of fish produced by the aquaculture cages. The island market or even the archipelago market cannot cope with the production of the aquaculture enterprises already installed in the Canary Islands, and the selling price for the main farmed species, 'dorada' and 'lubina', have decreased steadily in recent years. Restaurants, hypermarkets, and supermarket chains continuously buy fish from aquaculture producers, as they provide an almost stable year-round supply with prices that compete favourably with the best quality fresh demersal species. Also, aquaculture production is programmed to supply the commercial size fish (350-450 gr.) that is best adapted to demand from restaurants or hypermarkets. The greater part of Canarian aquaculture production is exported to the mainland.

Only a small group of the bigger *cofradías* or cooperatives in charge of fish marketing could perhaps in the future absorb the high fish volumes produced by these enterprises (Pascual 1999). For these organisations, which already sell many tons of fish and maintain commercial relations with different markets in the archipelago or on the mainland, the additional fish input, if well planned, may offer increasing stability.

This could probably augment the capacity to cope with drops in capture fisheries or with the surges in demand that fisheries cannot meet. Some of the inputs of aquaculture in the islands must be imported, such as the fry, the feed, and almost all of the equipment. Due to the specific fiscal conditions of the islands and their complexity, the collaboration of the *cofradías* or co-operatives could be extremely useful. Currently, we estimate that only with the support of these institutions and their marketing abilities would it be possible for aquaculture enterprises involving littoral fishermen to succeed. Also, in many harbours, the *cofradías* or fishermen co-operatives manage infrastructure and equipment that are potentially useful for the aquaculture activities of their members. The value of warehouses, cranes, forklift trucks, shipyards, ice factories, cold stores, cold trucks, hardware stores, et cetera, for these enterprises may be invaluable. But only a very small group of the biggest *cofradías* manage marketing, have these facilities, and could therefore help aquaculture initiatives.

Aquaculture and Investment Alternatives

We have already commented on the development of tourism in the coastal areas of the archipelago. Fishing communities have been extensively exposed to alternative economic activities associated with tourism, and have consequently modified their household economic strategies. The combination of different complementary activities has constituted a way of life that has attempted to maximise the complete use of the workforce and optimise economic opportunities. The actual situation and the investment options opened up to fishing-related households have changed in the last few decades.

However, there are some relevant limitations to the option of intensifying fishing activity. First of all, the availability of young people prepared to go fishing is limited. The larger boats, with a crew of more than four people, are frequently obliged to contract sailors from the mainland or even from Africa. In Las Palmas de Gran Canaria, the main harbour for the fleet that exploited the Saharan banks, almost half of the resident population involved in fishing was born outside the archipelago. This fact, related to the largest harbour of the Archipelago and the main base of the industrial fleet, illustrates the workforce deficit in this sector, the need to import workers, and also the general reduction of employed fishermen in this area. For instance, between 1991 and 1996 there was a 52.6 percentage reduction in the number of active fishermen born on the island of Gran Canaria. Their percentage in the total active fishing population has also dropped (see Fig. 3.1).

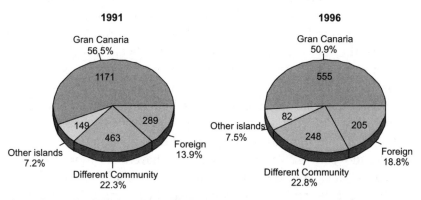

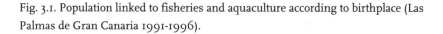
Source: Census 1991 and Population Survey 1996, data extraction by ISTAC to our request.

Fig. 3.1. Population linked to fisheries and aquaculture according to birthplace (Las Palmas de Gran Canaria 1991-1996).

In littoral fisheries the situation is similar. The reduction of the active fishing population in the last five years alone has been substantial, and in the youngest cohorts this reduction is even more dramatic. Workforce participation in the whole Canary Islands fisheries sector fell by more than 35 per cent from 1991 to 1996.

The options for intensifying littoral fishing are also limited by the difficulties in improving boats. The multi-annual guidance programs of the EU prevent investment in larger and more efficient boats, and the impossibility of fishing on the Saharan banks makes investment in larger boats (17-25 meters length) to fish tuna less profitable. In some areas, such as the north of Tenerife, the absence of fishing harbours has also prevented reinvestment, as boats near the settlements can only be used safely in the summer, when the sea is usually calm. The rest of the year the bad weather, with frequent large waves near the shore ('mar de fondo'), makes launching and beaching even the smaller boats a difficult and risky task. The larger ones must stay on land or in a harbour on the other side of the island for many months. Consequently, in those areas, reinvestment in more efficient boats is usually not a good option, as this means relocating or daily trips of many kilometres early in the morning.

Finally, the larger boats are particularly appropriate for pelagic fishing, especially tuna and sardines, but not for fishing demersal species. Smaller boats can manoeuvre more easily closer to shore or in shallow waters, and are less costly to buy and especially to operate. Their engines are less powerful, cheaper, and consume less fuel. The smaller boats can also go fishing with only one man, but the larger ones need at least two or three people. In some communities with a fishing harbour, like La Restinga in El Hierro, the initial tendency to increase the size and fishing capacity of the boats has changed for those reasons, and presently some of the larger boats are being sold. Tuna fishing is usually the main reason for increasing the size and capacity of the boats, because when a school of tuna fills a hold in an hour or less, incomes are accordingly high. But the tuna season is not regular, and there are often years when it is non-existent. In the last decade, bad years in many harbours have been more frequent than good ones, and the profitability of investment in larger boats has been greatly reduced. In some areas, however, reinvestment in larger boats has occurred, with the focus on fishing tuna and other coastal pelagic species. The European Union subsidies are the main reason for this improvement, but fishing strategies have not always changed according to the capacities of these new boats, which are frequently under-used. Investment in technical equipment is usually relevant, but limited in scope. Some technology is really useful (GPS, echo-sounders, radios), especially in boats with a bridge, but investment is always limited, especially in the smaller boats, and the possibility of upgrading the engine is always limited by the EU multi-annual fleet plans.

Investment of the economic surplus of the households is linked, in some areas, to alternative economic sectors. The impact of tourism development is also evident here. Two options have been particularly relevant: the investment in fresh fish restaurants and in apartments frequently built by the fishermen themselves. The littoral communities have received visitors for years, and not everywhere has this development process been fast and externally controlled. In many areas of the south west of Gran Canaria, Lanzarote, Fuerteventura, and Tenerife and even in some areas in the north, this has been the tendency, but the development of mass tourism is not evenly spread across the archipelago. In some coastal areas, such as on the island El Hierro, where there are no high volume tourist resorts and the number of beds is still low, the impact of mass tourism is negligible. In those areas, domestic tourism may be relevant, as Canary people like to spend their summer holidays in coastal zones of the island they live on or of the other islands. There is also a growing number of people from the mainland, as well as foreigners, who visit those areas not controlled by mass tourism strategies.

For local inhabitants, these new visitors progressively constitute a new economic alternative, and a source of social and cultural change. The possibility of offering accommodation in small apartments for those visitors has been a good option for the investment of fishing surplus. This investment has two major benefits. First of all, the long-term yield of the investment is good, as the appreciation of property is continuous in the islands due to economic growth, and near the shore this process is even more evident. Also, there are good short-term yields due to the rents obtained especially where it is possible to combine local domestic visitors in the summer and national or foreign tourism the rest of the year. The work involved in maintaining this business is minimal, as it is only usually necessary to clean the apartments quickly between different guests, a task that can be carried out by the women of the family, with the men carrying out the basic maintenance chores. It is not usual to offer the daily cleaning services typical of apartment complexes. Especially for domestic tourism, the stay period is longer than is usual in mass tourism, and may extend to fifteen days, a month, or even more, and frequently the same families repeat year after year in the same place, period, and even apartment.

The relevance of this domestic tourism is not covered adequately in many analyses or typologies of tourism, but in some of the coastal areas it is a crucial phenomenon that dominates the tourist economy, such as in Agaete (Gran Canaria), El Pris (Tenerife), or Las Playitas (Fuerteventura) (Pascual et al. 2001). An area free of mass-market tourism that possesses the charm of a supposedly traditional fishing community, where infrastructure is minimal, prices are low, and foreign people are rare, may attract domestic tourists and others seek-

José J. Pascual

ing an alternative experience. The development style in these areas adopts a slow or transitory pace that gives the local people the opportunity to undertake tourist development on their own, at least partially. The initial phases of the development of tourism in fishing communities like Caleta del Sebo (La Graciosa), Arguineguín (Gran Canaria), Valle Gran Rey (La Gomera), Agaete (Gran Canaria), Playa Santiago (La Gomera), and El Pris (Tenerife) have made it possible for local people to undertake business initiatives of various types (Pascual *et al.* 2001).

For example, in La Restinga, a small fishing community in southwest El Hierro with one attractive marine reserve where scuba-diving activities have grown steadily, the vast majority of the apartments are managed by people born on the island. We have estimated that there are more than two hundred beds on offer to domestic or foreign tourists: 31.8 percent of the apartments are the property of people who live in different villages of the island, 27.3 percent belong to permanent residents of this village, 22.7 percent belong to people born in El Hierro but who now reside on other islands, and only 18.2 percentage of the property belongs to foreigners (op. cit., data 2001). A consequence of the creation of marine reserves is the increased flow of tourists attracted by the natural values of the area assured by the official title of Marine Reserve. The activities of these tourists can have a significant impact on the protected area, but these tourists may also provide an economic alternative for productive units whose activities had been restricted to fishing. However, in many cases, and in the marine reserves of Canary Islands in particular, it seems that frequently some of the advantages of these new economic opportunities are not taken up by the locals but by the non-fishing population, or even by foreigners, who have an increasingly active role in such areas as diving clubs, restaurants, hotels, and boats for excursions.

In Valle Gran Rey (La Gomera), the process combining activities is even more evident. In the 1970s this was a community of fishing and agriculture activities, but tourism has progressively transformed economic strategies. First, the area was a popular destination for backpack tourism, but in the 1990s this was displaced by tour operators and apartment complexes. In the initial phases, fishing families tried to obtain complementary incomes by renting houses and apartments. In 1991 in Vueltas, the fishing neighbourhood of Valle Gran Rey, with a total population of 350, local residents offered 300 beds (MacLeod 1999:447-8). This process resulted in a drop of more than

50 percent in the productive units linked to professional fishing, and led to a rise in part-time and non-legal fishing activities by some of the people who left the activity professionally, but continue to fish and sell their catches through different channels. In Gran Tarajal (Fuerteventura), there have been similar processes, as can be seen in Table 3.3.

Table 3.3. Links of fishing-related households to tourist activities, Gran Tarajal (Fuerteventura), summer 2000

	[A]	[B]	%	[C]	%
Gran Tarajal	23	6	26	5	21.7
Las Playitas	8	4	50	4	50
Giniginamar	4	0	0	1	25
Tarajalejo	5	0	0	0	0
Pozo Negro	7	0	0	1	14.3
La Lajita	20	7	35	6	30
Ajuy	12	1	8.3	2	16.6
Total	79	18	22.78	19	24.05

A   Active fishermen; data from the Cofradía
B   Fishermen with apartment property in the household (included retired, not taken into account in A)
C   Other links of husband or wife to service activities, excluding apartment properties
Source : Fieldwork and data from the Cofradía, Pascual et al. 2001

The data show that there are differences in the combination of activities, but in almost all the settlements, taking only the fisherman and his partner into account, even without considering the activities of their family, the links to service activities are a relevant element in the economic strategies of the households. Investment in apartments and the strategies of economic diversification are clearly relevant in these areas. However, the differences between settlements are also evident. In those communities where ownership of land was diversified, as in Las Playitas or in La Lajita, access to apartment property has been possible, but in those areas such as Tarajalejo where the ownership of land was concentrated, and development centrally managed, it has been impossible. For households, the main advantages of constructing apartments are the permanence of the investment, low risks, high profitability, minimal maintenance, and independence from fishing fluctuations. It is, however, a capital-intensive strategy that is usually only feasible where the price of land is still low due to the sluggish pace of tourism development.

Other alternatives are not so capital intensive, at least in some phases, but are much more dependent on the work of the household. Fresh fish restaurants have, in some areas, been another investment alternative, one dependent on the fish supply from the boats linked to the household, at least in the initial phases of building up the business. The low captures of demersal species, greatly appreciated as quality fish, and the uneven commercial distribution of these species have elevated their prestige as a restaurant dish, a situation reinforced by concerns about the consumption of beef. In this context, these restaurants facilitate the consumption of almost the last supply of protein from the wild, guaranteeing freshness and solving the problems related to the preparation of a natural food not industrially processed. The ability to diversify by opening a fresh fish restaurant depends on certain conditions. First, and most important, is the possibility of renting or using premises in which to set up the restaurant. In some cases fishing families may start with a bar on the ground floor of their homes, or even with a grocery store that also serves alcoholic drinks. In some cases this activity can be transformed into a restaurant, even to the extent of using the housing area. These options in areas with developed tourism are less frequent, as the fishing-related populations may have already been displaced far from the shore. Second, the labour of family members must be abundantly available, as the work includes long hours organising the supplies, preparing and cooking the fish, serving the customers, attending to book-keeping, and so on. The activity cycles are also uneven, as the weekends and holiday seasons demand the participation of additional workers, and the extended family constitutes an invaluable resource for this. Third, the abilities of fishing populations to adequately prepare and cook the fish, according to species and size, cannot be underestimated. Typically, the women take on this role, although in Agaete several fishermen's sons also work as cooks. The Casa del Mar restaurant of Tazacorte (La Palma), for instance, has three women from fishing families as their cooks (summer 2000). The men usually prepare and clean the fish first, in some cases just on the beach. Fourth, the owners' activities as fishermen act as a guarantee of freshness, and their social bonds in the sector facilitate the fish supply from local communities or even surrounding areas when the catches cannot meet demand.

Fresh fish restaurants may increase the value of a scarce resource: the demersal species. Customers visit the restaurant to consume this product, but once in the restaurant will be tempted to consume many other goods. Even species that usually cannot be sold easily, as they are lesser known, or considered difficult to prepare and cook, will be served without a hitch. This diversification of economic activity offers an alternative investment strategy and an option for under-utilised household labour. For the first phase of the strategy, it is essential to continue the fishing activity, but the vast amount of work needed to run these family businesses means that it frequently becomes impossible to carry out both activities. Usually, one will be preferred, but which one may depend on the fishing or tourist situations.

Conclusions

Tourist development in the Canary Islands has progressively changed the way of life and the economic strategies of the littoral populations, particularly modifying the activities that fishing families traditionally combined in their households. The diversity of the interrelated economic and socio-cultural impacts of tourism is too complex to be fully explained here (Santana 1997). But we must remember that host communities are not passively modified by the forces of tourism and markets (Boissevain 1996:21), as local entrepreneurs can frequently select and develop successful strategies to cope with the new situations and economic opportunities, and people may use combinations of new activities to better their working conditions or standards of living. Changes in communities have obviously arisen not only from the impact of tourism, but also from transformations in many other aspects of society and culture. Particularly in those places where the pace of tourist development has been slow, and the impact of tourism neither displaced fishing-related populations from the shore nor led to a virtual monopoly of land ownership, the opportunities to invest in apartments or service-related businesses are still open to fishing families, and as we have shown, they frequently take advantage of those possibilities. Perhaps the main advantage of strategies that divert the investment of fishing surpluses into apartments, and especially restaurants, is the investment security and the distribution of risk across different sectors. People usually adopt risk-reduction technologies (Bailey *et al.* 1996:11) and frequently select investments in order to minimise and diversify risks, taking into consideration their available knowledge. The investment in service-related activities and infrastructure such as apartments, taking into account the almost continuous tourist expansion in the archipelago in the last few decades, may be a safe and attainable investment. Knowledge of this business – on a small scale – has slowly accumulated in many of the littoral populations through years of experience and contact with visitors.

Aquaculture may not appear so attractive to littoral fishing-related populations. Knowledge and information about this activity is scanty and partial in these communities, and it may seem to them that there is a monopoly in the aquaculture sector, involving biologists and investors external to fishing. The necessary knowledge of aspects such as the biology and physiology of cultivated fish are also beyond their qualifications (Bailey *et al.* 1996:6). In aquaculture the risks of investment are higher, and the permanence of the investment is much less than in apartments, for instance. Also, the risks are not so diversified, as a severe storm may adversely affect both fishing and aquaculture activities. Finally, the necessary investment for the installation of an aquaculture facility is much higher than the fishing surpluses available in most fishing-related households, requiring co-operatives or collective enterprises of some sort, and increasing costs like decision-making. This may explain why in the Canary Islands to date the participation of littoral fishing-related populations in aquaculture enterprises has been non-existent.[4]

It is especially meaningful to consider how the patterns of change in littoral communities in the Canary Islands have been linked to processes that go beyond the limits of local populations. The markets for canned tuna in mainland European countries, and Italy in particular, started the expansion of fishing in the south west of the islands. Later, with the growth of the tourism industry, millions of tourists came to the islands from northern European countries, the majority to the same south west areas because of their climate conditions. Finally, due in part to EU funds, aquaculture was also introduced in the south western parts of the main islands. Local populations have never been passive towards these globalisation processes (Pascual 2003). They continue to take opportunities, question aquaculture, develop alternative strategies, and combine economic activities in order to optimize individual knowledge and skills, household labour, and disposable financial capital.

Notes

1. This paper partly reflects the findings of the research project '*Modelo de desarrollo integral de poblaciones litorales: pesca artesanal, turismo y acuicultura*', directed by Jose Pascual and Agustín Santana, and financed by the Conse-

jería de Agricultura y Pesca of the Canary Islands Autonomous Goverment. The research team was composed of Jose Antonio Batista, Carmelo Dorta, Ramón Hernández, Álvaro Díaz, Beatriz Martín y Javier Macías. The paper also partly reflects the findings of the project 'Marine reserves and littoral fishing populations: impacts and strategies for sustainable development', REN 2001-3350/MAR, funded by the Ministry of Science and Technology of Spain and FEDER.

2. Decreto 155/2001 de 23 de Julio de 2001, B.O.C. 6 de Agosto de 2001 about the first sale of fish products; Orden de 1 de Julio de 2002, B.O.C. 5 de Julio de 2002, about allowed harbours for landing of fish products in the Canary Islands.

3. The boats or ships in Spain in order to be allowed to navigate need to be included in a register that is divided into several lists related to the activity developed by the boat. For instance, boats linked to professional fishing are included in the third lists and the boats that develop aquaculture activities must be included in the fourth list (Real Decreto 1027/1989, de 28 de julio, sobre abanderamiento, matriculación de buques y Registro maritimo).

4. Many of these arguments are not applicable, however, to capital and enterprises linked to fishing on the Saharan banks. The compensation given to ship-owners due to the end of the agreement with Morocco may result in investment in aquaculture. For instance, Agramar, one of the main canning companies in the islands, which had closed due to the end of the agreement, is one of the main shareholders in a large facility for fattening up tuna that was built in August 2001 in Lanzarote.

References

Aguilera, F., A. Brito, C. Castilla, A. Díaz, J.M. Fernández-Palacios, A. Rodríguez, F. Sabaté, and J. Sánchez
1994 *Canarias. Economía, Ecología y Medio Ambiente*. La Laguna: Francisco Lemus Editor.

Bacallado, J.J., T. Cruz, A. Brito, J. Barquín, and M. Carrillo
1989 *Reservas Marinas de Canarias*. Santa Cruz de Tenerife: Consejería de Agricultura y Pesca, Departamento de Biología Animal (ULL).

Bailey, C., S. Jentoft, and P. Sinclair
1996 Social Science Contributions to Aquacultural Development. In: C. Bailey, S. Jentoft, and P. Sinclair (Eds.), *Aquacultural Development: Social Dimensions of an Emerging Industry*. Boulder, Colorado: Westview Press. Pp. 3-20.

Boissevain, J.
1996 Introduction. In: J. Boissevain (Ed.), *Coping with Tourists: European Reactions to Mass Tourism*. Oxford: Berghahn Books. Pp. 1-26.

Cabrera Armas, L.G. and A. Díaz de la Paz
1991 La economía contemporánea. I. El proceso de consolidación capitalista y II. Las dificultades de la modernización económica. In: F. Morales Padrón, Francisco (Ed.), *Historia de Canarias*. Las Palmas de Gran Canaria: Editorial Prensa Canaria.

1992   Díaz de la Paz, A.
1993   Ecología y pesca en Canarias: una aproximación histórica a la relación hombre-recurso. *Ayer* 11:207-231.

García Cabrera, C.
1970   *La pesca en Canarias y Banco Pesquero Canario Sahariano.* Tenerife: Consejo Economico Sindical Interprovincial de Canarias.

Macías González, J., J. Pascual Fernández, and C. Dorta Morales
1999a   *Estudio sobre las potencialidades para el desarrollo de la acuicultura en los núcleos pesqueros tradicionales.* Las Palmas de Gran Canaria: Canaest Consultores-Consejería de Agricultura, Pesca y Alimentación (unpublished).

Macías González, J., J. Pascual Fernández, I. Lozano Soldevilla, J. González Pérez, J. Santana Morales, A. Díaz de la Paz, and A. Portillo Hanefeld
1999b   *Plan de desarrollo pesquero de Canarias. 1994-2004. Situación y perspectivas.* Las Palmas de Gran Canaria: Canaest Consultores-Consejería de Agricultura, Pesca y Alimentación (unpublished).

Macías González, J., J. Pascual Fernández, A. Díaz de la Paz, and C. Dorta Morales
2000   *Plan de Desarrollo Pesquero de Canarias 2000-2006: Segunda fase: programas operativos y actuaciones.* Las Palmas de Gran Canaria: Canaest Consultores-Consejería de Agricultura, Pesca y Alimentación (unpublished).

MacLeod, D.V.L.
1999   Tourism and the Globalization of a Canary Island. *Journal of the Royal Anthropological Institute* 5(3):443-456.

Pascual Fernández, J.
1991   *Entre el mar y la tierra, los pescadores artesanales canarios.* Santa Cruz de Tenerife: Ministerio de Cultura, Editorial Interinsular Canaria.
1999   Participative Management of Artisanal Fisheries in the Canary Islands. In: D. Symes (Ed.), *Southern Waters: Issues of management and practice.* London: Blackwell's Science, Fishing New Books. Pp. 66-77.

Pascual Fernández, J., A. Santana Talavera, J.A. Batista Medina, C. Dorta Morales, R. Hernández Armas, A. Díaz de la Paz, B. Martín de la Rosa, and J. Macías González
2001   *Pescatur: un modelo de desarrollo integral de poblaciones litorales.* La Laguna: Instituto Universitario de Ciencias Políticas y Sociales, Viceconsejería de Pesca del Gobierno de Canarias (unpublished).

Pascual Fernández, J.
2003   La actividad pesquera en Canarias en el contexto de la globalización. In: C. Bueno and E. Aguilar (Eds.), *Las expresiones locales de la globalización: México y España.* Mexico: Ciesas, Universidad Iberoamericana and Porrúa. Pp. 265-292.

Santana Talavera, A.
1997   *Antropología y turismo: ¿nuevas hordas, viejas culturas?* Barcelona: Ariel.

Webb, B.P. and S. Berthelot
1836   *Histoire naturelle des Iles Canaries.* Paris: Béthune (1836-1850).

4

Between the Sea and the Land: Exploring the Social Organisation of Tourism Development in a Gran Canaria Fishing Village

Raoul V. Bianchi and Agustín Santana Talavera

Introduction

This chapter explores social and spatial transformations in the fishing village of Playa de Mogán on the island of Gran Canaria (Canary Islands) influenced by the development of tourism over the last 40 years. It gives a brief account of the principal changes that have accompanied the shift from fishing and agriculture to a predominantly service-based economy centred around tourism. The issues raised in this chapter draw upon ethnographic fieldwork carried out by both authors (independently of each other) over a period spanning nearly 15 years, commencing in 1985 in the village of Playa de Mogán and two years earlier in the adjacent fishing village of Arguineguín. The principal focus presented here concerns an analysis of the changing social alignments amongst different segments of the village population in relation to the social organisation of production and consumption brought about by the emergence of a tourism economy. Overall, the authors concur with Meethan's contention that 'tourism is part of the process of commodification (or commoditisation) and consumption inherent in capitalism' (2001:4). However in addition the authors seek to demonstrate how the spread of capitalist social relations through tourism is mediated by locally specific social conditions which have given rise to an internally differentiated mode of tourism production and consumption. Thus, the chapter draws attention to the combination of social relations and spatial forms encompassed within the mode of tourism development in this particular locality, which demonstrates both universal and unique elements of tourism as a form of capitalist commodity relations.

Tourism Development in Gran Canaria: A Brief Summary

The historical development of tourism in the Canary Islands is rooted in the expansion of trans-Atlantic trade and has always been closely linked to foreign commerce and investment in the region. Regular tourist visits grew largely as a result of British commercial involvement in the growth of new agricultural exports (bananas, tomatoes and potatoes) during the last quarter of the 19th century and the subsequent establishment of regular steam-ship links between the Canary Islands and Northern Europe. These changes marked a qualitatively different phase in the nature of capitalist development, which became concentrated on the two main islands of Gran Canaria and Tenerife. The islands' agrarian bourgeoisie formed an alliance with foreign companies which helped finance the Port of Las Palmas and operated the shipping lines which facilitated the regular export of crops at competitive prices to the world market (García Herrera 1987).

The initial phase of tourism development on Gran Canaria lasted until the outbreak of the Spanish Civil War in 1936 and was largely concentrated in a number of luxurious hotels built with the assistance of British capital. The hotels were situated in the port city of Las Palmas as well as in the foothills to the south west of the capital. Rather than beaches or local culture, it was the exotic landscapes and, in particular, the mild (winter) climate that attracted these early visitors, many of whom came to convalesce from respiratory illnesses (González Lemus 2002:12-13). After the Second World War, mass tourism development received a significant boost, as the beach of Las Canteras in Las Palmas became the destination of Scandinavian, German and Belgian tourists, leading to the construction of a strip of shoreline apartment complexes and modern hotels. However, by the early 1970s tourism in Las Palmas had been eclipsed by the mass urbanisation of the southern coastline which gave rise to the macro-resort enclaves of Maspalomas-Playa del Inglés in the municipality of San Bartolomé de Tirajana and, subsequently, a series of resort complexes at the mouth of the narrow valleys along the coastline of neighbouring Mogán (Fig. 4.1). On the whole these were constructed with little regard for the environment, notions of authenticity or local culture. These developments precipitated massive structural

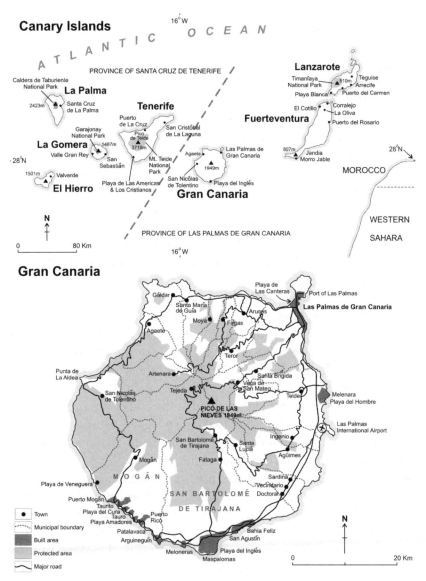

Fig. 4.1. The island of Gran Canaria with municipal boundaries and location of the village.

and spatial changes in the island's political economy. These changes were mirrored on the neighbouring islands of Tenerife, and later, Lanzarote and Fuerteventura. The service sector rapidly became the principal engine of economic development, as investors abandoned the agricultural sector and sought short-term profits in a speculative real estate-driven model of tourism development (Nadal Perdomo and Guitián Ayneto 1983).

Playa de Mogán: Between the Sea and the Land

Occupying much of Gran Canaria's arid and mountainous leeward face, the municipality of Mogán[1] covers an area of 172.43 square kilometres and comprises 11 per cent of the total surface area of the island. However, in 1999 the entire municipality was home to only 12,256 permanent inhabitants (out of a total 728,391), giving it a population density of 62.5 inhabitants per square kilometre, a figure considerably lower than the insular average of 459 (Istac 2000). Until the development of large resort complexes in Puerto Rico and Cornisa del Suroeste, the majority of the municipality's 'native' population resided in the wider and more fertile valleys of Mogán and Veneguera in the eastern half of the municipality. They have traditionally resided in the rural hamlet of Mogán, which is situated approximately 8 kilometres inland and has also been the seat of the municipal government since the 1830s, as well as the two fishing settlements of Playa de Mogán and Arguineguín.

The location of the municipality of Mogán on the arid and geographically isolated southwestern extremity of the island meant development of the area lagged behind that of the windward face of the island, which had been the focus of intense cultivation and settlement since the conquest of the island at the end of the 19th century. The development of Playa de Mogán also lagged behind that of the neighbouring municipality of San Bartolomé de Tirajana. However, during the late 18th and early part of the 19th century, a combination of forces including demographic pressures on the windward face of the island, declining agricultural productivity, and growing demands for agricultural produce forced many farmers and landless labourers to move southwards into Mogán in search of new lands to cultivate. The settlement of Mogán was also encouraged by the island council which, in an attempt to amortise public debts and modernise the agrarian economy, was keen to stimulate productive investment in the valleys of the island's southwestern face (Béthencourt Massieu and Macías Hernández 1977). As a result of these socio-demographic changes, a small but powerful local agrarian bourgeoisie began to take shape and soon monopolised much of the available land and water along the fertile valleys.

The emergence of a small cluster of rudimentary dwellings at the mouth of the valley of Mogán can be traced back to the late 1860s when migrants from the interior began to settle in this area in search of calm waters for fishing. During the latter half of the 19th century, and initially for short periods at a time (usually in summer), the area began to attract families from other parts of the island who engaged in subsistence fishing using small wooden boats and basic fishing techniques, in conjunction with the rearing of livestock and some agricultural activities. While most production was used for subsistence purposes, small surpluses were bartered in exchange for agricultural produce further inland and, later, transported by boat to a village some fifteen or so kilometres further east along the coast. From this village they were transported by road for sale in Las Palmas. In the early 20th century, the introduction of new fishing techniques and, the establishment of fish-salting warehouses (*factorías de salazón*) in which the catch was salted, preserved, and prepared for distribution by the Lloret and Llinares family, who originally from Alicante, led to rapid improvements in the productivity of fishing and the consolidation of a permanent settlement.[2] This was reflected in the dramatic expansion of the village population, which rose from 131 in 1920 to 341 in 1930, as people moved in from surrounding valleys and the rural interior in search of work. The *factorías* not only introduced new fishing techniques, as indeed did many of the new arrivals from other parts of the island, they also acted as a catalyst for the introduction of capitalist social relations into the artisanal fishing economy in Playa de Mogán by virtue of contracting fishermen to work on several boats which they owned. Nevertheless, pre-capitalist relations continued to exist in other areas of the local fishing economy where boats were owned and operated by the heads of different households and their respective kin. This did not, however, prevent artisanal fishermen from contracting extra crew members in return for a wage whenever necessary. These individuals were often referred to as 'hombres de la tierra' (men of the land) as they were usually drawn from the ranks of non-fishing families, although the boundaries between agrarian and fishing work were not clear cut, as will be illustrated below. Thus, from an early stage, peasant fishing households were integrated into an expanded network of commercial exchanges via the introduction of capitalist social relations through which the surpluses were distributed.

Although the majority of the village's inhabitants were engaged in fishing during this period, fishing was often combined with complementary wage-work, done largely by women, as agricultural labourers. They worked in fields adjacent to the village where members of the local *cacique* 'class'[3] had begun to plant crops for export (tomatoes then, later, bananas) between 1898 and 1900. These families com-

Fig. 4.2. The village of Playa de Mogán in 1994. The former residences of local cacique families can be seen in the foreground, adjacent to the shoreline. The cluster of predominantly fishermens' dwellings is also clearly visible, situated behind the tourist marina, the construction of which appropriated part of the waterfront.

prised a small but powerful local agrarian bourgeoisie which possessed the majority of the municipality's fertile land and water supplies, and whose members monopolised political power in the municipal government of Mogán, which dates from 1834-35. By the end of the 19th century, much of the land (approximately 70 hectares) in the lower part of the valley of Mogán leading towards the sea and Playa de Mogán, had become concentrated in the hands of two *cacique* families closely related through inter-marriage. The owners of these relatively large estates (although small in comparison with the *latifundia* of southern Spain) lived in larger, although not necessarily luxurious, houses situated along the valley floor and adjacent to the dense cluster of dwellings in which peasant and fishing families lived (Fig. 4.2). This pattern of settlement and urban development was to remain unchanged until the last two decades of the twentieth century and the construction of the tourist marina.

By the late 1940s, due to the tradition of partible inheritance, these two estates had been progressively broken up into a patchwork of small plots. More recently, the plots have been the source of protracted inheritance disputes, particularly where there have been potential profits to be made from speculative real-estate development

CHAPTER FOUR

linked to tourism. Whilst the cultivation of agricultural crops was situated on land owned by the local *cacique* classes, surpluses were sold directly to the British trading companies (in this case, Elder and Fyffes) who operated the boats onto which the crops were loaded. This company also financed the construction of packaging warehouses along the waterfront in Playa de Mogán, and in neighbouring valleys, which also provided a valuable source of employment for the women of the village. Playa de Mogán was linked by a rudimentary dirt track to other villages along the coast due to improvements made by the agricultural exporting firms during the 1930s, and the inauguration of a regular bus service between Las Palmas and the village of Mogán in the late 1940s. Prior to road and bus access, small wooden boats (*falúas*) provided transport for the majority of people and their products.

The improved productivity of fishing and the commercial expansion of export agriculture throughout the 1930s and into the post-war period continued to attract peasant families and labourers from other parts of the island. As a result the local population rose to 640 inhabitants in 1940, nearly double that of a decade before. Until the onset of tourism-related construction in the late 1960s dramatically transformed the structure of the local labour market, entire families, including the men, would often work as agricultural labourers during the winter months, and return to the sea in the summer for the more lucrative tuna fishing season. One of the characteristic features of the agrarian economy in the Canary Islands, and one that has enabled the social reproduction of 'artisanal' or 'craft' fishing communities, has been the proximity of such settlements to areas of export agricultural cultivation, which enabled fishing households to supplement their income through agricultural wage-work during low periods in the fishing cycle (Galván Tudela 1982:84). Such was the demand for labour in the local agricultural export economy that Santana Talavera (1990a:71) estimates as many as two hundred women were brought in to harvest and package the crops for export during the 1950s. Bountiful catches of tuna in the 1960s, in conjunction with the cultivation of new export crops such as aubergines, which had been introduced due to the declining profitability of tomatoes on world markets, enabled families to make substantial improvements to their rudimentary dwellings and increase their domestic savings. Fishing also continued to experience improvements in productivity as a result of changes in techniques and new technological inputs like engines and sonar equipment. Although the closure in 1975 of the remaining *factoría* in Playa de Mogán had a negative effect on the local fishing economy, fishing continued to provide a valuable livelihood for many, as well structure everyday social lives until the second phase of large-scale tourism construction began on the coast of Mogán in the 1980s.

Household Tourism Development in Playa de Mogán

From the creation of Mogán as a municipality in 1834-1835 until the construction of the first tourism resorts in this area in the late 1960s, established land ownership patterns structured the uneven historical development of capitalism in the village and surrounding areas. The social divisions between those who owned the land and those who worked the sea and, to some extent the land, were relatively marked, with the owners of the *factorías* occupying an intermediate social status. During the 1960s, the development of an extensive infrastructure of urban tourism enclaves along the southwest coastline of the island began to lay the foundations of the present geography of tourist production in Gran Canaria, the epicentre of which is located in the two tourism municipalities of San Bartolomé de Tirajana and Mogán. At this time Playa de Mogán was still sparsely populated and relatively inaccessible, and thus, for the moment, spared the full brunt of the tourism-related changes taking place further east. However, during the late 1960s and early 1970s, approval was given to commence construction of a number of urban resort enclaves along the coast of Mogán, of which the largest, in Puerto Rico, has around 22,000 bed spaces. These new developments began to draw villagers towards the growing number of employment opportunities in tourism and construction.[4] In addition the decline of agriculture[5] as a complementary source of income for peasant households and the increasing availability of work in construction and tourism expanded the temporary (and sometimes permanent) daily migrations of young people beyond the village. It also had the effect of enlarging the proportion of the village population subjected to capitalist wage relations. As a result of the uneven territorial expansion of tourism, which was centred principally on the large conurbations of Maspalomas-Playa del Inglés and Puerto Rico, the population of Mogán, particularly in the western reaches of the municipality, suffered a decline. While the population of Playa de Mogán remained relatively stable during the 1960s, many small hamlets disappeared altogether.[6] Increasingly, their populations moved to villages adjacent to the resorts, such as the 'sister' fishing village of Arguineguín, where new sources of employment were more easily available. As tourism construction spread further west along Mogán's coastline, population decline across the municipality as a whole began to reverse (it had fallen from 5,357 in 1960 to 4,919 in 1970), and the number of permanent inhabitants increased to 5,871 in 1975 and 6,608 in 1981 (Cabildo Insular 1986:11).

Although no new tourism-related construction took place in Playa de Mogán until the early 1980s, these changes, in particular the improvements to the coastal road, precipitated a number of important socio-economic transformations within the village itself. By the late 1960s the village began to experience a gradual increase in the number of visitors, referred to locally as '*los ipis*' (hippies) due to their distinctive appearance compared with the more conservative dress of the by now relatively familiar 'mass tourists', who had come in search of a rustic 'peasant authenticity' that could not be found in the urban tourism enclaves rapidly spreading along the coast in the adjacent valleys. The first encounters between local inhabitants and these early visitors took place in the narrow alleyways and intimate spaces of the fishing quarter, where they would drink with locals and often sleep out in the open. Rudimentary lodging facilities had existed in the past, mostly to accommodate visiting merchants and the labourers who had built the *factorías*. However, by the 1970s no hostels or guesthouses of any description existed, prompting one or two families to rent out rooms in their domestic dwellings to these northern European visitors. Despite their proclivity for naked bathing, usually in the neighbouring bay, and smoking marijuana, their relaxed attitudes and relatively small number meant that these 'hippy-tourists' were for the most part easily accepted by locals who saw them as a source of entertainment and welcomed their custom. As in Mykonos (see Stott 1996:291), this tolerance could perhaps be attributed to historic links to wider patterns of international trade and contact with a variety of associated foreign merchants. Also, as Pérez-Díaz (1998:151) reminds us, hedonism was very much part of the 'moral traditions' of the peasant classes in Spain. This is a view confirmed by the Canary Island anthropologist Pascual Fernández, who points out that fishermen in the Canary Islands have a well-earned reputation for drinking and partying (1991:223). The view amongst many of the wealthier, landowning families, particularly those resident in the village of Mogán, that fishermen and their families had a tendency to display immoral behaviour[7] underlined a marked social division which separated the inhabitants of these two villages.

In a process resembling that observed by Cornélia Zarkia (1996) on the Greek island of Skyros, inhabitants of a more marginal social status were the first to come into contact with the visitors and accommodate their needs for food, drink, and a place to stay through a variety of opportunistic entrepreneurial initiatives. Initially, the response to this low level of tourist activity was accommodated by one or two existing grocery shops which often doubled as bars. As recalled by a Danish painter who arrived in the late 1960s in search of inspiration and who has since set up a string of commercial establishments, including a restaurant and art gallery, the choice was largely restricted to rum, 'hot coca-cola' (as there were no refrigeration facilities), sardines, and bananas. However, in 1969 the first registered bar-restaurant was opened by the descendant of peasant farmers from the neighbouring valley of Veneguera who, together with his wife, had been one of the first inhabitants to convert part of their home into rooms-for-let (Bianchi 1999:165-6). By the early 1970s half-a-dozen or so similar establishments, mainly rudimentary bars with basic restaurant facilities, had opened in recently abandoned agricultural buildings or in converted grocery stores. In the late 1980s the number of household enterprises providing lodging facilities reached a peak when several small guesthouses opened in a separate neighbourhood a short distance inland from the main fishing quarter. By this time Playa de Mogán was no longer a well-kept secret, and the economic expansion of Gran Canaria's tourism economy meant that numerous foreign residents and entrepreneurs had begun to move into the village and open several bars and restaurants. A combination of increasing competition, rising property prices and a lack of space in the fishing quarter meant that without substantial savings or the ability (and willingness) to borrow significant levels of capital, it became increasingly difficult for former peasant and fishing households to open commercial tourist establishments.

The existing framework of social relations mediated the development of these early tourist enterprises. However, the 'informal' nature of these early tourist commodification processes – the conversion of existing dwellings from *use* values into *exchange* values – led to different degrees of social mobility which subsequently began to challenge the dominant patterns of ownership and power in the village. These changes not only brought about the (partial) commodification of households and other use values, but they also signalled the

CHAPTER FOUR

transformation of the social relations upon which the emergent tourism economy was to be based. In particular, in the absence of intermediaries such as tour operators at this stage, the social organisation of tourism production could not be subordinated to the monopsony[8] powers of the traditional elites. A new (entrepreneurial) class was beginning to emerge from amongst the half a dozen or so peasant households who had started letting rooms or opening small bar-restaurants specifically for tourists, thus transforming the material basis of social relations between the inhabitants of the fishing quarter and the landowning classes who, although living in close proximity, inhabited very different social worlds. Tourism thus acted as a social force for the dissolution of the semi-feudal relationships of inequality built upon the local *cacique* class's monopoly of economic, political, and social power in the locality. The reasons for this particular pattern of early socio-economic advancement perhaps give us some insight into the specific productive arrangements encompassed within tourism, given the type of social conditions prevalent in southern European societies at this time. With one or two notable exceptions, most fishing households continued to fish, although sons and daughters were now being attracted to the prospect of more stable and less arduous (but not necessarily lucrative) employment in construction and/or tourism. Indeed, according to Pascual Fernández (1991:102), fishing families were ill suited to adapt to the new economic circumstances and would continue to work at sea until things got really desperate.

Similar research in other southern European/Mediterranean societies has revealed that tourism often leads to a rapid inflation in land-property values and thus produces a speculative real-estate-driven model of development underpinned by a rentier capitalist class of former agrarian landowners (cf. Zarkia 1996; Smith 1997; Selwyn 2000). Initially, however, this cycle did not take effect in Playa de Mogán, although one or two landowning households did become involved in the running of bars and restaurants in the early to mid-1980s. There were two reasons for this. First, the local *cacique* classes were traditionally more concerned with professional employment; indeed many of the younger generations had moved to Las Palmas for this reason. Second, as the initial social exchanges took place for the most part in the fishing quarter, landowners did not have the 'relevant' means of production immediately at their disposal. They did, however, extract rent from shopkeepers, to whom they leased property in the fishing quarter, and sold defunct warehouses to some of the 'new' peasant-tourism entrepreneurs referred to above. Nevertheless, as emphasised by Smith (1997), control of land is a central component in the creation of a rentier capitalist class in any tourism economy. A combination of unfavourable economic circumstances throughout the 1970s and several high-profile construction scandals during the 1980s, including a case which involved the chief planning officer of the local council, himself a descendant of a well-known *cacique* family, delayed construction of larger-scale tourism infrastructure on the flat valley floor, land which had been sub-divided amongst the numerous heirs to the original agricultural estate. However, once the bitter internecine disputes over the inheritance and partition of the agricultural estate had been resolved in the late 1990s, earlier plans to develop the valley adjacent to the fishing quarter were revived.[9] Before that, however, plans were already afoot to develop a commercial tourism marina and fishing harbour along the seafront of the fishing quarter.

The 'Urbanisation' of the Sea and the Marina of *'Puerto Mogán'*

While the early stages of tourist visitation in Playa de Mogán had benefited an existing stratum of self-employed shopkeepers and a new 'class' of peasant entrepreneurs who opened facilities *for* tourists, the construction of a marina-fishing port on the village waterfront signalled a major transformation in the social and spatial arrangements of village life. Although construction did not commence until 1983, plans had already been drawn up in the early 1970s to develop port facilities for fishermen as part of a wider concern for the future of artisanal fishing fleets in Spain. These plans were precipitated by competition from larger commercial fleets and the loss of fishing rights in the 'Sahara fishing bank' as a result of the decolonisation of Spanish Sahara (Macías Hernández 1982:40). However, the actual impetus for the construction of a port in Playa de Mogán was triggered in 1972 by a conflict between fishermen and a foreign resident, over the use of the beachfront adjoining the latter's property on the other side of the bay from the fishing quarter. Fishermen had traditionally used this area to repair their nets and carry out other tasks of routine maintenance. Although the seashore was ostensibly public property (*dominio público*), the lack of official delineation between the shore and the hinterland had enabled the owner to claim the right of expropriation under Spanish law (*expediente de dominio*) and annex part of the beach where the fishermen gathered.

The enclosure of this space understandably angered local fishermen who subsequently submitted a petition to the council for the construction of a fishing port. In 1974, along with plans to allow for the construction of tourism facilities on the agricultural land adjacent to the fishing quarter, the construction of a port *and* marina were approved by the council, only to be superseded by another set of more detailed plans drawn up in 1975 (Cabildo Insular 1989). It is not clear precisely when and by whom it was decided to incorporate a marina into the plans for a fishing port. However, during this period most of the remaining areas of flat coastal land had also been granted planning permission for tourism development. The combination of Gran Canaria's increasing dependence on tourism, the prime location of Playa de Mogán and its characteristic fishing quarter made it a prime target for tourism development and speculative real-estate investment. After having already approached the municipal council the previous year, a consortium of mainly Spanish investors who had financed a number of tourist marinas on the Costa del Sol was provisionally granted the contract to go ahead with the construction of the commercial marina in March 1979. However, as a detailed inquiry by the island council points out (Cabildo Insular 1989), this was a full two years before the central government authorities in Madrid had granted the council the authority to do so (27 February 1981).

The development of the marina and its tourism infrastructure was thus of dubious legality and, furthermore, took place in the absence of any strategic municipal planning instruments.[10] Such was the extent of collusion between the private company and certain key interests in the municipal council that the commercial interests of investors began to marginalise the collective interests of fishermen and the village as a whole. The section of the marina which according to the terms of the concession granted by the Ministry of Public Works in Madrid was to remain in the public domain (gardens, access routes, open spaces, et cetera) had been annexed and converted to a tourist function. Moreover, the provision of adequate infrastructure and facilities for fishermen lagged behind the construction of the tourist marina and facilities (two-storey apartments with additional space for bars, restaurants, and retail outlets), contrary to the terms of the concession. In particular, the public section of the marina set aside for the fishermen lacked electricity, refrigeration, storage space for nets and other equipment, and, most importantly, a winch to enable boats to be pulled out of the water for repairs and maintenance. Moreover, the fishing port was only allocated 46 moorings (in comparison with over 200 for tourist craft), thus restricting the future growth of the local fleet (although this was not the only cause). According to some local fishermen, the council consistently blocked their attempts to ensure that adequate infrastructure was built and local training provided for locals to enable their transition to the new employment in tourism. To date, the village council has provided no public housing and few opportunities for adequate training to prepare locals for work in the tourist trade.

There is no doubt that the mixed marina-port should have led to substantial improvements in the fishing economy. The port facilitates the unloading of the catch, eliminates the need to drag boats up onto beach as used to be the case, reduces maintenance costs and labour requirements, gives boats greater protection from storms, and creates an area in the village (albeit smaller than was envisaged) specifically demarcated for fishing and associated work. However, the eventual configuration of the mixed marina-port infrastructure and the absence of any effective counter-weight to the interests of private investors demonstrates the existence of continued tensions between these two economic sectors. Beyond the pragmatic concerns related to the adequate distribution of benefits in the marina-fishing port lies a series of tensions which reflect deeper struggles over the organisation and use of space. The tourist marina and associated pleasure infrastructure reflect the new spatial and symbolic arrangements of capital through which new sources of value are created in the tourism economy. It can be seen as an extension of those processes that have been simultaneously occurring in the new urban spaces of consumption at the 'centre' (cf. Meethan 2001:20-25). On the other hand, the fishing part of the marina, although incorporated into the symbolic economy or, rather, 'illusory apparatus' (Harvey 1990:344) of this tourist space, is still ordered by a distinctive use of space and social relations configured by the workings of the fishing economy.

The construction of the marina not only began to increase the scope and intensity of linkages into wider circuits of capital and power, it also laid the foundations for increasingly capitalist forms of ownership and exchange in the village as a whole. The purchase and development of the prime waterfront site proved attractive to international capital[11] for two reasons. First, the actual cost of development was substantially underwritten by public investment. Second, the marina offered myriad new opportunities for speculative investment under the guise of promoting 'quality tourism' during a period in which the standardised coastal mode of tourism production was increasingly suffering under the weight of its own internal contradictions here and across mainland Spain (cf. Williams and Montanari 1995). In this regard, the marina operates as the aesthetic focus within the new symbolic economy of tourism consumption in so far as it constitutes both part of the 'product', as well as the new means of production to be bought and sold in a constantly expanding international tourism market.

The transformation of the waterfront has not only extended the village into the sea, it has changed the uses of existing space. It has stimulated the gentrification of the fishing quarter itself and, more recently, the urbanisation of the valley floor where construction has recently begun on a third phase of tourism development. The local uses of the space for fishing and associated work and social activities have been shifted to the new purpose-built quay away from the epicentre of the village. Although still lucrative for some, fishing has now been overshadowed by the bars, restaurants, cafes, boutiques, suppliers, and accommodation facilities that support the capitalist enterprise economy introduced by the marina. This has also given rise to an increase in both temporary and permanent foreign resident populations. Some of these foreign residents have formed a small entrepreneurial class owning or managing a variety of capitalist tourism enterprises[12] both inside and outside the marina. This class employs the labour of a highly segmented workforce, which will be discussed further in the following section.

The events in Playa de Mogán should not be seen in isolation from the changing economic and political contexts both in Spain and in the wider European tourism economy of the 1980s and 1990s. The restructuring of the coastal mode of tourism development towards the end of the 1980s was accompanied by the continued enclosure of the littoral, particularly by new urban forms such as marinas, as well as the extension of tourism into rural areas (Selwyn 2000). In Spain these developments have been encompassed within planning legislation at both national and regional levels that claims to advance a 'new' model of 'quality tourism' underpinned by principles of sustainability (Yunis 2000). However, marinas, regarded by many policy-makers as a central component of this model, have been the subject of numerous criticisms due to their adverse impact on coastal eco-systems, as well as the convenient cover they provide for speculative property development in the 'post-mass tourism' era (see Garrido 1994). The spatial arrangements of tourism development in this case also illustrate, to some extent, the distinctive relationship of the state (particularly at local levels) to the market in southern Europe. Here the emergence of democratic political institutions has tended to follow, rather than precede, the development of capitalist market mechanisms (cf. Sapelli 1995). In areas like Mogán, a combination of agrarian underdevelopment and local clientelism thwarted the development of a robust civil society. This facilitated the flagrant abuse of municipal power by local political classes in alliance with foreign capital and a local rentier capitalist class, which has emerged in the context of tourism. Rather than act as a constraint on market forces, local politicians, many of whom descend from or are close to landowning families, have exploited the increase in autonomy and planning jurisdiction conferred upon municipal governments by the 1978 Constitution. Their principal aim has been to regulate access to strategically placed assets, including beachfront land and commercial premises in the marina, and thereby convert their political capital into economic gain in a latter day form of 'primitive accumulation' (cf. Marx 1974 [1887], Part 8). On many occasions, this has brought municipal councils, in Mogán and across the region, into direct conflict with the state bureaucracies (regional and national) formed after 1975. The final section of this chapter will examine the consequences of Playa de Mogán's insertion into a more complex web of market relations for the social organisation of household, patterns of entrepreneurship, and labour relations.

Configurations of Tourism Enterprise and Patterns of Employment

The tourism economy and labour market are influenced by an increasingly diverse range of commercial enterprises characterised predominantly by capitalist relations of production. These coexist with a smaller, yet equally diverse, number of *independent family enterprises* embedded within the expanded market economy, but in which capital-labour relations are less established. The pattern of tourism development described above produced a local entrepreneurial stratum that has exploited its own resources by taking tourism into its ambit without undertaking any significant form of capitalist investment. Rather, the enterprises have drawn on the resources of household economies by reclassifying and/or diversifying the usage of individual dwellings (meeting the requirement for fixed capital) and by extending the utilisation of family labour in order to meet the needs of the enterprise(s). Not only do these developments involve little or no capital investment, they have not been fully subsumed by the market in so far as capitalist wage relations have not entirely dissolved hierarchical family loyalties. Furthermore, they are predominantly concerned with the reproduction of the family unit rather than the maximisation of profits. This does not mean to suggest that there is not considerable variation amongst them. Indeed, some of these enterprises have managed to generate rather large surpluses, often re-invested in the acquisition of property. At the same time, the village has attracted a small number of foreigners who have settled in the fishing quarter and opened a number of bars and restaurants for tourists and, in the case of a long-established Danish artist who settled in the village in the 1960s, an art gallery. Some of these are situated in the marina itself, whereas half a dozen or so are situated in a number of converted buildings in the fishing quarter. Nevertheless, despite sharing some attributes of local enterprises, in so far as they are usually family-run, the social and cultural ties to the village are of an entirely different order and somewhat disconnected from the deeper, historically mediated relations of community interaction.

It is one principal characteristic of the independent family enterprise that it serves multiple purposes beyond the fundamental need to secure the material well-being of its members. In particular, it combines both the use values and the exchange values of resources within the same operation, more often than not within the same physical location, a feature enhanced by the proximity of the place of work and the place of residence. This has been a vital factor in the ability of the family economic units to reduce their costs of material production and reproduction, thereby enabling them to compete with the increased scale and scope of capitalist tourism development within the village. Indeed, the articulation between the capitalist and household economies has given rise to a series of social relationships whose consequences demonstrate the dangers of over-simplifying the processes of tourism development and presenting them in opposition to putative notions of the 'local'. Yet, these local developments are also underpinned by and, in part, premised upon the multinational investments involved in the transformation of the waterfront and the creation of the marina project. Whilst the entrance of national and international investment into the proliferation of tourism enterprise increases the competitive pressures within the local tourism economy, the resultant transformation of the built environment of the village acts as a further magnet for tourists and ensures a relatively steady demand for rooms, food, and other services.

Occupational pluralism has been a more or less permanent feature of each household since the planting of agricultural crops for export began at the beginning of the last century. The progressive tertiarisation of the village and wider economy has brought individuals and households into a diverse network of labour/capital relationships within the modern service economy. The enlargement of the use of family labour within the provision of tourism services thus also combines with the simultaneous proletarianisation of members of the household unit. Household members may have entered into wage relations as cooks, cleaners, waiters, receptionists, gardeners, et cetera, whilst continuing to carry out a number of duties in the family enterprise. Indeed, not only did qualitatively different relations of production intersect within a particular household, but individuals could find themselves situated in a wider network of labour relationships where more than one job was undertaken throughout the working day (for example, by combining work in a hotel or supermarket during the day with work in the family restaurant during the evening).

The locally specific conditions of development in the village have also constructed the experience of employment in particular ways. The structure of the tourism labour market has changed as the social composition and organisation of production have shifted. It has also been mediated by the gendered relations of employment as well as the increasingly cosmopolitan nature of the migrant and temporary workforce that has risen rapidly since the late 1980s. Responses to the affluence brought about by the flourishing of tourist enterprises are manifest in generational social mobility, amongst women in particular and young adults in general, allying them to the changing patterns which challenge the economic dominance of the established elites. This mobility requires the recruitment of a replacement workforce to cover the tasks previously undertaken by the children and relatives of the enterprise owners. For instance, the owners of a bar-restaurant, one of the most common forms of locally owned enterprise, may increasingly depend on the recruitment of wage labour as their children enter professions or seek employment elsewhere. This replacement of non-wage family labour with waged labour produces two important contributions to the social configuration of the village. First, the village has witnessed increased social mobility within the younger generation and a change in their awareness of educational and cultural registers. Second, as the number of tourism-related businesses in the marina and village itself has expanded, so has the demand for workers, stimulating an influx of a wider variety of people endowed with myriad cultural attributes and skill categories.

Initially, there were relatively few opportunities for employment in the village itself, although the marina did employ a small workforce of female cleaners which was drawn from amongst a number of peasant households in the village. The expansion of demand for workers in the wider economy during the 1960s and 1970s provided a number of different opportunities, often at good rates of pay and with permanent contracts. Indeed, Santana Talavera (1990a:33) estimates that up to 40 percent of the local workforce abandoned fishing to take up permanent jobs in the tourism and construction sectors during the late 1980s. In particular, these sectors absorbed those young men who had not yet completed their apprenticeship in the fishing sector or who were not able to fish all year round due to a lack of adequate resources at their disposal. Working in the tourism sector offered a regular wage and a relatively more secure form of employment. In general, the opportunities afforded to male members of the village were greater than those for women, who bear the burden of domestic labour and child-rearing unless elderly female kin are able to look after children while their mothers are away at work. Many men have been able to re-deploy skills acquired as fishermen or boat mechanics either as crewmembers on sport fishing/excursion boats or as general maintenance men in the marina. However not only do these pursuits fail to guarantee higher rates of pay than can be earned during a good fishing season, but sport fishing has led to a certain amount of tension between those who remain in the artisanal fishing sector and those who have chosen to sell their knowledge (and labour) to the private boat operators. The latter are referred to by the former as *ladrones de la pesca*, literally 'fishing thieves' (see Santana Talavera 1990b:33-36). Moreover, despite local fishermen's undoubted knowledge of the sea and familiarity with boat maintenance, young foreign workers, members of an itinerant labour force, are often preferred as maintenance workers or crew on pleasure yachts. This tends to confirm Gubbay's (1997:82) findings that 'what counts as skill or credentials depends not on their inherent qualities but rather the demands by employers for particular sorts of workers'. In this case, foreign workers can exploit their familiarity with the tourists' own cultural register as well as work for lower rates of pay given that they are only passing through the village and seeking to fund their onward travels (see Bianchi 2000).

The growth of opportunities for the young, especially amongst a minority who have benefited from higher levels of education,[13] has allowed them to move into administrative and supervisory jobs. These positions occur in the larger developments and within the smaller retail and tourism establishments introduced by absentee capitalist proprietors. For instance, in Playa de Mogán there is an increasing requirement for work in supermarkets, boutiques, and other small retail enterprises principally located in the marina. These posts are often confined to those who have recently left school or else filled by young workers from the larger urban areas, who may have more experience, language abilities, and high school qualifications. Moreover the employment of young women in particular from outside the village appeals to the owners of small retail establishments in the marina because it conforms to certain metropolitan standards of customer service, and reinforces tourist expectations of the type of 'quality tourism' that Puerto Mogán is said to represent. In this case, those employed in such establishments often conform to a socially constructed, transnational norm which underpins the notion of 'women's work' in tourism (see Kinnaird et al. 1994) and which therefore dictates the ability of local women to negotiate work in capitalistic tourism enterprise in the marina and elsewhere.

In general, those without access to employment or a stake in an independent family enterprise have become dependent upon a range of semi-skilled wage-work in tourism due to their generally low educational attainment and low levels of expectation conditioned by the experiences of the recent past. A uniform service-oriented working class has thus not arisen in Playa de Mogán. Rather, those working in tourism might best be referred to as what Gaviria (1974) called 'los braceros del turismo' (tourism labourers) or rather, a 'heterogeneous strat[um], occupying the same contradictory position within the relations of production, but disarticulated by varying power bases' (Callinicos 1989:163).

Conclusions

The transformation of Playa de Mogán from an isolated, peasant fishing village visited by explorer type tourists into an urbanised tourism resort integrated into the international market occurred over a relatively short period, during which time new social alignments of power have emerged. Whilst the influence of tourism has been mediated by the prevailing social structure and social organisation of the fishing and agrarian economies, it has nonetheless brought about dramatic changes in commodification, a process which structures differential access to resources and defines the nature of appropriate knowledge and skills in the post-agrarian service economy. Tourism opened up the possibility for the partial commodification of household resources in the form of 'rooms-for-rent' and precipitated the emergence of a cluster of independent family enterprises to provide a range of local services for tourists. For the most part, these enterprises are owned by a local entrepreneurial class consisting of a formerly less well-off strata of inhabitants, with little or no access to agrarian or fishing means of production, including land, other than the meagre dwellings in which they lived.

It should also be stressed that tourism neither introduced villagers to the 'monetized calculus of market exchange' (Smith 1997: 202) for the first time, as is often implied by certain critics of tourism, nor entirely submerged households into the realm of commodity capitalist relations. Whilst the conversion of households into independent family enterprises and the availability of wage-work in the service sector have integrated members of the same household into qualitatively different relations of production, the household still remains a vital reproductive unit and a means of securing a stable livelihood for many. Yet the pressures of proletarianisation will likely increase in tandem with the pace and scale of hotel and apartment construction by coalitions of local landlords and foreign investors, both locally and in adjacent areas. The reproductive capabilities of local households, particularly those of young couples, are further undermined by a lack of space and restrictions on building new and affordable housing (an exception is made, ironically, for tourist apartments!), property inflation fuelled by gentrification, and an influx of outsiders looking to purchase second homes.

One or two members of the landowning classes, who for decades had monopolised economic and political power in this locality, also opened eating and lodging facilities in the village. Nevertheless, tourism enables independent family enterprises to supply services directly to tourists and thus has eroded the monopsony powers of the landowning classes. This has transformed the hierarchical social divisions upon which the relations between those who worked the land and sea and those who owned the land were based. However, the emergence of new entrepreneurial classes in tandem with the social mobility brought about by tourism has not altogether dissolved the underlying inequalities that characterised the agrarian-fishing economy. Ultimately, the disproportionate access to freehold land (in the valley) of the former landowing *cacique* families, few of whom continue to live in the village, has been easily converted into property-based capital.

The unfettered encroachment of capital into the built and cultural environments of the village demonstrates how the rapid development of a modern tourism market economy, in the absence of robust political institutions through which asymmetries of power can be counter-balanced by public intervention, may well threaten the fragile advances of independent family producers and the social advances afforded by tourism employment. Only recently has the establishment of democratic procedures through which tourism planning takes place, in particular the advent of a pluralistic system of governance incorporating checks and balances between local, island, regional, and national governments, begun to constrain the profit-seeking influence of the peculiar alliance between municipal politicians, local landowners, and 'external' capital. Contrary to many assumptions underlying models of development in the radical and conservative camps, the emergence of independent family enterprises is not a transitional phenomenon but rather structured by the changing historical circumstances of development that have shaped the particular configurations of capitalism in this locality. This is perhaps even more so in the context of a tourism economy in which the processes of commodification, the means of consumption, and the configurations of labour and capital are equally diverse.

Notes

1. Mogán is the second largest municipality on the island of Gran Canaria after San Bartolomé de Tirajana, with a surface area of 333 square kilometres.
2. There is some discrepancy in the dates given for the establishment of the *factorías* in the village. The historian Francisco Suárez Moreno (1997:162) claims that they were established in 1911, but, Santana Talavera (1990a:64) suggests that they did not in fact open until 1924-5.
3. The term *cacique* has often been applied to groups of powerful local notables who monopolised economic and political power, particularly in rural parts of Spain as well as Latin America, during the passage from feudalism to agrarian capitalism in the 19th century (see Carr 1982:366-379).

4. In 1955, the percentage of the working population employed in agriculture and fishing was 59 per cent, with a further 5.3 per cent employed in construction, and 23.5 per cent in the service sector. By 1975 these figures were 21.1, 11.1, and 55.9 per cent, respectively (Alcaide Inchausti 1981:65).
5. The total surface area under irrigated cultivation (*regadío*) in Mogán fell from a peak of 567 hectares in 1963 to 270 hectares in 1983 (Suárez Moreno 1997:200).
6. The population of Playa de Mogán fell from 690 to 614 permanent residents during the period 1950-1960, and gradually rose again to a peak of nearly 700 in 1986.
7. Amongst other reasons, this was probably due to the fact that womenfolk would often remove their clothes when helping in certain manual tasks which took place on the seashore, such as the repair of fishing nets.
8. Monopsony powers refer to those instances where powerful middlemen, acting on behalf of a single buyer, control access to the international market (see Narotzky 1997:195-6). To some extent, the fishing economy (controlled by the *factorías*) and certainly the agricultural exports (controlled by a single *cacique* family in alliance with British export companies) were characterised by these relationships of exchange. The household tourism economy, however, enables direct producers (independent family enterprises) to deal directly with the international market (in the form of the tourists themselves), albeit during the initial stages of development.
9. Planning permission for the development of the valley floor had already been granted by the Provincial Government of Las Palmas in 1974.
10. The municipality of Mogán did not approve its standard planning guidelines (*normas subsidiarias*) until 1987. At the time of publication, it is striking that a municipality of such considerable touristic importance has yet to approve a General Plan, the principal instrument for the rational and ordered regulation of land use.
11. In 1994, five years after the completion of the marina, a consortium of Italian and British investors purchased approximately 50 per cent of the bed capacity and other commercial establishments in the marina, which were converted into time-share properties and subsequently re-christened the "Venice of the Canaries". It is also worthy of note that local residents continue to refer to the village as Playa de Mogán while the authorities and developers tend to use the term Puerto de Mogán to refer to the entire locality.
12. Those locales which are not directly owned by the proprietors of the bars, restaurants, and other tourist services are leased from a variety of property companies and banks who own the freehold in the marina (which itself was granted for a period of 50 years from 1981).
13. The majority of the tourism workforce is less than 35 years of age and, in most cases, had until recently only completed basic secondary schooling (*Enseñanza General Básica*).

References

Alcaide Inchausti, J.
1981   Estructura y Evolución de la Economía Canaria. In: *Canarias ante el Cambio*. Santa Cruz de Tenerife: Instituto de Desarollo Regional, Universidad de La Laguna. Pp.61-79.

Béthencourt Massieu, A. and A. Macías Hernández
1977   Expansión del Cultivo y Conflictos Sociales en Gran Canaria en el Tránsito del Antiguo al Nuevo Régimen: Una Aproximación Histórica. In: *Historia General de las Islas Canarias* (4), Las Palmas de Gran Canaria: Ediciones Edirca. Pp. 237-361.

Bianchi, R. V.
1999   *A Critical Ethnography of Tourism Entrepreneurship and Social Change in a Fishing Community in Gran Canaria*. Unpublished Ph.D. Thesis, London: University of North London.
2000   Migrant Tourist-Workers: Exploring the 'Contact Zones' of Post-Industrial Tourism. *Current Issues in Tourism* 3(2):107-137.

Cabildo Insular de Gran Canaria
1986   *La Movilidad Geográfica de la Población de gran Canaria'. Anexo, Plan Insular de Ordenación de Gran Canaria* (draft). Las Palmas de Gran Canaria.
1989   *Informe sobre Actuaciones Urbanísticas en el Municipio de Mogán*. Las Palmas de Gran Canaria: Oficina Insular de Planeamiento.

Callinicos, A.
1989   *Against Post-Modernism: A Marxist Critique*. Cambridge: Polity.

Carr, R.
1982   *Spain: 1808-1975*. 2nd Edition. Oxford: Clarendon Press.

Galván Tudela, A.
1982   Aspectos Sociológicos de las Comunidades Pesqueras Canarias. In: *II Jornadas de Estudios Económicos Canarios: 'La Pesca en Canarias'*. La Laguna: Secretariado de Publicaciones de la Universidad de La Laguna. Pp. 81-96.

García Herrera, L-M.
1987   Economic Development and Spatial Consequences in the Canary Islands: the Role of Cities in a Peripheral and Dependent Area. *Antipode* 19(1):25-39.

Garrido, C.
1993   El Turismo Cinegético: Un Negocio de 'Armas Tomar'. *Mediterranean Magazine* 39:7-10.
1994   Desastres a Toda Costa. *Mediterranean Magazine* 42 (April-May):6-20.

Gaviria, M.
1974   *España a Go-Go: Turismo Charter y Neo-Colonialism del Espacio*. Madrid: Ediciones Turner.

González Lemus, F.
2002   *Del Hotel Martiánez al Hotel Taoro*. Tenerife, Puerto de la Cruz: Búho Ediciones.

Gubbay, J.
1997   A Marxist Critique of Weberian Class Analyses. *Sociology* 31(1):73-89.

Harvey, D.
1990   *The Condition of Post Modernity*. London: Blackwell.

Istac
1997b *Evolución de la Economía Canaria. 1996*. Las Palmas de Gran Canaria: Gobierno de Canarias, Instituto Canario de Estadística.
2000   *Evolución de la Población Canaria, 1991-1999*. Las Palmas de Gran Canaria: Gobierno de Canarias, Instituto Canario de Estadística.

Kenna, M.
1993   Return Migrants and Tourism Development: An Example from the Cyclades. *Journal of Modern Greek Studies* 11:75-95.

Kinnaird, V., U. Kothari, and D. Hall
1994   Tourism: Gender Perspectives. In: V. Kinnaird and D. Hall (Eds.) *Tourism: A Gender Analysis*. Chichester: John Wiley. Pp. 1-34.

Machado Carrillo, A.
1990   *Ecología, Medio Ambiente y Desarollo Turístico en Canarias*. Santa Cruz de Tenerife: Gobierno de Canarias, Servicio de Publicaciones.

Macías Hernández, A.
1982   El Sector Pesquero en la Economía Canaria del Pasado Inmediato (1800-1970). In: *II Jornadas de Estudios Económicos Canarios: 'La Pesca en Canarias'*. La Laguna: Secretariado de Publicaciones de la Universidad de La Laguna. Pp.13-40.

Marx, K.
1974   [1887] *Capital, Vol. 1*. London: Lawrence and Wishart.

Meethan, K.
2001   *Tourism in Global Society: Place, Culture, Consumption*. Basingstoke: Palgrave.

Nadal Perdomo, I. and C. Guitián Ayneto
1983   *El Sur de Gran Canaria: Entre el Turismo y la Marginación*. Las Palmas de Gran Canaria: Centro de Investigación Económica y Social.

Narotzky, S.
1997   *New Directions in Economic Anthropology*. London/New York: Pluto Press.

Pascual Fernández, J.
1991   *Entre el Mar y La Tierrra: Los Pescadores Artesanales Canarios*. Editorial Interinsular Canaria.

Pérez-Díaz, V. M.
1998   *The Return of Civil Society: The Emergence of Democratic Spain*. Cambridge, MA: Harvard University Press.

Santana Talavera, A.

1990a *El Sol Siempre Va a Estar Ahí (Antropología y Turismo en Canarias)*. Unpublished Ph.D. Thesis, Tenerife: University of La Laguna.

1990b Turismo, Empleo y Dependencia Económica. Las Estratégias de las Unidades Domésticas en dos Poblaciones Pesqueras (Gran Canaria)', *Eres (Antropología)*, Vol. 2:25-38.

Sapelli, G.

1995 *Southern Europe since 1945: Tradition and Modernity in Portugal, Spain, Italy, Greece and Turkey*. London and New York: Longman.

Selwyn, T.

2000 De-Mediterraneanisation of the Mediterranean? *Current Issues in Tourism* Vol 3(3):226-245.

Smith, M. Estellie

1997 Hegemony and Elite Capital: The Tools of Tourism. In: E. Chambers (Ed.), *Tourism and Culture: An Applied Perspective*. Albany: State University of New York Press. Pp. 199-214.

Stott, M.

1996 Tourism Development and the Need for Community Action in Mykonos, Greece. In: L. Briguglio *et al.* (Eds.), *Sustainable Tourism in Islands and Small States*. London: Pinter. Pp. 281-305.

Suárez Moreno, F.

1997 *Mogán: De Pueblo Aislado a Cosmopolita*. Gran Canaria: Ilustre Ayuntamiento de Mogán.

Williams, A. M. and A. Montanari

1995 Tourism Regions and Spaces in a Changing Social Framework. *Tijdschrift voor Economische Sociale Geografie* 86 (1):3-12.

Yunis, E.

2000 Tourism Sustainability and Market Competitiveness in the Coastal Areas and Islands of the Mediterranean. In: A. Pink (Ed.), *Sustainable Travel and Tourism*. London: Green Globe 21/IGC Publishing. Pp. 65-68.

Zarkia, C.

1996 *Philoxenia*: Receiving Tourists – but not Guests – on a Greek Island. In: J. Boissevain (Ed.), *Coping with Tourists: European Reaction to Mass Tourism*. Oxford: Berghahn Books. Pp. 143-173.

5

Tourism, Kinship, and Social Change in Sennen Cove, Cornwall

Michael John Ireland

Introduction

This chapter examines the changes brought about in the social structure of Sennen by the continued development of tourism in the local
economy. Sennen Parish is situated in the extreme southwest of
England on Land's End peninsula (Fig. 5.1), approximately eight
miles from Penzance and 290 miles from London. The parish covers
approximately 2,300 acres of predominantly plateau land between
250 and 300 feet above sea level. The north and north-western
boundary is formed by Whitesand Bay, which comprises the beach of
Sennen Cove and the granite cliffs washed by the Atlantic Ocean. To
the southwest the Atlantic meets the English Channel, the most
prominent point along this coastal boundary being the promontory
of Land's End, a national tourist attraction that features in this study.
Inland the parish is bounded by parts of the parishes of St.Leven (to
the southeast), St.Buryan (to the east) and St.Just (to the north).

The population of Sennen at the time of my fieldwork was 739
(1981 Census). Today (2003) the population is given as 840 for the
parish as whole (http://www.cornwall.gov.uk/Facts/facts8.htm).

The inhabitants of the parish do not live in one village, but are dispersed among eleven townships and one fishing settlement. These are
the townships of Escalls, Trevorian, Trevear, Mayon, Treeve (Church-
town), Trevescan, Trevilly, Skewjack, Brew, Bosvine and Penrose, and
the fishing settlement of Sennen Cove. The majority of the population
live close to the A30 road in Mayon, Treeve and Trevescan and in the
council housing situated between Mayon and Escalls.

Anyone who has stayed in Sennen either as a resident migrating
from another area or as a visitor who has spent regular holidays in
the village will be aware of the existence of kin ties. I was made aware
of the significance of the social structure of Sennen in the Penwith

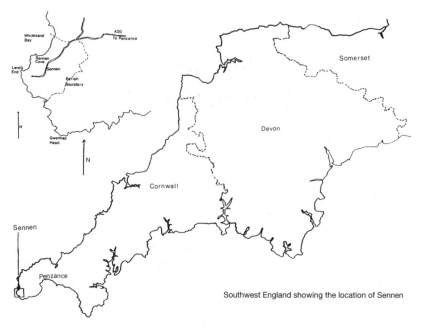

Sketch map showing the parish of Sennen

Southwest England showing the location of Sennen

Fig. 5.1. Map Southwest England with inset of Sennen Parish.

district on a visit to Penzance during the first few weeks of my field-work. A waitress in a cafe, after learning that I was working in Sennen, asked, 'How do you get on with the Covers?' The intonation in her voice was such that I felt I could expect some difficulty. At that time I was unaware of the contemporary significance of the term Cover.

Similar conversations with people from other communities on the Land's End peninsula suggested to me that the Covers were per-ceived to be in some way different from their fellow Cornishmen. Among the folklore that surrounded the Covers was a reputed stutter in their speech, supposedly the result of inter-marriage. First-cousin marriages were purported to have been common among earlier gen-erations. This was in part a consequence of their reluctance to 'marry out of the Cove', that is to marry into the families of the farming com-munities of the Land's End plateau. Finally, more than once it was suggested to me that the Covers had descended from the Spanish. The question this raised was: What was the validity of these claims? The task that confronted me was to piece together an accurate picture of kinship and social structure in the parish. Two methods of enquiry were adopted: the use of historical data, primarily the Census returns

CHAPTER FIVE

Fig. 5.2. Covers outside the Lifeboat House in Sennen Cove. *Back Row.* John George, Pender George, Stephen Roberts, Henry Penrose, Albert George, John Ellis, Mathew George Ellis. *Middle Row.* Sam Pender, Willy George, Alfred George, Stephen Trenary, John Pender, Thomas George, George George, Robert Frances Pender. *Front Row.* Mathew George, William James Penrose, Richard Penrose, Willy George, Edward Nicholas, Tom Pender and Steve George. (Source: W. J. Pender, Sennen Cove, c1910).

and parish registers, and genealogical interviews supported with personal documents and photographs from local people. From this information I was able to construct a number of kinship charts.

This view of the social and spatial structure of Sennen has its historical basis in the primary occupational groups, farmers (Overhillers) and fishermen (Covers), who dominated the social structure of the parish in the nineteenth century. The picture that emerged from the census data of 1871 and 1881 was a community divided by the strategies adopted to recruit and retain its labour force in order to sustain the local economy. Fox (1995:81) notes that economic activities that require a 'large labour force of males' who must be trained leads to the males remaining in the locality. In communities like Sennen where fishing forms an important sector of the economy, wives are taken from sisters in other family groups within the village, or they are brought in from other parishes. Evidence for both strategies can be found in the kinship systems of Sennen Cove (Fig. 5.3).

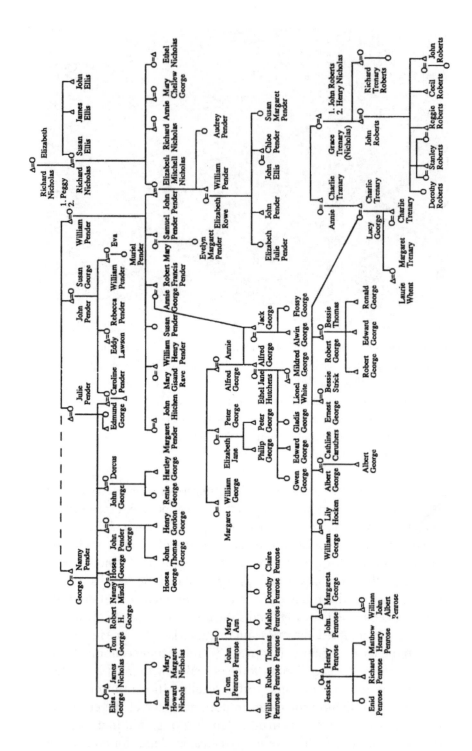

Fig. 5.3. Genealogy of the Covers, showing kin sets.

This is in direct contrast to an economy where skills are readily transferable from one location to another as in the case of farming, where neither sex is tied to their place of birth, and all that matters is that there are enough males and females in the farm household to carry out the work (Fox 1995:81). Statistical evidence for this kind of social and economic organisation in Sennen was provided. This showed that in 1881, 96.8 percent of the fishermen in the parish had also been born there, whereas only 52.5 percent of the farmers and 25.5 percent of the labourers had been born in Sennen. Toward the end of the nineteenth century, we saw that the simple dichotomy between occupational groups had begun to breakdown, and a small but important group of entrepreneurs was earning a living from visitors to Land's End. The growth of tourism brought women a recognised place within the local economy.

One of the problems I have tried to overcome is to present the social structure in such a way so as not to lose sight of the interdependence between kinship, stratification, and local institutions. A schematic outline of the changes in the social structure of Sennen which have taken place mainly since the end of the 19th century, is charted below (Fig. 5.4).

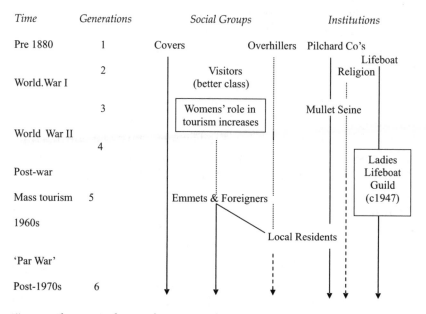

Fig. 5.4. Changes in the social structure of Sennen measured against historical and generational time.

Everyday Life and Work in Sennen

The retention of relational boundaries between Covers and Over-hillers into the late 20th century would seem to have as much to do with business acumen and prosperity as it does with ties of kinship. In other words, rules governing social intercourse have developed because of perceived differences in wealth. Evidence for this view can be found in the respective group perceptions. Whenever I asked an informant to tell me about his or her social group, reference was routinely made to family histories and personal experience. The following extracts from my field notes demonstrate this point.

Louise Chellew, once a farmer's wife at Escalls, recalled her grandfather's relationship with the fishermen. She told me, 'Relations with the Covers *were* not very good'. Her initial explanation rested on rumours of inbreeding and racial prejudice. She continued to explain the reasons for her grandfather's attitude saying, 'A lot of Covers stammered in their speech, that was supposed to come from the Spaniards.' Other reasons for her grandfather's suspicion of the Covers included measures taken by the fishermen to relieve their poverty.

This was illustrated when Louise related a story from her childhood about her father. As a farmer at Escalls, she told me, he would grow a field of turnips on the farm. At that time it was commonplace for every two or three Covers to own a donkey cart, and she recalls that on moonlit nights, 'The donkey carts got up into the turnip and cabbage field, if there were two or three of them (Covers), they weren't beyond anything to get a load. The feeling wasn't very good'.

In general, the farmers or Overhillers were more enterprising than the Covers, and some made the transition from tenant farmer to landowner. Mr Humphries, a retired farmer who had made this transition described the asymmetrical relationship between farmer and fisherman that existed in his father's time. He told me the Covers supplied labour for the farmers. He gave the example of Henry Penrose (Captain Enny), who used to work three days a week for Aunt Alice, and said his Grandfather George not only bought the Covers' labour but also sold them services. As his son put it, 'He pulled fish and coal for the Covers'. The entrepreneurial activities of the Overhillers extended to acting as 'accountants' for the Covers. One farmer and landowner in Sennen told me about William Vingoe, also a farmer, who 'used to count the money for their (the Covers) fish'.

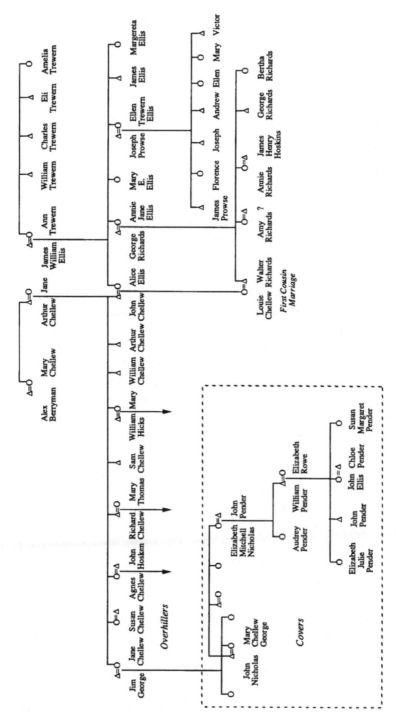

Fig. 5.5. Geneology of the Chellew – Ellis – Richards kin sets showing their link to the Covers through the Nicholas – Pender kin set.

Past memories assist in retaining the relational boundaries between the two communities today. Some informants tried to account for the differentiation that exists, while others offered no explanation. One middle-aged man, himself a farmer and former entrepreneur in the tourist trade at the Land's End, described the Covers as, 'coarse eaters and drinking men with an unfamiliarity with money'.

It is interesting to note here that men are the subject of derogatory remarks but not the Cove women. Women, as will be shown later, appear to act as intermediaries, not only between Covers and Overhillers but also between visitors and local people. However, that is not to say that women hold neutral views with regard to relational boundaries between Covers and Overhillers. One woman, a retired farmer's wife, gave no explanation for differentiating between the two groups. When asked how she saw the Covers she said, 'People in the Cove are strangers'.

The failure to acknowledge the existence of kin ties between the two groups was just as strongly voiced by a Cove woman, now married to a man from 'up the hill'. Mrs Jago, formerly a Roberts, told me that she 'never accepted people up Escalls, they were like foreigners'. Nevertheless, Cove women had to sell their labour and their husbands' fish to the farming families. For example, one woman recalled that in the past women had cut corn for a Land's End farmer for sixpence a day. These same women had also sold fish to the farmers of Land's End, Trevescan and the nearby town of St.Just.

However, relationships between the two occupational communities were not always as hostile as we might be led to believe. In an economy that still had elements of subsistence agriculture among the Covers, the granddaughter of one of my informants related that she was allowed to keep a cow on the farm of an Overhiller in exchange for labour on the farm. What is not in dispute is the way in which the economic resources of the Cove were jealously guarded. Richard Pender, a Cover, told me, 'Overhillers couldn't get a share in the mullet. Some married into the Cove but still couldn't get a share'.

The Mullet Seine is an institution that still forms an important boundary between Covers and the outside world, not just the Overhillers. The Covers continue to guard this resource from the seascape, but the scarcity of land in the Cove made them more dependent on the farming community for seasonal work and food.

Irrespective of the resources available to the two groups, a fundamental difference existed between the fishermen and the farmers with regard to their mode of economic organisation. The farmers hired labour, sometimes from the Cove. In contrast, the nature of fishing as an activity meant that crews were closely related through kin ties. Early photographs show Cover families crewing boats, but later recollections show that this practice was only common up until World War II. Between the two world wars inshore fishing in Sennen experienced a decline and with this decline began the gradual depletion of fishing crews that had provided such an enduring social boundary.

The prosperity of the fishing community depended not only upon the success of catches enjoyed throughout the year but also on external variables. The decade from the mid-1920s to 1930s was a period of particular hardship in the Cove, resulting in seasonal migration to other fishing grounds, and for some of the Covers this became a permanent move. The Roberts family of Sennen illustrates this point.

I interviewed Reggie Roberts, a member of the family now living in Padstow, about his recollections of leaving the Cove in the mid-1920s. He told me it was 'very rough and hard'. His father John Roberts had been left a widower with seven children to bring up. Reggie, his three brothers and his father crewed the family fishing boat the 'Ardencraig'. The significance of the 'Ardencraig' is that it had a motor, whereas most boats used when catching crabs (crabbers) in Sennen at that time were sailing boats.

The decision for the Roberts family to leave Sennen Cove came from a chance conversation with Richard Nicholas, another Cover, who had been fishing off Padstow some twenty years earlier. Subsequently, Nicholas' contacts enabled him to arrange accommodation in Padstow for the Roberts family.

Easter 1924 saw the departure of the Sennen crews in their boats for other fishing grounds. Three boats left for the Scilly Isles: The Titania, crewed by Nick Nicholas, Tom Nicholas and Willie Trenary; the Meteor, crewed by John George (Ebby's Jack), Mathy Nicholas and Edmund George; and the Mizpah, crewed by Richard Nicholas, John Penrose, John Nicholas and Tom Nicholas (Enny's Tom).

On Easter Monday the Roberts family left Sennen Cove for Padstow. Their original aim was to return to Sennen at the end of the season, but only one brother returned to live in the Cove. The other two brothers, Reggie and Stanley, married Padstow women. The pattern had been very different twenty years earlier, circa 1900, when fishermen from Sennen had visited Padstow, married local women and brought them back to the Cove.

What the Roberts family recognised with their departure from Sennen Cove was that the community could no longer retain its traditional occupational base, founded on fishing and farming, with men as dominant breadwinners. Within the local stratification system Covers and Overhillers represented two status groups. Their status is ascribed by birthplace and the occupation of the family to which the individual belongs. The recognition or denial of the existence of kin ties between these groups serves to define a relational boundary between them. As fishing gradually declined and farming became less labour-intensive, the stratification system of the parish became more complex, with the result that there was an identified change in the economic position of women.

Women and Tourism

Women have always played a 'hidden role' in the economy, and the role of the Sennen woman suggests no significant differences for Covers or Overhillers. In my fieldwork I have shown that as visitors began to discover the parish and take holidays there, some women undertook paid housekeeping duties. Other women developed their entrepreneurial skills by providing hospitality for the visitors for profit. Through their work with the early visitors, women achieved status as an identifiable socio-economic group within the parish. The relationship between local women engaged in providing hospitality for visitors is important because it demonstrates the existence of a market. The market relationship between women and what local people call 'the better class of visitor' is important because of the contact between class and status groups. In engaging in this relationship, women acted as intermediaries between the local people and visitors. The growth of this relationship also freed women from some of the 'ties and obligations of local community structure' (Giddens 1978:164).

The accounts given by Sennen women of their work with visitors identify three cultural themes: their perceptions of the visitors, the nature of the host-guest relationship and the type of hospitality provided. The following account of women's work is relevant to the period prior to World War I and up until the early 1980s. What is apparent is that women's work and the nature of their relationships with visitors changed over time as a result of a perceived change in the social and economic distance between the two groups.

CHAPTER FIVE

Three stages in the way hospitality was provided can be shown to exist, namely: taking lodgers, providing bed-and-breakfast, and letting self-catering accommodation. Lodgers, also referred to by local people as 'the better class of visitor', were the predominant visitors until the beginning of World War II. Bed and breakfast and eventually self-catering accommodation became the main modes of hospitality for the middle and working class visitors to the parish during the post-war period. This trend of gradual disengagement from close contact with the visitors occurred as the perceived class base changed, and this is recognised by local women working with tourists today. Mary, a Cover involved in providing accommodation for tourists, likened these changes to that of her own family's past involvement with visitors. She recalls, 'Yes, I can remember the posher people staying with Auntie Audrey (Pender) and my Granny (Elizabeth Mitchell Pender) and then more bed and breakfast ... Everybody had them – and it went to like chalets, small places and other self-catering'.

Women's work at each stage of this development can be illustrated through their own accounts.

Tourists and Change to the Local Stratification System

Lodgers or the Better Class of Visitor

Local perceptions of the better class of visitor can be assessed from remarks made by women whose families had been involved with the first visitors to the parish. Margaret Trenary described the Lodgers as a better class of person. 'We treated them really special, early visitors were the type of person you could look up to.'

From her remarks it is not hard to detect elements of respect and deference to the Lodgers.

A farmer's wife who had taken visitors to the parish for over thirty years held similar views about visitors to the Cove. She told me, 'Cove people started with visitors very early. So if anybody came to the Cove they would be Gentry'.

This deferential behaviour gives rise to the use of another phrase with cultural significance. Today when discussing the early visitors, locals still talk about 'going out to sleep'. This means that host families slept in temporary accommodation for the duration of the visitor's stay. Mrs Hutchens, a Cover, told me that in the 1920s and 1930s houses would be rented out to 'big families' (big referring here both to the perceived class position and to the number in the household). Covers slept in attics above washhouses from May to September. The visitors frequently adopted the local family and returned to the same household year after year.

Margaret Trenary gave me a detailed account of her family's relationship with the better class of visitor. She said,

> Well, you see the women, they took the visitors in during the summer time to help keep them all in the winter; 'cause the fishermen didn't earn any money then you see. It was through the women taking in these visitors you see that enabled them to live well; otherwise they could never have survived. It was the women that looked after the visitors, the men had nothing to do with them. I lived up there with that headmaster of Cheltenham College (he had a house built overlooking the Cove). We went to live with him. Mother went there as a housekeeper. She looked after the visitors in his house, that were masters from different Colleges, all summer.

Margaret Trenary talked about her relatives' involvement with the visitors. Her aunts all took visitors from Easter to September each year, this meant they would 'go out to sleep'. She told me, 'They would sleep in the kitchen or anywhere you see ... the house would be taken over; they (the local women) were like servants to the visitors you see'.

Nevertheless, she felt that the lodgers, '...respected the people they stayed with, although they came to stay with fisher people, they didn't take the mickey out of them'.

Margaret compared this respect for one another with the relationship between visitors and local people which exists today saying, 'Now the people if they come staying, they are always trying to take the mickey out of the Cornish people'.

The deferential relationship that existed between the Cove women, local families and visiting families fostered a loyalty between hosts and guests expressed in mutual adoption. Margaret recalled some of the visiting families and their hosts.

> Well, you see there was the Brownfield family, they used to come with the Pender people and they'd take the house. Then there was the

CHAPTER FIVE

Fords, who used to be in Mrs Chopes, and Alfred Warren's mother had another family. Mother had Mrs Sibs from Birmingham, butchers they were; they all used to come year after year.

I shall return to the relationships that developed between the lodgers and their local hosts later in this chapter. At this point we need to examine the type of hospitality provided for the lodgers by the local women's own accounts.

Sennen people were (and still are) very proud of the fact that they provided food and accommodation for a class of people they respected and with whom they would not otherwise have come into contact. Local Cove women customarily asked each other questions such as, 'How many lodgers you got in?' This question was common in the Cove and is still recalled by younger women today. Mary recalls a relative, Mary Trahair saying, 'You always exaggerated; implying that you had more lodgers than you actually had in'. Qualifying her remark with, 'I don't know where it got us' (meaning she did not know what the exaggerations had achieved).

Her remark is an indication of how much personal comfort the Covers gave up for the lodgers. The charge for full board in the pre-war period was modest, as low as £1.00 per room, and for this it was explained, 'Covers provided full board, breakfast, mid-day meal, evening meal and something before they go to bed'.

The work involved in providing hospitality for the lodgers can be appreciated from the comments of Cove women whose families took visitors. Each phrase has a cultural significance. Mrs Hutchens, a Cover, explained what 'carrying water' meant.

She told me, 'Women would go to the visitors' bedroom and knock on the door to provide them with fresh water to wash in their jug and basin'.

Margaret Trenary described the hard work entailed in this apparently small task when she said,

> The women used to carry all the water; used always see the women with buckets of water; they used to have to fill the jugs with clean water and throw away all the water they (the Lodgers) had washed in. I mean the poor things they never stopped.

She continued outlining the services provided to the visitor.

They always had a tray of tea in bed before they came down; and then they'd have their breakfast and then they'd go out in the morning sometimes and come back in and have lunch; they'd have afternoon tea and then a cooked evening meal; so the women were going all day.

The kind of hospitality provided for the visitor changed gradually as legislation effected a change in the social characteristics of holidays in the country as a whole. These changes were recognised by local people, who thought, '...because of holidays with pay ... down came all the riff-raff after the war'.

The perceived change in the type of visitor coming to Sennen corresponds with a change in the type of accommodation offered, to that of bed-and-breakfast style.

The Post-War Visitor

This perceived change in the visitor type was not immediately obvious, accounts from those who provided hospitality suggest only a marginal change. The most significant change seems to have been that 'going out to sleep' had stopped being a precondition to taking in visitors. Local people now shared their homes with bed-and-breakfast guests.

Sennen women's perceptions of post-war bed-and-breakfast visitors can be drawn from the accounts of three local women; a retired farmer's wife, a widow and a young housewife.

Mrs Nicholas had been taking in bed-and-breakfast guests, since about 1940 at their farm situated on the parish boundary of Sennen and St.Just. She thought the wartime and post war visitors were mostly professional types.

Mrs Beachfield, a widow who had kept a guesthouse in Sennen Cove from 1954 to 1981, was very clear about the change in her clientele, saying,

> Well, really then there was a better class of visitor than what we get now; I used to have the Director of Rothmans tobacco people; but now (1981) you see it's the ordinary, well like ourselves, working class people that come; well, it's been a gradual change; it's gradually changed over the years. Well, those people like I had from Rothmans. I can tell you who else I had; the Editor of the *Daily Mirror*, he and his wife came for years and their children. You see people, they come

down here; they sort of book in for bed-and-breakfast, because they knew no facilities were here for that sort of thing. Where else could you go for an evening meal?

The provision of bed and breakfast accommodation by local women still existed in Sennen at the time of my fieldwork, but was being replaced to a large extent by self-catering units.

Mrs James, a Cornish woman in her early thirties, who had originally come from St.Ives and had been living in Sennen for 12 years, still did bed-and-breakfast. She explained to me that her mother was also in the holiday trade, and she had therefore been brought up with visitors all her life. When she was first married, she used to take external employment during the winter then 'take the summer months off to do bed and breakfast'. Her customers were mainly families.

Her husband was very clear about how he saw the differences between the working class visitors and what he described as the 'upper crust' families about whom Mr James said,

> Your upper crust families, the ones that think they are well to do. The children just run wild; don't have any manners. They (the parents) creep out of the house. When the visitors sat in the lounge he complained that they would pretend to read a book.

He compared their behaviour with that of the working class visitor saying, 'You could tell they are working class.' The implication in his next comment seemed to be that they had better manners. He said they would ask, 'Could we have the T.V. on?'

The preceding paragraphs have illustrated through the accounts of some local people that there had been a gradual but irreversible change in the type of visitors who came to Sennen.

The involvement of women with the visitors can be seen as important in identifying the emergence of new relational boundaries between visitors and local people. By entering into a host-guest relationship with the visitors, women established their own rules of hospitality. This relationship allowed men to maintain a social distance and thus preserve their local identity. We need only note here the way in which Cove men perceived work with the visitors.

Richard, a Cover whose wife and sister both took in visitors, saw the transition from bed and breakfast to self-catering accommodation as desirable. He said of contemporary visitors, 'They are out there, and they are out the way'. Referring back to the period when his wife took in visitors as bed and breakfast guests and he worked as a carpenter, he said disapprovingly, 'You would come home, and they would be in the kitchen'.

From my conversations with Richard, it seemed that he preferred the relationship of mutual respect that existed between the better class of visitors and the Covers. Territorial boundaries were unwritten and had rarely been transgressed, the result being that good relationships have endured.

However, from the remarks made with regard to post-war visitors, it is clear that they do not enjoy the same degree of deference afforded to the lodgers by the locals.

Women's work with the visitors to Sennen makes us aware of the dynamics of the local stratification system. Women have established their position as breadwinners in the household.

Visitors as Part of the Local Stratification System

Visitors have become a semi-permanent feature of the local stratification system, so much so that local people have placed them in a crude rank order. Expressions of deference indicate that the lodger, the better class of visitor, was someone to be 'looked up to'. In sharp contrast, post-war visitors are seen as equals or inferior to their hosts. Cornish people refer to the latter groups by such derogatory names such as emmets, foreigners or Andy Cap's and, in doing so, confirm a perceived lower status.

The argument I want to put forward is that the locals' perceptions of the visitors whilst on holiday are replicated by the positions they subsequently occupy in the local stratification system when, upon retirement, they take up residence in a previous holiday destination. This idea can be better understood by reference to figure 5.4.

The position occupied in the local stratification system upon taking up residence in Sennen can be predicted from the relationship developed with the indigenous population on recurrent holiday visits. The most important single indicator of local residents' positions in the village stratification system appeared to be their social class as perceived by their hosts whilst on holiday.

The validity of this argument can be tested in two ways. First, from the hospitality afforded the visitor when on holiday in Sennen. Second, by observing the degree to which the visitor integrates into local institutions once resident. This process of positioning within the local stratification system is not passive. Among the post-war visitors in particular, evidence exists to show a certain amount of predatory behaviour (Ireland 1987:90) in the areas of property acquisition. The behaviour was countered to some extent by the strategies of local people, who made properties more accessible to those people they thought would fit in. In the diagram (Fig.5.4) I have shown this process through the emergence of a new social group in the parish in the post-war period, that of local residents. This term is intended to describe two visitor groups, the better class of visitor and the emmet or foreigner.

Local Residents

Recollections of three local residents who came to Sennen as lodgers or better class visitors during the pre-war period serve to illustrate their negotiations for position in the parish. A process that, in the case of these families, spans almost eighty years and details the hospitality afforded them by local people and their involvement in local institutions.

Miss Lydia Hampton is the granddaughter of a professional man who had first come to Sennen in the 1890s and had stayed with a local family at Badgery Terrace, in the Cove. Twelve years later in 1902 her grandfather bought the land from a farmer in Escalls to build Miss Hampton's present house in Sunny Corner. After the house had been constructed, the Hampton's spent every holiday in Sennen until World War II. These holidays lasted for five or six weeks, including the whole of August. Miss Hampton's remarks illustrate how the holiday home gradually became a permanent home. Her grandfather used the house for summer holidays, but never retired there; it was very much a holiday home. Later, in 1938, her father retired to Sennen, and Miss Hampton has consequently lived permanently in Sennen since 1959.

Miss Hampton's background shows the social and material status of the better class of visitor. Until the age of thirty-two she had not worked in paid employment. She said, 'Before the War, I just lived at home'. Like many upper middle class women during World War II, she joined the Women's Voluntary Service, and this took her to the Far East working in Army Welfare. After the war, and until her move to Sennen, she was a House Matron at King's School, Canterbury. The attraction of Sennen for Miss Hampton is clear from her lifestyle. She never goes to Penzance shopping, but prefers to deal with local family businesses that provide a delivery service. The family has traded with the same local shop for over eighty years. Her account confirmed the respect the local people say exists between them and the better class of visitor. When she bought another property in the village the local reaction was, 'Thank God one of the old crowd have got it'. This remark, together with Miss Hampton's views of modern visitors as 'having just bad manners' are important indicators of the changes in the social structure of the parish in the postwar period.

Mr Brownfield, a retired headmaster of a public school for boys in Windsor, first came to Sennen as a three-week-old baby. He told me, 'I was christened at Sennen church, that was in 1906. My father and mother had been down here one year before that'. Talking about his early memories of holidays in Sennen, Mr Brownfield said,

> I can remember my father writing out a cheque for sixty pounds, I think it was the amount which covered the return fare from Windsor for the four of us ... train fare to Penzance and five weeks board and lodging down here as well ... The type of visitors were purely professionals ... a lot of them were school masters or clergymen and that sort of thing. I remember once in Sennen Church the local Parson had to preach to, I think it was, something like four headmasters and three bishops!

Asked about their relationships with local people he said,

> We always got on very well with the people, and so did my parents. I always think that the Cornish don't resent foreigners providing they behave in a reasonable manner, and don't go chucking their weight about as though they own the place. We always got on extremely well. I used to play on the sand with the fishermen's children. I think they enjoyed having us to be quite honest. Because apart from anything else we were a source of income, much needed at that time.

I asked Mr Brownfield to explain why he returned to Sennen to re-
tire. To which he replied, 'Well wherever I have been ... I've always
said, I wonder what it is like at Sennen today? We had a bungalow up
at Rock (North Cornwall) for about eight years. I suppose its somewhere you have enjoyed yourself as a child. The only thing is, I don't
know whether it might have been a bit of a mistake coming here, its a
little bit at the end of the world. At any rate I suppose I've got roots
here, because although I spent sixty years at Windsor, it is not the
same Windsor today, or even when I retired it was sixteen years ago
you see. As much as I like Windsor and I like to see my old boys, if I
had lived in Windsor I could have never ever known peace.'

Although local people would describe Mr Brownfield as one of the
better class of visitors now settled in Sennen, his perceptions of local
people were more egalitarian. He describe his relationship with local
people as follows,

> Well personally I always get on well with everybody. I have always
> considered them equals. I never considered any difference at all you
> see. I don't really regard them in any sort of special light. Except in
> the fact that they are old friends because I know them.

My final case study is Miss Constance Edmonds. She has been associated with Sennen for at least as long as Mr Brownfield, who had
told me that Miss Edmonds' father, a Clifton School master, had
come to Sennen at least one year (c1905) before his parents. Miss
Edmunds disclosed little about her own migration to the parish except to tell me about her family's first holiday.

She told me her family first came to the Cove on bicycles looking
for a place to spend their holidays. At that time there were no facilities for catering to visitors and no recognised tourist trade as such.
'Then you just lived in the Cove with families. This meant having all
your meals with the families, that is, full board.'

A host and guest relationship seems to have built up between the
families and the Covers, resulting in the exchange of gifts.

Miss Edmonds illustrated this point by saying that the Covers
would send you a lobster, and in return the visitors may send some
clothes that could not be obtained locally. She agreed with Mr
Brownfield that there was real affection between host and guest.

The better class of visitor who has become resident in Sennen has
found acceptance among local people. Respect for each other and

good manners are valued by both groups, as is loyalty to the social and economic institutions of the parish, whether they be in the village shop or the church. Their accounts also display a common belief about contemporary visitors as being people lacking in manners and in respect for the local way of life. As a consequence, although the visitors and subsequent migrants may hold a higher social status or possess greater economic power outside the parish, within Sennen they were perceived to occupy a lower position within the local stratification system.

One of the reasons for the post-war visitors' perceived lower status within the village is a response to their behaviour when on holiday. The local perception of emmets behaviour is complex and is based on verbal and non-verbal actions. These include general mannerisms, accent and strategies used to 'find out' and 'get in'. 'Finding out' is the cover term used by local people to describe what are often the preliminary stages of predatory behaviour. 'Getting in' usually refers to the successful purchase of a second or retirement home in the parish.

These terms can be operationalised through the use of a case study of a professional couple's career cycle that culminates in the purchase of a second home. The case study shows they possess a totally different set of values to local people and the pre-war visitors who are now resident.

The Cartwrights first came to Sennen Cove in 1950 and rented a holiday-home not far from their present cottage, near the harbour. Their holidays were taken out of season for six weeks from the end of May. They changed to the traditional holiday period as their family reached school age at about the same time other professional families began to frequent the Cove.

The mention of the fact that their holidays included lobster fishing illustrates in a small but important way how they encroached upon rather than contributed to the local economy. The Cartwrights were aware that the local fishermen resented their lobster fishing excursions. They said, 'if we got five lobsters we always used to cover them'.

This suggested they felt the need to disguise the catch from local fisherman, although it was their stated opinion that they did not interfere with the indigenous population.

The penultimate stage in the holiday home owner's career cycle begins when the holiday destination is regarded as more than just a place to spend a vacation. For the Cartwrights this was the point when they began to see themselves as local residents.

They said, 'In a sense we don't regard ourselves as visitors. We regard it (Sennen Cove) as a second home. We have embraced the area as a spiritual home'. Mr Cartwright explained how they bought their 'spiritual home'.

He told me, 'It took us a long time to get our hands on it (their present cottage). We had to go for tea, then one day she (the local woman who owned the property) said we could have it'.

The culmination of the holiday-home ownership cycle comes when they reach the end of their working lives and consider retirement. The movement of visitors from their permanent residence and place of work to one of recreation requires an adaptation in material terms. The need for a change coupled with a dissatisfaction with their present holiday cottage as a permanent retirement home was clearly felt by Mrs Cartwright, who complained that the fisherman's cottage in general was awful.

It is at this point in the cycle that predatory behaviour by the visitors reached its final stage. In local terms the visitor is seen to have succeeded in 'getting in'. The precise way in which this is achieved, of course, varies from case to case. In an attempt to buy a more suitable property in the Cove, the Cartwrights approached another retired migrant who owned a larger house in the same row of cottages.

This attempt at 'getting in' meant extending their predatory behaviour to a former businessman from Surrey. Mr Ashford, then in his late eighties, said that, 'Only in the last 18 months to 2 years have I mixed with them socially. One day they just knocked on the door and asked would I like to have a sherry?'

Looking back over the Cartwrights' holiday career cycle, this sudden wish to socialise with Mr Ashford may be interpreted as a repetition of earlier predatory behaviour, the taking of tea with the old lady to gain their first foothold in the Cove.

From this case study it is possible to abstract certain characteristics of the holiday-home owner cycle, from purchasing a second home to becoming a local resident. They do not see themselves, nor wish to be seen, as visitors. They regard *their* holiday village as *home*, but maintain a social distance between themselves and the host community. Predatory behaviour is exhibited through sudden 'friendships' between previously unacquainted parties and the temporary crossing of social boundaries that may occur in order to secure a property.

The boundaries between local residents like the Cartwrights and the Covers can be recognised from their accounts of each other. The local people's reaction is to almost welcome this social differentiation and to ridicule the behaviour of the local residents. Mary, a Cover, summarised the locals' perception of local residents as a social group. She said,

> Those people they don't want nothing to do with the likes of us, do they? ... but most of 'em like these 'Cartwrights'. Oh they are total snobs, aren't they? They got no interest in anything down here, more than their little small circle of friends and their dinner parties. They got no interest in neighbours unless they want something.

She continued giving an example of the way in which the local residents tried to recreate the competitive environment of southern England in Sennen Cove. 'Well, they got their own circle. Well, for instance all them cottages are more or less the same size ... might be two foot here or two foot there.' She recalled the story of Molly's dinner party to illustrate her point. She said, 'Molly used to say hers was the biggest house in that row.'

When Molly was invited to a dinner party at the cottage of another local resident, the host came to the door and said to the other guests already there, 'Oh, it's the people from the big house'.

Mary's concluding remarks indicated the difference in values between the local people, the better class of visitor and the local residents. A more subtle differentiation was detected through the discussion of food. She recalled another example of the Crossmans fish pie, saying, 'there is droves of them in the summer, they don't just have a bit of dinner or something. They'll have a "huge" fish pie or a "huge" stew. It's just like we have here everyday, we don't say anything about it. But to hear them talk you'd think it was something special'. The post-war visitors who became either residents or holiday home-owners are a heterogeneous group. What unites them is their holiday career cycle and their contrasting experiences of Sennen first as visitors and then as owners of property. Table 5.1 sets out the holiday career histories of nine local residents.

Table 5.1. Holiday career cycle of local residents moving to Sennen after the war

Family	Place of origin	1st visit to Sennen	Bought holiday home	Became local resident	Time lapse (Years)
1	Surrey	1956	1964	1976	20
2	Glous.	1962	1982	-	20
3	Midlands	1962	-	1977	15
4	London	Not given	-	1978	-
5	Avon	Not given	-	1978	-
6	Services	1966	-	1976	10
7	Midlands	1967	-	1970	4
8		1950	1980	-	30
9	Kent	1961	1982	-	21

One of the most interesting deductions to be made from the table is the average period of time that elapses between the visitors' first holiday in Sennen, buying a property and taking up permanent or semipermanent residence in the village. The average time lapse is 17 years. Given that many local residents were in their 50s or early 60s when this took place, the first visit to Sennen is likely to have been as a family holiday.

At the time of my fieldwork most post-war local residents had owned property in Sennen for an average of five years. From the accounts of their experience in that period this had given them enough time to appreciate their position in the local stratification system. They saw themselves in one of three categories: incomers, outsiders or emmets. The realisation that these were derogatory terms that placed them below the better class of visitor and the Covers and Overhillers was apparent from their comments. One woman from Bristol said, 'We are all Emmets.' She continued, 'I don't like the Cornish people. If they like you, that's it. If they don't, that's it!'

Only in one case did a complete lack of perception of place within the local social structure emerge. Mr 'Fox', who came originally from the West Midlands, said, 'I consider myself a Cornishman now, because we have adopted them (the people of Sennen)'.

This adoption was not reciprocal; tolerance would be a more accurate description. One local woman described how she saw Mr 'Fox' and his family. She said, 'I am friendly with Mrs Fox up there (Mayon) but we don't have one thing in common. We are only friendly because my daughter and her's is friendly. But apart from that ain't got one thing in common with her at all. She thinks we are a bit of a rough crowd down here (Sennen Cove)'.

Women in particular became identified as mediators between the major categories in a way that had not been possible between Covers and Overhillers despite marriage. The provision of hospitality brought women into contact through a formalized set of relationships with their guests. Some of these guests were eventually to become local residents within the parish.

Institutional Forms

In this section of the chapter I want to deal with a new set of relationships that provides structure to the day-to-day life of non-visitors who live in Sennen. These include the local people themselves and the categories of local resident already described. The problem faced by this now heterogeneous community is how to conduct relationships in a non-holiday setting.

We began by examining the dichotomous relationship between the Covers and the Overhillers. I then sought to show how the social structure of Sennen gradually became more complex as a result of internal and external economic and social change.

Three institutional forms can be observed within the parish: the Lifeboat, Mullet Seine, and the Church. Each institution is characterised by differing degrees of 'openness' in relational terms.

Whilst on holiday in Sennen visitors were assigned a place in the local social structure as guest, although the rules of behaviour toward these guests changed over time, as local perceptions of the visitor altered. For example, I have noted an inverse relationship between the visitors' perceived social distance from their hosts and the mode of holiday accommodation. Taking in 'lodgers' who were usually seen to be 'the better class of visitor' was replaced in the post-war period with accommodation for visitors in self-catering units, thus socially and physically distancing the visitors from their host.

The Lifeboat is a complex institution of which the boat is actually only a small part. The 'Lifeboat' brings into contact, but does not bring together, three groups: the local men who crew the boat; the women of the Ladies Lifeboat Guild who are almost exclusively local residents; and the management committee, which is an alliance of retired naval personnel and local councillors.

The Mullet Seine refers to the organisation of local labour and capital to secure the large shoals of fish that follow a migratory route around the coast from November to March. Because of the volume of fish the shoals realise, fishing is organised on a communal basis. Originally, a man's right to a share in the Mullet Seine required that he was a Cover by birthright. The contemporary Mullet Seine operates along similar lines. However, today men are also expected to purchase a share in the net. The Mullet Seine is essentially a closed institution. The Seine provides a vehicle for much of the history attached to fishing and the Cove.

The Church provides an occasional meeting place for all parties, through formal worship and staged events.

The Sennen year is punctuated by a series of events organised annually along familiar lines. Events such as 'Lifeboat Day', a visit from the St.Buryan male voice choir to the lifeboat house, and the Church Fete all provided potential points of contact between Sennen people, local residents and visitors. Other events are prepared each year but are never supposed to be public, the prime example being the catching of mullet in the Cove. These events provide a focus for the different social groups in the parish, and their personal identity, whether local resident or Cover, can be expressed through them.

Each event is linked to one of the local institutions. The argument put forward is that the alliances and divisions that form part of the social structure of the parish can be identified through the analysis of these events. My starting point is the involvement of the local residents in the lifeboat.

'Getting in the Lifeboat' – The Ladies Lifeboat Guild

When Sennen people talk about getting in the lifeboat, they do not mean it literally. What they are referring to are the local residents who join the Ladies Lifeboat Guild. Fund-raising committees have raised funds for the Royal National Lifeboat Institution in the Land's End district since the mid-1930s. An account of the annual flag day for the Sennen Cove Branch (R.N.L.I. record books 14.3.35) records almost £75.00 being raised in contributions. The programme for the day included the selling of flags, the launch of the lifeboat and a country dance in the lifeboat house in the evening. Details of the collectors make interesting reading, because there is a distinct lack of

Cornish names among the list. This small piece of evidence gives support to the view of Sennen people that the institution is the province of outsiders.

Prior to 1947 fund-raising for the Lifeboat was organised from Penzance. It was not until November 1947 that a branch of the Ladies Lifeboat Guild was formed in Sennen Cove.

The aims of the present day Ladies Lifeboat Guild are broadly similar to their predecessors, to raise funds for the R.N.L.I. The proceeds of their efforts are paid into a central fund. In addition, the Sennen Cove branch has a comfort fund, which provides for the needs of the Sennen Cove lifeboat crew.

The current membership rules no longer require a subscription to be paid, but a commitment to spend a certain amount of time on the souvenir stall is essential. Membership of the Guild totalled 20 women at the time of my fieldwork, of which only two were Sennen women.

The Branch organises a series of events throughout the summer period, from May to September. In 1980 the Guild raised £10,000, a third of which came from the sale of souvenirs.

Local Perceptions of the 'Lifeboat'

To the visitor the Lifeboat is the centre of the community, but to Sennen people and local residents it does not symbolise village unity. Rather it symbolizes the differentiation and conflict which exists between social groups in the parish.

Sennen people's perceptions of the 'Lifeboat' appear to be based on two factors: their dislike of outsiders' involvement in village life and competition with locals for scarce resources, that is, the monies spent by visitors. Their dislike of outsiders is not just an expression of native xenophobia but is based on the social relationships between them. An indication of the content of these relationships can be gained from locals' comments about the lifeboat (see Fig. 5.6.).

Hugh, a member of the Lifeboat crew, first made me aware of the divisions within this institution, when he told me,

> The Lifeboat women have a stall which sells souvenirs. When there is a dinner (to which the crew, committee and ladies guild are invited)

Fig.5.6 Sennen Cove Lifeboat (Source: M.J. Ireland 1982).

> it's them (local residents) who are first and foremost, not the actual
> crew. All they get is two pounds eighty pence a call out.

The Ladies Lifeboat Guild in particular provides a niche for women who have moved into the parish. Phil, another member of the crew, summed up the view of the Guild that there was 'not a local woman in it'. My own observation of some of the events the Guild organised tended to confirm this view. At a Lifeboat Garden Party held at the end of July, it was noticeable that the stalls were run almost entirely by local residents. Sennen women supported the event as customers.

At a similar event, the Cornish Fayre, the lack of involvement by local women in the activities of the 'Lifeboat' was even more marked. The Cornish Fayre takes place in August each year in a car park close to the boathouse, where local resident women dress in what they consider to be traditional Cornish costume. To the visitor this display of pageantry may appear convincing, but an examination of old photographs of the wives of Sennen fishermen makes clear the lack of authenticity of this event.

The visitors who are drawn to this event are not presented with Cornish culture as it is understood by the Sennen people, but with a touristic version. Probably the greatest irony in this presentation is that local residents, who were themselves holiday visitors to the parish, are now engaged in presenting a commoditised version of

Cornish life to a new generation of tourists. The primary reason for this is that local women have actively pursued a policy of disengagement from both the local residents and the holiday visitors, except for the provision of holiday accommodation.

Whilst the 'Lifeboat' provides a purpose for local residents to use their skills in the organisation of events throughout the summer, its real function is to raise funds for the parent institution the Royal National Lifeboat Institution. It is this economic function that provokes resentment amongst Sennen people. Objections to the fund-raising activities of the 'Lifeboat' come from two quarters: local people with a business interest in tourism and those who would like to see monies from the visitors more equally distributed among local projects.

James, a local entrepreneur with business interests in self-catering holiday accommodation and in food and souvenir retailing in Sennen Cove, complained that the 'Lifeboat' stall that is opposite his shop undercuts his prices, and as a result he employed fewer local people in his shop. This kind of perceived unfair competition is by no means unique to Sennen. What is more localised is the economic impact of the 'Lifeboats' fund-raising activities on local institutions. For example, Mrs Pender, a local woman, told me that the 'Lifeboat' had raised £400 at their Harvest Festival at the First and Last Inn. She contrasted this with the amount raised at the Church Fete, which was only £140.

In the pre-war period Lifeboat day was only once a year at which time local people and visitors made their donations to the R.N.L.I. Today, as one local man put it, 'Lifeboat day is everyday', referring to the marketing activities of the Ladies Guild.

Social Relations at a 'Lifeboat' Event

The Setting: The St.Buryan Male Voice Choir Concert in the Lifeboat House

Each year the Lifeboat organises a concert given by the St.Buryan male voice choir and held in the boathouse at Sennen Cove. The Lifeboat provides the focal point of the evening. Temporary seating is arranged for the visitors and for local people on the available floor space. The boathouse has three levels, each providing some space for seating. These include the entrance area with its steps leading down to the second level and main floor area, and the 'well', a rectangular area open to the slipway at one end and partially occupied by the hull of the boat.

The second level accommodated the majority of guests for the concert. The 'well' had limited seating and an obscured view of the lifeboat deck on which the choir stood to sing.

The concert is an extremely popular event with both local people and visitors. I had been advised to arrive almost one hour early if I wanted a seat. This advice proved correct for shortly before the start the boathouse appeared to be full except for a few seats in the 'well' and two or three in the front rows of seats on the second level. The latter positions would have given an unobstructed view of the lifeboat and the choir.

The evening brought into contact three groups prominent in the social structure of the parish: Sennen people, local residents and visitors. The situation I want to examine focuses on the nature of social relations between members of two of these groups, Sennen people and local residents. The participants in the events of the evening were Mr Richard Pender, a Cover and former crew member of the lifeboat, his wife Honor, a Cornish woman who had married into the Cove, and Mr Lacey, a local resident who was also the administrative secretary of the Lifeboat committee. Mr Lacey acted as the master of ceremonies for the evening and conducted the choir.

Two small incidents occurred during the evening which help us to understand why Sennen people distance themselves from the 'Lifeboat' and the local residents who organise the fund-raising events.

Incident One

Although Richard Pender had told me to arrive early to obtain a seat at the concert, he failed to take his own advice. Mr and Mrs Pender arrived late. Almost all the seats were taken except three, two rows from the front. Richard and his wife naturally went to occupy these seats. Before they had the opportunity to sit down, Mr Lacey intervened. He told the couple, 'They (the seats) are reserved for some friends.'

Mr and Mrs Pender eventually found a seat down in the 'well' at the top of the lifeboat slipway. From this position it would have been almost impossible to see the choir.

Incident Two

Throughout the evening Mr Lacey presented himself with reverence and authority over the audience and the choir. At 8:45 pm there was an interval in the concert. At this point Mr Lacey made announcements and presented certificates for long service to former Lifeboat crew-members. Richard was presented with a certificate. He accepted it from Mr Lacey with deference.

Prior to the concert ending, Mr Lacey told the audience that 'many people here tonight regard Cornwall as their second home'. The effects of their colonisation seem not to be fully appreciated.

Analysis

These incidents illustrate the lack of understanding of Sennen peoples' feelings by local residents. Mr and Mrs Pender were after all guests at a ceremony. Richard was to be honoured for long service to the Lifeboat, the very institution that on a local level gave meaning through the fund raising events to their lives. Instead of being given a place of honour as a mark of respect for his service, Richard and his wife were symbolically and actually seated lower than the local residents and visitors.

While publicly Mr Pender behaved in a deferential manner toward Mr Lacey during the presentation, privately these incidents had only served to sharpen the divisions between Sennen people and local residents. Support for this view came a few days later from Mrs Pender, when we talked about the evening. Referring directly to the reserving of seats for 'outsiders' by Mr Lacey, Mrs Pender openly questioned in her own mind 'whether or not we are locals!' She compared their treatment in the boathouse with that which they received at Lifeboat dinners. She described the way they were treated by the local residents in the 'Lifeboat' as like a Sunday school outing – patronising!

The Mullet Seine

The importance of the Mullet Seine as an institution in Sennen arose as a result of the loss of the pilchard shoals to the coast (see Fig. 5.7).

Fig. 5.7. A good catch of pilchards, Sennen Cove (Source: W.J. Pender, Sennen Cove).

The Mullet Seine still embodies many of its traditional customs and practices. Here, historical and situational analysis is used to explain why the Mullet Seine has remained such an important institution for over a century.

The Mullet Fishery in the Nineteenth Century

Local papers began to report large shoals of grey mullet being caught off Sennen Cove from the 1880s. Grey mullet were high value fish commanding a market price of between 14 shillings and 1 pound 2 shillings a score (*Cornish Telegraph* 2.3.1882 and 13.4.1882). Their value seems to have been realised on the London and Paris fish markets (*Cornish Telegraph* 6.4.1882).

The quantity of mullet caught in Whitesand Bay each season was estimated to average between 17,000 and 18,000 fish (*Cornish Telegraph* 2.3.1882). Based on an average price of 15 shillings a score, the mullet seiners could have expected an income of between £634 and £675 a season. It is not surprising that a report in the *Cornish Telegraph* (4.3.1879:4) informs the reader that, 'The recent good catches of grey mullet at the Cove have quite revived the spirits of the fishermen.'

Even quite small quantities of mullet were worth catching. The *Cornish Telegraph* (26.1.1882) reports,

> The first catch of mullet for the season was effected last week at the Longships, when about 120 were secured. These fish are esteemed highly in the Great Markets and are likely to realise a good price.

In April 1882 mullet were fetching as much as 1 pound 2 shillings a score. In the following seasons (*Cornish Telegraph* 1.3.1883:5) both the forces of the sea and the market place were set against the Covers. The difficulties encountered by the Covers and the losses they sustained were reported in the *Cornish Telegraph* (8.1.1885) with the headline 'Sennen – a great loss of mullet.' The report notes that about 10,000 fish were enclosed off the Gywnver sands. The *Telegraph* goes on to report, 'In hauling ashore this immense quantity, the cork rope broke, and all but 500 fish escaped'.

The financial loss was particularly hard for the Covers in view of an already unsuccessful pilchard season.

These illustrations have been chosen to shed light on more recent events, known locally as the 'Par War'. In this incident cultural knowledge that had been passed down through generations of Sennen fishermen that had resulted in making them cautious was mistaken for lack of expertise by the Par fishermen.

The Par War

The Par War, as it became known locally, began because a group of fishermen from Par in Southeast Cornwall attempted to challenge the Sennen fishermen's right to exercise this custom. The first incident in the war occurred at Gywnver Beach, on Sunday, January 10th, 1960.

An account in the *Cornishman* (14.1.60) tells us that the first incident in the 'Par War' took place in the afternoon, while the Sennen fishermen were clearing the beach in readiness for the landing of the mullet. Aware of the difficulties their kin had experienced in landing large quantities of fish on this beach (cf. *Cornish Telegraph* 8.1.1885), the Covers had removed heavy boulders. The fish could then be hauled in with the aid of a tractor.

The paper reports that 'to the Covers' surprise, a party of four or five men arrived with a jeep towing a small boat on a trailer, containing a small net' (*Cornishman* 14.1.60). The Covers realised this equipment would be inadequate to secure the shoal. They attempted to persuade the Par men not to launch the boat. The *Cornishman* reported,

> an altercation ensued, during which it is stated that the boat (belonging to the Par fishermen) was wrested from its trailer and overturned on the beach. In due course the visitors left without having put their boat in the water.

Some days later this incident was reported in the national press (*Daily Telegraph and Morning Post* 18.1.1960).

Mullet. What Mullet?

The mullet fishery in Sennen Cove after the 'Par War' became even more secretive. The *Sunday Independent* (1.4.73) carried a headline 'The Great Mullet Mystery' and suggested a catch of large shoals of mullet that season was 'just a fisherman's tale'. This was one mystery that was relatively easy to solve. I was able to examine the records of the Fishery Office at Newlyn, which gave the weekly and monthly totals of fish landed at Sennen Cove. The records are valuable for a number of reasons. First, they dispel the myth posed by the 'Great Mullet Mystery' of 1973. Second, they show that newspaper reports and the remarks of my informants with regard to the value of the catches are reasonably accurate. Although the figures I was able to obtain for the mullet caught were incomplete, it was possible to get a good idea of the true value of these fish to the Covers.

Table 5.2. Mullet landed in Sennen Cove and recorded by the Fisheries Office at Newlyn for the period January 1969 to April 1980

Date of Catch	Weight in stone	Value of fish sold
January 1969	552	£1,027
April 11th 1969	1360	£2,237
March 18th 1972	2264	£2,415
March 21st 1973	1230	£2,565
March 16th 1980	10	£ 85
April 13th 1980	602	£2,783
" " "	253	£1,104
" " "	288	£1,124

Table 5.2 shows 1980 to have been a particularly good year for the mullet. The total value of the catch for the season was £5,096. This would be shared among an estimated eight shareholders. When casual help had to be employed, sums said to be approximately £50 per man were paid. The shareholders themselves could expect to receive anything up to £500 for their work.

The mullet season of 1982 provided a social drama enacted over three incidents, which occurred between March and May that year. The incidents brought together three important local institutions: Kinship, the Lifeboat and the Mullet. What I hope to show through these events is that kin ties and obligations contracted through involvement in local economic institutions demonstrate conclusively that the Lifeboat is not, as often supposed, the centre of the community.

The mullet fishery is supposed to be a secret activity that you only hear about after the fish have been caught and sold. The reasons for this secrecy in the past were based on superstition and kinship, although now tax evasion would seem to be the prime factor. A local fisherman who features prominently in the incidents once reminded me on my mentioning of the mullet, 'No one should ever know'. While another Cover whose kin ties can be traced back to the fishing families of nineteenth century Sennen Cove, said, 'You would hear it had been shot (the mullet seine net) but that's all'. Jacob concluded with a remark that had greater significance to the following incidents than I thought possible. He told me that there may be thirty people helping, but not all would get a share.

The first incident catalogues the activities leading up to the preparation for the catch.

Incident One: The False Alarm

I had noticed fishermen watching for patches of mullet in the bay from the cliff tops above Sennen Cove since the end of February. It was not until almost one month later (24.3.82) that the first shoal was sighted. I was alerted to the preparations being made to secure the shoal.

Later I walked out to the Cove and noted three boats on the slipway around which were a large group of men loading nets. I approached them and was told, 'They spotted a patch this morning.' There were at this time still 'watchers' below 'Fernhill' on Stone Chair lane.

The night and early hours of the following morning were full of tension and excitement with the impending mullet catch. Two punts with nets aboard moored in the bay in readiness. This was because the tide was on the ebb (7.45am).

The boats had been placed there to avoid missing the shoal because of the difficulty of launching at low water.

Four 'watchers' appeared in the garden of 'Fernhill' to signal the location of the shoal. As the tide ebbed a fisherman brought a punt from the harbour slip to the end of the Lifeboat slip. This was to allow the fishermen to row out to the punts carrying the nets should the shoals be sighted.

A possible 'disruption' to the mullet shoal occurred as a group of visitors carried a large inflatable boat to the water in Whitesand Bay principally for use by skin divers. An outboard motor was attached, which, had it been used, might have scared the fish. This is an important point with regard to the effects the visitors have on the traditional economy of the Cove.

At the harbour men were gathering on the wharf. There was obviously much conversation and chat about the mullet. One Cover said, 'Got to have some rules. It's like someone coming into your field and wanting a share of potatoes.' He was obviously not very keen on persons who had not bought a share turning up to help, with the expectation of some reward without investing capital.

Expectations that a shoal of mullet might be caught in the Cove continued for almost a fortnight after the first sighting. The nets were left aboard the boats in readiness. Even so, the life of the Cove had to continue. The second incident took place immediately prior to the Lifeboat practice evening, 13 days after the first shoal of mullet had been sighted.

Incident Two: Lifeboat Practice

This incident is difficult to describe in the abstract, so pseudonyms have been used to give meaning to the tensions and conflict between the 'Mullet Seiner's, some of whom were members of the Lifeboat crew, and a young Cove man ('Nick') who was marginal to this group. My first indication of any trouble was when I heard Peter threaten to 'smash Nick's face in'. He was standing on the wall surrounding the Lifeboat house entrance shouting after Nick, 'I'll smack you in the mouth'. Nick came running away from the Lifeboat house in fear. Dissent had been caused by Nick shooting a net that might have been used to catch mullet. This coincided with the Lifeboat meeting. Before leaving the scene I noticed a fresh face with the slip gang, Charles Tonkin. Charles' presence was to prove important as a source of evidence.

Later that evening I joined James Trahair and Charles Tonkin in the 'Old Success' Inn. We discussed the dispute over Nick's net and the mullet.

Charles had been at the Lifeboat house that evening after the practice. He told us how Nick Pascoe was ordered by Humphrey Stevens (the Coxswain) to stand down from the Lifeboat crew. At this point a bye-law in force for the period October to March, which prohibits any other method of fishing than by seine net between Aire Point and Irish Lady, was mentioned. Doubt was expressed as to whether or not this law was still in force.

The point Charles was trying to make was that Humphrey should not have allowed the subject matter of the net to influence the Lifeboat meeting. However, during the meeting matters had escalated. Charles told us, 'Then while the meeting was on, there was tap on the door of the Lifeboat house'.

Charles continued. 'I didn't see who it was, but Humphrey and Peter rushed to put their 'oilers' on and left the meeting.' Charles assumed this was to cut the net which Nick had out, but had no proof. Both James and Charles were of the opinion that it was 'he up there who was behind it'. They were inferring that the man responsible for the disruption of the meeting and the removal of the net was Edmund Warren, whose family had been prominent figures in the Mullet Seine for some years.

Shortly after this incident I met Honor, a local woman from the Cove. She told me that her daughter had told her that, 'Sarah (Nick's wife) came around and said that nine men were chasing Nick around the village last night'.

Honor's analysis of the situation was that Nick was in the wrong to break an unwritten rule, which was to 'put a net out when the mullet were about'.

On enquiring if Nick had phoned the police about being pursued, she said, 'Yes, but [that] they were unable to do anything.' This was because although Humphrey had removed the net belonging to him, they had not damaged it.

Fig. 5.8 Unmeshing the catch on the slip at Sennen Cove (Source: M.J. Ireland 1982).

Incident Three: The Catch

Almost outside the official season a small shoal of mullet were caught. They were only enough to fill three fish boxes, but were of good size.

The small fishing boats were hauled up on to the slip, and the Mullets Seiners were busy taking fish from the mesh of the net. To my left and directly below the wharf stood two fishermen, 'Joe Pender' and 'George Beachfield'.

It is a well-known fact among the Covers that the Penders have no part in the Mullet Seine. The positioning of the two groups of men on the harbour slipway was an indication of this quiet feud.

To my surprise one of the Seiners threw a fish across to George and Joe for bait in their crab pots. This acted as a signal for the other fishermen in the Mullet Seine to try to engage Joe in conversation but there was little or no response. The Mullet Seiners felt guilty about their monopoly.

Analysis

The contemporary mullet fishery is much smaller than at the time of the Par War, yet it retains some of the features that make it a recognizable institution within the local social structure.

Among the group of men gathered to load the nets in preparation to catch the mullet, four important Sennen family names appear, Nicholas, Trenary, George and Roberts. Figure 5.3 shows the Georges, Trenarys and Roberts to be closely related through ties of kinship. The Nicholas family are linked through the Penders, who are significantly related to the Georges.

It is evident that the rules governing who can hold a share in the mullet are based on two criteria, one based on ties of kinship and the other on capital invested. All the men assembled in the first incident could satisfy the former, but not everyone could afford to invest. 'Nick' had not bought into the Mullet Seine, yet still hoped to share the catch.

The conflict that developed as a result can accurately be described as a 'threatened outbreak', (Gluckman 1969:217) carefully controlled so as not to break the law. The actual encounter between the two fishermen outside the Lifeboat house described in the second incident can be seen as a relatively unimportant event on its own. What is important is the emergence of a leader among the mullet seiners who had the power to enforce sanctions and disrupt the lifeboat. Historically, the Warrens have defended the right of Covers to catch mullet against external threats, shown through the Par War. Today, they continue to command the support of the Covers over the mullet, even when there is disagreement on an individual basis.

This cohesion is shown by a member of the Pender family's reaction to Nick's behaviour. They agreed he had broken an unwritten rule by putting a net out independently of the Mullet Seiners.

Gluckman (1982:216) has noted that, 'Conflicts are a part of social life, and custom appears to exacerbate these conflicts: but in doing so custom also restrains the conflicts from destroying the wider social order'.

The third incident was of symbolic value to the Mullet Seiners because it allowed them to exercise publicly their right to catch the fish. The incident is more important for what it can tell us about alliances and divisions within the kin sets of the Cove. As had already been noted, the Mullet Seine as an institution represents most of the major kin groups in Sennen Cove, both past and present, with the exception of the Penders. Their exclusion is a result of an unresolved dispute between them and the Warren family. The details of the dispute were never made clear. What is important is that it was possible to observe the consequences through the mullet catch.

Incident three shows the 'Warren' and Pender families to be rivals for the dominant position of respect and authority in the Cove. This was demonstrated by the fact that only after Johnny 'Warren' threw a fish to Joe Pender did the other members of the Mullet Seine attempt to engage him in conversation. The incident showed the Lifeboat coxswain to be subordinate to Johnny 'Warren', since he only attempted to speak to Joe Pender after the fish had been thrown.

Conclusion and Discussion

This chapter has used the ethnographic present to convey the importance of kinship in a community that has undergone over a century of change through the combined forces of the tourism and fishing industries. The intention here is to add a postscript to the original ethnography using recent fieldwork undertaken in Sennen Cove (April 2003).

The chapter began with a 'statement of the structure of the society' (Mitchell 1964:xii) drawn from genealogical interviews and documentary sources. Mitchell (1964:xii) maintains that such a statement is an essential prerequisite for the use of the extended case method or situational analysis.

Sennen immediately prior to the development of tourism in the parish had a stratification system made up of two status groups from among the local population, the Covers and the Overhillers. These status groups can be accurately described as communities (Weber 1982:391). As a consequence of the growing importance of tourism to the local visitor, the social structure became more complex with the addition of 'classes,' used here in the Weberian sense to denote those people who 'represent possible and frequent bases for communal action' (Weber 1982:388). In this context the concept of predatory behaviour has been developed to explain the acquisitiveness of visitors with regard to property in the parish. Before examining the usefulness of this concept in explaining visitor behaviour, the chapter sought to highlight the important role women play in the changing social milieu.

Women were found to have acted as intermediaries between the local men and the visitors, through the provision of hospitality. The relationship has been shown to be one based on market principles. Hospitality necessarily involves social relations between host and guest. What has been shown here is that the socio-economic position of the visitor and their host has converged over time. This convergence has been demonstrated in local people's descriptions of the visitor. The post-war period has seen a shift away from the 'better class of visitor' to those perceived as being 'the ordinary working class people that come'.

As the visitors and their hosts have moved closer together structurally, the social distance between them has increased. This inverse relationship has been most clearly demonstrated through their increased physical distance when on holiday, expressed through a movement from taking in lodgers to providing self-catering accommodation.

Property remains an essential prerequisite to the continuity and social significance of kinship in Sennen Cove today. Women continue to act as intermediaries in the local tourist industry by adopting a more aggressive entrepreneurial role. This role has two important dimensions. Women with kin ties in the Cove now have property rights and actively invest in holiday accommodation. Continuity of ownership by a kin set is secured for future generations by 'family meetings' at which the inheritance of property is agreed to pass to female members on the death of the patriarch. The entrepreneurial role of these women also has a more pragmatic side. They employ agencies to let the properties bequeathed to them. The effect is to increase still further the social distance between Covers and tourists. It is now no longer necessary for a Cover to ever meet their 'guests'.

The chapter has shown that some visitors follow a career to become local residents, one of the most interesting facets of their holiday career engaging in what I have termed predatory behaviour. This concept has been developed from observations made in the field, to explain the calculative behaviour of some visitors to intervene in the local property market. Predatory behaviour is characterised by the visitor gaining information about a property likely to become vacant in the parish, *before* the sale becomes public. This is achieved through gaining the confidence of local people.

The day-to-day life of the non-visitor (local people and local residents) has been explained with reference to the institutional forms which give meaning to their lives. My use of the term institution corresponds closely with Leach (1982:234), who included not only 'customary arrangements' but also the 'personnel who are involved in those arrangements'. My study of local institutions has been directed toward the local residents engaged in fund-raising for the lifeboat. Case material has shown that they are packaging and selling themselves as a commoditised version of Cornish culture.

The behaviour of local women in distancing themselves from the Lifeboat is similar to their relationship with the visitor when on holiday. The observed behaviour of local women adds support to the view already expressed that the way visitors are perceived and related to on holiday is replicated when they become local residents. In this context Van Velsen (1964:xxvi) has said that situational analysis puts the reader in a better position to evaluate the ethnography, 'when several or most of the actors appear again and again in different situations'.

My analysis of the mullet as an institution returns the reader to the starting point of the chapter, the significance of kinship to present-day behaviour. The case material showed the lifeboat to be secondary in the minds of the Covers when they had to make a choice whether or not to protect an economic resource (the mullet) that had been their birthright for generations. The mullet dispute united families with unresolved differences, the Penders and Warrens, over an unwritten rule that should not have been broken. Today, the mullet remain significant to the Covers not so much for their value as a catch, but as a symbol of the tensions that continue to exist between kin sets.

The analysis of these incidents adds substance to a point made by Fox (1984) that the study of kinship is the study of what a person does and 'why they do it, and the consequences of the adoption of one alternative rather than another.' Kinship remains an important indicator of belonging and cultural continuity in Sennen Cove. This has only been possible because kin groups have adapted their traditional lines of inheritance and descent to ensure their continuity in the face of social changes brought about through tourism.

References

Cornish Telegraph
1879   Report on Mullet Catch *Cornish Telegraph* 4.3.1879:4.

1882   Report on Mullet Catch *Cornish Telegraph* 2.3.1882:4.
1882   Report on the Mullet Fishery *Cornish Telegraph* 6.4.1882:5.
1882   Report on the Mullet Fishery in Sennen Cove *Cornish Telegraph* 13.4.1882:4.
1883   Report on the Mullet Fishery *Cornish Telegraph* 1.3.1883:5.
1885   Report on Mullet Catch *Cornish Telegraph* 8.1.1885:5.

Cornishman
1960   '£2,000 Mullet Shoal at Sennen Defended' *Cornishman* 14.1.1960:7.

Daily Telegraph and Morning Post
1960   Police Prevent Clash in Fishermans "War" *Daily Telegraph and Morning Post*.

Fox, R.
1984   *Kinship and Marriage: An Anthropological Perspective*. Cambridge: Cambridge University Press.
1995   The Land: Use, Ownership and Inheritance. In: *The Tory Island: a People of the Celtic Fringe*, University of Notre Dame Press. Pp. 82-126.

Giddens, A.
1978   *Capitalism and Modern Social Theory: an Analysis of the Writings of Marx, Durkheim and Weber*. Cambridge: Cambridge University Press.

Gluckman, M.
1982   The Peace and the Feud. In: L.A. Coser and B.Rosenberg (Eds.), *Sociological Theory: a book of readings*, New York, Macmillan. Pp. 215-217.

Ireland, M.
1987   Planning Policy and Holiday Homes in Cornwall. In: M. Bouquet and M. Winter (Eds.), *Who from their Labours Rest? Conflict and Practice in Rural Tourism*. Aldershot: Avebury.

Leach, E.
1982   *Social Anthropology – Fontana Masterguides*. London, Fontana Press.

Mitchell, J.C.
1964   'Forward' to *The Politics of Kinship*, by J. van Velsen. Manchester University Press. Pp. xxiii-xxix.

Sunday Independent
1973   The Great Mullet Mystery *Sunday Independent*.

Van Velsen, J.
1964   Note on the Situational Analysis. In: *The Politics of Kinship*. Manchester: Manchester University Press. Pp. xxxiii-xxix.

Weber, M.
1982   Class and Status In: Coser L.A. and B. Rosenberg, *Sociological Theory: a Book of Readings* (5th Edition). New York: Macmillan. Pp. 387.

Websites

Cornwall County Council
2003   Fact and Figures: Socio-Economic Statistics for Cornwall (http://www.cornwall.gov.uk/Facts/facts8.htm) Accessed 28/07/03.

6

Evaluating Contrasting Approaches to Marine Ecotourism: 'Dive Tourism' and 'Research Tourism' in the Wakatobi Marine National Park, Indonesia

Julian Clifton

Introduction

The establishment of marine protected areas (MPAs) in developing countries is perceived as solving problems of over-exploitation of marine resources whilst also offering opportunities to promote alternative sources of income for local communities through tourism-related activities (Boersma and Parrish 1999; Gubbay 1995). These activities, commonly referred to as nature-based tourism or ecotourism, constitute one of the fastest growing sectors of the travel market (World Tourism Organisation 2002). Increasing consumer choice and spending ability in developed countries has led to an expansion of destinations catering to tourists demanding increasingly remote and unspoiled locations. Whilst the definition of ecotourism itself is subject to debate, most writers accept the following description:

> ...[ecotourism is] environmentally responsible, enlightening travel and visitation to relatively undisturbed natural areas to enjoy and appreciate nature and any accompanying cultural features both past and present that promotes conservation, has low visitor impact and provides for beneficially active socio-economic involvement of local populations (Ceballos-Lascurain 1996).

This definition highlights the fact that although ecotourism should cause minimal disturbance to the natural environment, it should also bring about economic and social benefits to local communities. The degree to which ecotourism fulfils these objectives is to some extent dependent upon the ability of government departments with jurisdiction over protected areas to influence the development of ecotourism activities. In developing countries, this ability is severely restricted by a lack of resources, leading to many protected areas being labelled 'paper parks' as a result of the lack of managerial control over activities within them (MacAndrews 1998).

In analysing the impacts of ecotourism in developing countries, attention has progressed from a focus on purely economic or environmental benefits to an approach which adopts a development-oriented perspective (Scheyvens 1999). This latter approach emphasises the need to facilitate community development through ecotourism in a manner that empowers the local community in a number of ways. Economic benefits are therefore seen not just in terms of total revenue but also with regard to the numbers of people involved and the extent to which these benefits are distributed within communities. The development approach focuses on socio-cultural impacts. For example, whether ecotourism improves community cohesion through activities such as investing in communal facilities and reinforcing the value of local traditions and the awareness of the natural environment. Attention is also paid in this analysis to the impact of ecotourism on local people's ability to influence decisions regarding the management of the protected area. These impacts can be analysed in terms of their capacity to empower the local community in economic, social and environmental terms.

This paper will utilise a development approach to examine two contrasting tourism operations in a marine national park in Indonesia which both advertise themselves under the banner of ecotourism. The analysis will demonstrate the contrasting impacts of ecotourism and identify issues related to the effective management of ecotourism in developing countries. It is hoped that this will serve to underline the need to critically assess the value of marine ecotourism in terms of its impact on local communities and their ability to actively contribute and participate in the management of their local environment.

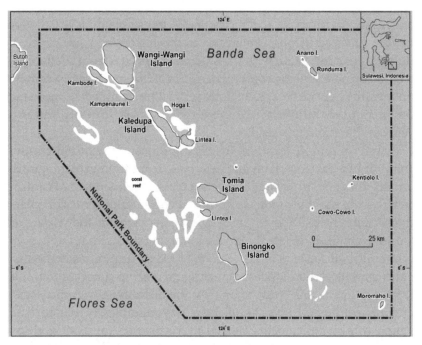

Figure 6.1. Location of Wakatobi Marine National Park.

Background to Case Study Area

The Wakatobi Marine National Park, located in the Tukang Besi islands of southeast Sulawesi, Indonesia (Fig. 6.1) covers a total area of
13,900 km² and was officially designated in 1996, making it one of
the largest and newest marine national parks in Indonesia. The park
encompasses the four major islands of Wangi-Wangi, Kaledupa,
Tomia and Binongko, which support a total of around 80,000 people, as well as sixteen smaller uninhabited islands and atolls. Arable
and pastoral activities are mainly practised by the Wakatobi ethnic
group, which constitutes around 92 percent of the islands' population. The other group in the area are the Bajau or 'sea gypsies' who
are scattered throughout coastal environments of Southeast Asia.
These communities rely almost exclusively on marine resources for
food, fuel and building materials, whilst engaging in small scale trading of surplus fish catches with the Wakatobi. Surveys conducted by
overseas non-governmental organisations in the early 1990s highlighted the threat to marine biodiversity posed by the increasing use
of destructive fishing practices by local communities subject to competition with outside fishermen, a factor common to many areas in

Indonesia (Cesar *et al.* 1997). Proposals to establish an MPA were further justified through reference to the historical significance of Sulawesi in connection with the studies of Alfred Russel Wallace, as well as the potential to promote marine ecotourism in such a remote and relatively pristine area of Indonesia. This resulted in the rapid designation of the area as a marine national park in 1996, within 3 years of the initial proposal.

Given its remote location, which until recently required a minimum of two days overland and sea travel from the nearest regional airport, it is not surprising that ecotourism is limited to two centres of activity in the Wakatobi. Despite their contrasting modes of operation as detailed in Table 6.1, both operations promote themselves as 'ecotourism' in publicity materials, justifying this with references to economic and social benefits reaching local communities in their vicinity as well as their strategies relating to marine conservation. It is the intention of this study to analyse the differing economic, social and environmental impacts of these two examples of ecotourism, which will be henceforth referred to as 'dive ecotourism' and 'research ecotourism', reflecting their core clientele and main activities.

Table 6.1. Characteristics of two ecotourism operations in the Wakatobi Marine National Park

	Dive ecotourism: Wakatobi Divers, Tomia Island http://www.wakatobi.com	Research ecotourism: Operation Wallacea, Hoga Island http://www.opwall.com
Ownership	Swiss-owned company	UK-owned company
Year established	1995	1996
Operating season	10 months (March–December)	3 months (July–September)
Clientele and origin	Experienced divers / photographers; predominantly from USA and W. Europe	University students, almost all from UK & Ireland; specialising in marine biology / geography
Visitor capacity	22 (2000)	120 (2001)
Cost of visit	US$2700 for 2 weeks including return flight from Bali	US$2400 for 4 weeks; US$3250 for 6 weeks excluding all flights
Number of employees	6 foreign, 22 local	25 foreign, 29 local

Despite the vastly differing visitor capacity of the two operations, the total number of visitors to both is relatively similar. Whilst the capacity of the dive ecotourism operation has remained stable since its inception, its resort facilities are booked up for the duration of its open season, giving rise to a total of around 480 visitors per year. In contrast, whilst the research ecotourism operation is only open to coincide with the university summer vacation in the UK and Ireland, there has been a rapid increase in total visitor numbers during this period from 50 in 1995 to 300 in 2001.

Furthermore, in July 2001 the construction of an airstrip on the island of Tomia was completed. The presence of the airstrip, which had been privately financed by the dive ecotourism operation, reduced the travel time from Bali to Tomia from two days to four hours. The implications of this with regard to the future development of ecotourism within the region will be discussed later in this paper. It is also worthwhile to note that there is very little personal or professional contact between the owners of these two ecotour operations in the Wakatobi.

Methodology

Field research was conducted for two periods of eight weeks, one in 2000 and one in 2001. This was initiated through a series of interviews with the owners and employees of the two ecotour resorts. The interviews explored a range of issues including daily operations, product marketing and the relationships between local communities and national park authorities. These were followed by interviews with local employees and individuals from communities located in close proximity to the two ecotour resorts. These interviews focused upon the extent to which economic and social benefits were reaching local communities and the nature of any perceived problems associated with the presence of the ecotour operators. Interviews were conducted with the assistance of locally based translators and, in the case of the Bajau, questions were phrased in the Bajau dialect in order to ensure accuracy of response. Participant observation provided insights based upon informal discussions with a range of informants, together with notes of activities and interactions between local residents and overseas visitors. Secondary sources of information were also utilised in the research. Analysis of available financial records from the ecotour operators was conducted to obtain additional economic data, and the socio-cultural impact of the ecotour operators was also addressed through analysis of web-based publicity material.

Results and Discussion

Economic Impacts

The annual expenditures of the ecotour operators on locally obtained goods and services was determined through interviews and analysis of financial records. For the purposes of this study, 'local' was defined as goods or services that were obtained from the island where the ecotour operator was based. The data are summarised in Table 6.2.

Table 6.2. Local spending associated with two ecotourism operators in Wakatobi Marine National Park

	Dive ecotourism local spending year 2000 (US$)	Research ecotourism local spending year 2000 (US$)
Accommodation	-	9210
Local staff salaries	10560	3500
Food and drink	500	3900
Non-food items	-	4210
Total	11060	20820

It is apparent from Table 6.2 that whilst the dive ecotourism operation is open 10 months per year in comparison to the 3 months during which the research ecotourism operation is active, the latter spends approximately double the total quantity of income on locally derived goods and services. In order to put these data into perspective, the average monthly salary in this region of Indonesia is in the order of US$40, hence the total spent by the research ecotourism operation is equivalent to the monthly wage of 520 people. This is primarily due to the policy of renting accommodation provided by local landowners in order to house individuals. The research ecotourism operation is also dependent upon local suppliers of non-food items, primarily related to the operation and maintenance of dive boats, which are supplied by a village co-operative shop.

These practices have wider implications in terms of the distribution of economic benefits within and between local communities. In the case of the dive ecotourism operation, the reliance upon food imported from outside the local area means that financial benefits are essentially limited to the 22 local staff who are employed by the ecotour operator. However, in the case of the research ecotourism operation, in addition to the direct benefits experienced by employees, a large number of local individuals also benefit indirectly through use of the co-operative, whose participants will receive some additional income when profits from the co-operative are returned to its members. Furthermore, the purchasing policies of the research ecotourism operation ensure that economic benefits reach both ethnic groups in the local community. The landowners supplying accommodation are all members of the majority Wakatobi ethnic group, whilst the minority Bajau are the people from whom fresh fish are purchased on a daily basis.

However, there are certain constraints and potential problems associated with the incorporation of local communities into the economic activities of ecotourist operators. It is inevitable that the communities in close proximity to the ecotour operator will experience greater opportunities to realise economic benefits to the detriment of more distant communities. This may generate resentment against both the ecotour operator and those communities enjoying a greater share of the economic benefits. Furthermore, during the course of this study, a limit on local purchases had to be imposed in order to avoid excessive use of local markets and a concurrent inflation in prices or shortage of supplies. There is also a potential danger in an excessive reliance of the local communities on the research ecotourism operator as a source of income, as this activity only operates for a limited period of time each year. This could lead to overcapacity in terms of producing and supplying goods when not required by the ecotour operator, whilst in the longer term it is possible that the neglect of other income-generating activities could lead to a loss of skills and knowledge, particularly in the farming sector. An additional problem relates to the rental of locally owned accommodation, which has resulted in a sharp increase in building activity as the numbers of 'research ecotourists' have increased in recent years. In legal terms, the Department of Forestry, as the lead authority in Indonesia's national parks, is charged with ensuring that building activity takes place within designated zones, whilst the Department of Tourism is responsible for ensuring that buildings conform to appropriate designs. However, both of these departments are severely restricted in terms of budgetary allowances at the national and provincial level, and as a result there is no effective monitoring or control of building activity within the marine park. Consequently, the increase in building activity can have environmental implications with regard to wastewater disposal and can result in a considerable degree of visual intrusion. Finally, questions need to be raised about the financial stability of ecotourism in the longer term, which will depend upon a range of economic, social and political factors at the international level as well as the fortunes of the individual ecotour operator. If visitor numbers decline, it is likely that the financial losses experienced amongst local individuals and communities will cause disaffection and possible opposition to any alternative proposals to develop ecotourism in the area, with potential consequences for the longer term viability of the marine park.

Socio-Cultural Impacts

When evaluating the impact of ecotourist operations on the social and cultural fabric of local communities, a distinction can be drawn between direct and indirect effects. The former refers to the consequences of interaction between visitors, local communities and the ecotour operator itself with regard to the maintenance or otherwise of local institutions, traditions and values. The latter refers to the image of the local community projected by the advertisements of the ecotour operator. The way in which ecotour operators portray local people will influence the expectations of visitors and thereby affect the nature of subsequent social interaction with local communities.

Direct Impacts

The direct socio-cultural impacts of ecotourism are largely dependent upon two factors: the willingness of local communities to accommodate the presence of foreign visitors and the nature of informal social contact between the two groups. The first factor may be considerably influenced by the extent to which local communities benefit in economic terms from the presence of ecotourists, a relationship that has been explained elsewhere through the use of social exchange theory (Ap 1992). The second factor is reflected in local residents' attitudes towards ecotourism. In the present context these attitudes were found to be markedly different for the two types of tour operations. Both factors were addressed through discussions with individuals living in close proximity to the ecotour operations and with the operators themselves. With regards to the dive ecotourism organisation, visitors are offered the opportunity to undertake small organised group tours of the nearest Bajau fishing village and observe activities promoted as traditional sarong and boat manufacturing. Residents did not perceive these tours as offering a regular source of income through the sale of handicrafts or food produce because the tours occurred too infrequently and without prior notice. Whilst the operator does purchase occasional supplies of fish from the Bajau settlement, again these were seen to be too infrequent to present a reliable or significant source of income to individuals. With regards to the employment of residents in the dive ecotourism operation, research demonstrated that jobs in maintenance and catering available to local residents were taken almost exclusively by individuals from the mainstream Wakatobi ethnic group and not from the Bajau group. As discussed below, the nature of these types of employment may reinforce any existing stereotyped images of both visitor and local resident, with little opportunity for informal exchange and interaction.

It can therefore be concluded that in the case of the dive ecotourism operation, the potential for mutually beneficial social interaction between visitors and local communities in Tomia and the Bajau in particular will be extremely limited. Taken alongside the restricted range of economic benefits outlined above, it is perhaps to be expected that attitudes towards ecotourism held by local residents may be characterised by apathy or negativity. Such attitudes were found in the Bajau fishing community in connection with the designation of a no-fishing zone around the dive ecotour resort. The no-fishing zone was created in 1995, predating the establishment of the marine national park itself. This restriction was imposed in order to safeguard the reef adjacent to the dive resort from the perceived threat associated with local fishing activity and destructive fishing practices such as cyanide and bomb fishing in particular. Such threats are commonly attributed to nomadic fishing communities such as the Bajau on account of their propensity to venture over large distances in fishing activities and their perceived immunity to the consequences of overfishing and destructive fishing practices (Hopley and Suharsono 2000). Whilst this may have been the case in the past, the 'true' nomadic Bajau are increasingly rare in Indonesia and elsewhere in Southeast Asia, primarily due to direct and indirect state pressure to conform with an image of mainstream modern society (Hope 2002). This process of sedentarisation has resulted in contemporary Bajau settlements such as those visited in the course of this study being built on stilts over reef flats, where individual houses are connected by a series of raised walkways and bridges. It is therefore questionable as to whether the exclusion of all artisanal fishing activity regardless of the technique utilised can be justified in terms of marine resource conservation alone. The interests of the dive ecotourism operator in terms of guaranteeing visitors sole access to 'undisturbed' coral reefs appear to be paramount in this case, to the detriment of the local fishing economy and the relations between residents and the ecotour operator. The legal implications of this are addressed later in this paper, but it is important to note at this stage that the designation and subsequent strict enforcement of the no-fishing zone without local consultation provides a basis for ongoing resentment towards the existence and activities of the dive ecotourism operation within the local community.

The extent of social contact between visitors and local residents is therefore considerably restricted because most overseas visitors encounter local people working primarily in maintenance and cleaning roles for the dive ecotour operator. Those tourists who do visit local villages do so in a highly formalised and structured manner. As highlighted by Teye *et al.* (2002), it is important to recognise that employment within tourism should not be assumed to generate support for the industry, as individuals working for a tourist operator may well hold negative attitudes as a result of their experiences. Whilst there was no direct evidence for this in the current study, it does appear that employees' attitudes may contribute to the negative opinions held by local people.

Conversely, the extent to which positive socio-cultural impacts can be generated through economic benefits and maximising the opportunity for informal contact between visitors and local communities is reflected in the opinions held by local people in contact with the research ecotourism operation. Surveys of local residents in both 2000 and 2001 indicated a near unanimous level of support for the continued operation and expansion of the research ecotourism operation, with respondents referring to the range of economic as well as socio-cultural benefits associated with its existence. As stated earlier, there is opportunity for both ethnic groups to benefit in economic terms from the activities of this ecotour operator through formal means such as providing food, labour and accommodation. During 2001, it was noted that additional economic benefits are increasingly being realised on an informal basis by members of the Wakatobi ethnic group through providing tours of the island of Kaledupa and the Bajau ethnic group through canoe trips around the village of Sampela.

CHAPTER SIX

Both of these are offered to overseas visitors as a weekend recreational pursuit and involve a wider cross-section of the local communities, with young people and children often being at the forefront of these activities. Thus, the local community has welcomed developments that facilitate the wider distribution of economic benefits. Such developments are in accordance with economic principles of ecotourism, as they will lessen the possibility that benefits are restricted to a few individuals in positions of power within local communities.

In addition to these formal and informal means of generating income, local residents stressed the impact of the research ecotourism operation on local culture and society as a reason for their continued support. Perhaps the most significant factor in this sense relates to the accommodation policy pursued by the research ecotourism operator. The majority of visitors are housed on the island of Hoga in accommodation built specifically for this purpose by local residents who often live nearby and undertake daily maintenance of the property. In addition, a number of visitors are housed in rooms rented from local families. As visitors stay for a minimum period of two weeks up to a maximum of eight weeks, this provides ample opportunity for informal social contact and interaction with the families of hosts or landlords. Personal observations recorded numerous instances of visitors conversing with local individuals, playing with children or engaging in sporting activities. The latter was particularly evident during national holidays such as Independence Day, a highlight of which was organised competitions between local teams and those composed of visitors.

It is also important to note the significance of the research activities undertaken by the visitors to the research ecotourism operation, the vast majority of whom are university students. Many of these projects involve working with fishermen, women and children from both ethnic groups as part of research programmes. The projects often relate to socio-economic aspects of local communities as well as their relationship with the national park authorities and the park's impact upon local livelihoods. Consequently, visitors spend a considerable amount of time interviewing individuals in their homes and other informal settings as well as accompanying fishermen during their daily activities, all of which will serve to acculturate the visitors to the local environment and, it may be assumed, increase local communities' acceptance of them. Some of these activities are particularly oriented towards community development. They include the provision of English language classes for adults in their homes and for children in schools, the implementation of a census for villages and, in Sampela, the provision of birth control services for those women wishing to participate. These programmes are recognised as valuable by local communities and serve to generate support for this type of ecotourism activity. Local residents expressed an awareness that their villages and, particularly in the case of the Bajau, their culture represent a significant attraction for overseas visitors staying and working in the settlement.

Taking these opinions into account, it can be seen that this form of ecotourism is potentially beneficial in terms of social capital and community development in a number of ways. One area of concern may be expressed with regard to adverse socio-cultural impacts of Western visitors, which have been noted elsewhere as particularly significant in remote or rural communities in developing countries. This may take place gradually through a process of commodification or loss of cultural authenticity (Sharpley 1999) or as a result of cultural and value differences generating conflict and hostility (Reisinger 1994). Such processes have not been noted in the current case study, however. This could reflect the fact that the current scale of research ecotourism activity is relatively small, and total numbers of visitors are limited. Furthermore, surveys of visitors have indicated a high level of awareness of potential adverse cultural impacts and a willingness to conform to local societal norms and values (Galley and Clifton, forthcoming). Although the situation may change in the future, there is little indication that adverse socio-cultural impacts have been taking place thus far.

Comparison of these two examples of ecotourism therefore highlights the positive contribution which research ecotourism can make to local communities. In particular, close informal interaction can raise local communities' awareness of the distinctive nature of their values and customs in comparison to those of foreign visitors. Research ecotourism can also add to the social capital of the community through improving their knowledge of the natural environment and their expertise in foreign languages. In contrast, the limited potential for contact between local individuals and visitors in the dive ecotourism operation, in combination with the relatively limited economic benefits available to local communities, has generated an atmosphere of apathy or distrust which needs to be addressed.

Indirect Impacts

These findings are borne out by an analysis of publicity material available on the websites of the two ecotour operators, which is the main source of advertising for these companies. The analysis compared the language and images used to describe the local community and visitors' interactions with local individuals. This is important because these projections of the local community influence visitors' pre-conceived notions of the local community, thereby either reinforcing or combating stereotyped images of indigenous communities. Furthermore, they influence visitor behaviour by implying that visitors may act as passive consumers of local culture, or on the other hand, they may emphasise that visitors are guests of the local community and are expected to act accordingly.

A distinct difference is evident in the portrayal of the local communities and visitor behaviour in the websites of the respective ecotour operators. The dive ecotourism website utilises phrases such as *'experience the culture!', 'the natives are friendly – no-one is begging or pestering visitors'* and *'it is possible you will be the first tourist some villagers have ever seen'*, which are supplemented with images of local individuals in traditional dress performing a ritual dance. The research ecotourism website, by contrast, uses images of local individuals alongside their houses alongside quotes such as *'you will be working, travelling and socialising with ordinary Indonesians', '[the people are] very welcoming, friendly and interested in you'* and *'you will need to adapt to the social and cultural standards'*. It is evident that visitors to the dive ecotourism operation may expect to receive samples of local culture if they so require, thereby demoting the local community to a subservient position and implying that local people will be in awe of foreign visitors to some extent. This perspective, which could be characterised as a neo-colonial attitude toward indigenous culture, stands in stark contrast to the ideas projected by the research ecotourism publicity, which stresses the need for the visitor to adapt to local norms and values and presents images assumed to represent daily life amongst everyday Indonesians. Although the research ecotourism depiction is simplistic, with little attention to the widespread problems of poverty, education and healthcare within this region of Indonesia, it is clearly far more congruent with ecotourism principles in terms of respecting local cultural values and ensuring local people are not disadvantaged in any way as a result of ecotourism activities.

Environmental Impacts

The third area of analysis of ecotourism impacts in the Wakatobi is the management of the marine national park. As stated earlier, many protected areas in developing countries are beset by financial problems that inhibit the implementation of management plans designed to ensure conservation and sustainable use of resources within the protected area. However, the development of ecotourism within national parks such as the Wakatobi requires a high degree of financial investment and commitment to the region on behalf of the ecotour operators. For example, the construction of an airstrip financed by the dive ecotourism operator. In the face of management uncertainty, ecotour operators will inevitably seek to ensure that the quality of their principal environmental assets is maintained in order to secure their investment in ecotourism. This is manifest in several areas of activity within the Wakatobi and has considerable implications for the local community's ability to become empowered in decision-making activities affecting their local environment.

In order to secure their investment in the Wakatobi, both ecotour operators have established organisations that are partly or wholly financed by the ecotourism operation. The ecotour operators justify the existence of these organisations, or 'trust funds', by explaining the need to expand their areas of activity in order to ensure the continued conservation of the wildlife in the marine park. They refer to the inability of the park authority to undertake such activities. These activities include providing educational material to local communities highlighting the importance of coral reefs as fish spawning grounds and training local people to monitor reef quality and disseminate information to other members of the community. Given the availability of qualified staff and the reliance of both ecotourism operations on overseas visitors, these activities would seem to represent a logical step in facilitating community involvement in environmental management.

However, the trust funds are also active in other areas. In terms of enforcement, the trust funds are increasingly important in supplying fuel to park rangers in order to enable them to mount patrols. As the proportion of funding supplied by the ecotour operators increases, the patrols will be under more pressure to strictly enforce rules applying to fishing activity in the vicinity of the ecotour resorts in order to ensure the resorts attract overseas visitors. This is illustrated in the case of the dive ecotourism operation, which has built a base specifically for the park rangers in close proximity to the resort. It is possible that local communities affected by the more rigorous application of park rules could become alienated from the principles of marine conservation and less likely to participate or collaborate with park management in the future. Furthermore, the question is raised as to whether the activities of small-scale fishermen are the main threat facing the biodiversity of the park, which also experiences incursions of trawlers and larger fishing vessels based outside the marine park. These cause considerable damage both to reefs and to fish stocks.

A final area of concern relates to the establishment of no-fishing zones that are now present over the fringing reefs adjacent to both ecotour resorts. These zones, as noted earlier, generate negative opinions in the case of the dive ecotourism resort. However, opposition to the zones has not yet become apparent with regard to the research ecotourism operation, primarily because the operator adopted a process of ongoing consultation and dialogue with local communities concerning the nature of enforceable restrictions. Aside from effects on the local fishing community near to the dive ecotourism resort, there are wider management implications which need to be addressed. The designation of no-fishing zones by ecotour operators amounts to an assumption of the role of the Ministry of Forestry, which under national law is responsible for allocating resource use within protected areas. It is therefore apparent that the authority of the legally empowered institution in this area is being undermined to some extent by foreign-owned organisations that are not accountable to local communities. Furthermore, no-fishing zones should theoretically be imposed where intensive fish spawning takes place in order to protect stocks (McClanahan and Kaunda-Arara 1996). It is therefore quite likely that the current location of these no-fishing zones reflects the interests of ecotourism more than those of marine environmental management. Finally, the exclusion of fishermen from one area often results in increased fishing effort being directed elsewhere, which could cause a decline in fish stocks in other locations. The provision of alternative income-generating activities such as seaweed farming or fish farming would help alleviate this situation. However, given the lack of funds available for management, it is likely that the responsibility for this would fall to the ecotour operator, again raising the question as to whether such duties should remain with the ecotourism industry.

Given the current political and financial situation of Indonesia, it is unlikely that funding of protected areas will change significantly in the near future. Meanwhile, the growth in the ecotourism market is likely to strengthen the ability of ecotour operators to influence park management in the ways described above. Park managers may avoid implementing decisions opposed by the ecotour operators. This could therefore lead to a situation where management decisions increasingly reflect the interests of ecotourism rather than local communities, leading to the disempowerment of local communities in terms of their ability to contribute to the management of protected areas.

Conclusions

This case study has utilised a development-oriented perspective to analyse the impacts of two forms of ecotourism operating within a newly established marine national park in Indonesia. It has demonstrated that despite the similar labelling of these two activities, they are associated with contrasting economic and social impacts with regard to local communities. These impacts reflect the philosophy of the ecotour operator as well as the nature of the ecotourism activity. They underline the need for a critical analysis of differing forms of ecotourism in order to aid planning of those activities that can most benefit local communities. It is apparent that activities classified as 'research ecotourism' in this study offer considerable potential and could well serve as a model for future developments, particularly in remote locations suited to the needs of this sector of the market. The present study has also highlighted that economic benefits can be equitably distributed amongst local communities with relative ease, but that increased integration between the local economy and the ecotourism industry can lead to a range of potential problems. The study has also demonstrated the value of assessing how ecotour operators present local communities to their potential market, as this will reflect the emphasis placed by the ecotour operator on generating significant lasting financial benefits within local communities. Because of the difficulties experienced by government authorities responsible for the management of Indonesia's protected areas, attention has also been drawn to the increasing influence of ecotourist operators in this respect and its significance with regard to the future role of local communities. These findings highlight the need for planners and managers to ensure an appropriate mix of ecotourism activities is promoted within protected areas in order to generate benefits to local communities whilst maintaining a range of attractions to the visitor market. It also underlines the need for a code of conduct to be developed which will ensure the ecotourism industry can be held accountable for its actions. This is particularly important in light of the increasing attention paid in the literature to principles of co-management of protected areas, which are intended to address the issue of lack of managerial capacity through a sharing of responsibility between managers and local communities (Christie and White 1997). The influence of ecotour operators on park management merits attention in this debate in order to design appropriate models that facilitate the distribution of management responsibilities between park authorities, local communities and ecotourist organisations.

References

Ap, J.
1992   Residents' Perceptions on Tourism Impacts. *Annals of Tourism Research*
19:665-690.

Boersma, P.D. and J.K. Parrish
1999   Limiting Abuse: Marine Protected Areas, a Limited Solution. *Ecological Economics* 31:287-304.

Ceballos-Lascurain, H.
1996   *Tourism, Ecotourism and Protected Areas*. Gland: IUCN.

Cesar H., C.G. Lundin, S. Bettencourt, and J. Dixon
1997   Indonesian Coral Reefs – an Economic Analysis of a Precious but Threatened Resource. *Ambio* 26(6):343-350.

Christie, P. and A.T. White
1997   Trends in Development of Coastal Area Management in Tropical Countries: from Central to Community Orientation. *Coastal Management* 25:155-181.

Galley, G. and J. Clifton (forthcoming)
The Motivational and Demographic Characteristics of Research Ecotourists: a Case Study of Operation Wallacea Volunteers in South-East Sulawesi, Indonesia. Submitted to *Journal of Ecotourism*.

Gubbay, S. (Ed.)
1995   *Marine Protected Areas: Principles and Techniques for Management*. London: Chapman and Hall.

Hope, S.
2002   *Outcasts of the Islands: the Sea Gypsies of South-East Asia*. London: Flamingo.

Hopley, D. and Suharsono
2000   *The Status of Coral Reefs in Eastern Indonesia*. Townsville: Australian Institute of Marine Science.

MacAndrews, C.
1998   Improving the Management of Indonesia's National Parks: Lessons from Two Case Studies. *Bulletin of Indonesian Economic Studies* 34(1):121-137.

McClanahan, T.R. and B. Kaunda-Arara
1996   Fishery Recovery in a Coral Reef Marine Park and its Effect on the Adjacent Fishery. *Conservation Biology* 10(4):1187-1199.

Reisinger, Y.
1994   Social Contact between Tourists and Hosts of Different Cultural Backgrounds. In: A.V. Seaton (Ed.), *Tourism – the State of the Art.* Chichester: Wiley. Pp. 743-755.

Scheyvens, R.
1999   Ecotourism and the Empowerment of Local Communities. *Tourism Management* 20:245-249.

Sharpley, R.
1999   *Tourism, Tourists and Society* (2nd edition). Huntingdon: ELM Publications.

Teye, V., S.F. Sönmez, and E. Sirakaya
2002   Residents' Attitudes Towards Tourism Development. *Annals of Tourism Research* 29(3):668-688.

World Tourism Organisation
2002   International Year of Ecotourism, http://www.world-tourism.org/ sustainable/IYE-Main-Menu.htm (2 December 2002).

7

Fishermen and the Creation of Marine Parks: Northern Sporades (Greece), Northern Cap de Creus (Catalonia), and the Iroise Sea (France)

Katia Frangoudes and Frédérique Alban

Introduction

The three examples of national marine parks to be presented here have been chosen for the following reasons: their set-up procedures differ, the objectives underlying their creation differ, and the points of view held by the respective fishing communities vary. The three national marine parks are the National Park of the Northern Sporades in Greece, the Northern Cap de Creus Nature Park in Spain, and the National Marine Park of Iroise Sea in France. The establishment of the three parks was based on three different initiatives in which affected fishing communities played, or did not play, significant roles. Here, we will briefly present the context, the reasoning, and the decision-making mechanisms that led to the classification of these areas. This will lead us to present the fishermen's positions regarding these parks. The data used to illustrate this report originate in fieldwork undertaken in 2000. The purpose of this fieldwork was to explore the impact of these marine protective measures on local fishing activity and to record how fishermen perceive the measures.

The National Marine Park of the Northern Sporades in Greece

The first steps towards classifying the island of Alonisos and the surrounding area started in 1988. Four years later, the park was created by presidential decree. This was the first national marine park to be created in Greece. Inland national parks had been in existence since the 1940s. The speed of the process by which the marine park was created raises a number of issues.

The project of creating a marine park in the Northern Sporades was put forward by an environmental non-governmental organisation (NGO), MOM (Hellenic Association for the Study and Protection of the Mediterranean Seal), with the aim of saving the seal, *Monachus monachus*, which is in danger of extinction. According to the President of MOM, the island of Alonisos is the ideal spot for the creation of a national marine park because the surrounding islets shelter a dozen seals, because tourism has little effect on the area, and because coastal fishing is the island's main economic driver. He stated that 'not all the Greek islands can become a Santorini or a Corfu'.

In 1988, MOM organised an international meeting on the island of Alonisos. Several European environmental NGOs and European civil servants attended. The project to save the seal population undertaken by MOM received unanimous support at the end of the meeting. Following the meeting, the Greek NGO was the beneficiary of European and international funding for the protection of the seals. The creation of a national park seemed the best protective measure, as this would not only protect the seals, but would also protect the marine ecosystem, which is said to be exceptional.

European Union funds were used to build a veterinary health centre for the seals and to purchase a boat to be used for scientific research and for monitoring the park. The national park was officially inaugurated by a presidential decision, May 16, 1992.

The MOM president stated that

> at the end of the 1980s, none of the Greek authorities fully understood the issue of marine parks ... This is still the case, in spite of the park's creation. We still await regulations governing park management.

Indeed, although the park was created eight years ago, no management body has been established. The Environment Ministry put MOM in charge of monitoring the park.

We (MOM) are the only people to observe changes in the park's eco-system and to monitor it. We use our boat to do this, as the maritime authorities only have a dinghy.

MOM took responsibility for carrying out a study into the type of management body that should be created and the role it should play.

We have decided to do this because the Environment Ministry is incapable of doing it. We are thinking on the basis of three different institutional frameworks: the United States, France, and Germany. None of these three exactly fit our circumstances and so I believe we should combine them.

The Park's Surface Area and its Local Impact

The park has a surface area of 2200 km². This includes zone B (678 km²), which has minimal protection and is situated between the islands of Alonisos and Peristera; zone A, which is strongly protected, and lies between the islands of Kyra Panaya, Yura, Skantzoura, and Psathura; and a high protection zone around the island of Piperi. This latter island is totally prohibited for fishermen, day-trippers, or anybody else. Only a few scientists have the right to go there. On this island many coves and rocky cliffs shelter a small seal colony and most of their mating places.

Agreeing upon or Imposing a National Marine Park

The creation of a national park profoundly changes local life, as pro-tection for the ecosystem requires controls on anthropogenic activity. With inland national parks, there is always the concern of limiting the number of visitors and, above all, of stopping them from walking wherever they please. How can these restrictions be shifted to an off-shore area? Local fishermen must be convinced of the importance of the strict rules. We examine now how MOM has convinced fisher-men to accept the reduction of their fishing territory.

MOM's Views on Fishing Communities and the Fishing Industry

In its statements, MOM agrees that the success of the park and its protected areas depends on the integration of all parties into the creation process, including the authorities. As one respondent said 'When we go anywhere, we discuss our plans with the local authorities. These are the only people capable of judging whether or not our proposals properly fit into the local situation. For him, the island's fishermen live from tourism, and the park will help in the development of this activity, as it will attract all the more tourists'. He reasons that fishermen not only sell their fish to the tourists, but they also rent out rooms and organise trips out to sea in their boats. Consequently, they can only benefit from the park, even if their fishing territory is reduced.

MOM is pro-coastal fishermen but against towed gears and seines. The Alonisos fishermen have the same preference, as they operate vessels between 4 and 12 metres in length and use fixed fishing gears. A MOM staff person said,

> We were lucky, because Alonisos does not have medium-scale fishing vessels, so from the very beginning it was quite easy to bring the coastal fishermen on side. We told them we were going to outlaw all trawlers and seines. They supported us because it was in their interests to do so.

However, MOM also posed a different argument, that the fishermen compete with the seals because "fishermen want to sell fish, and seals want to eat fish. In the past, seals found sufficient fish but nowadays this is not possible because of decreasing stocks. A seal needs to feed on approximately 150 fish every day..." (MOM). MOM clearly perceives a conflict of interest between the seals and the fishermen that arises from their common dependence on a scarce resource.

The fishermen of Alonisos have difficulty in selling their catches due to a market shortfall. They are well known throughout Greece thanks to the marketing efforts made by their co-operative. Tourists only come for two months of the year, and for the other ten months fish must be shipped to Athens, which is an eight-hour trip, mostly by ferry.

Tension between MOM and the fishing co-operative could rise on this issue. MOM regards this tension as inevitable, as 'everyone looks out for their own interests...'. MOM says that today, 'if there were an island referendum deciding on the park's future, only 20 percent would vote for the park. Fishermen would be the first to vote against'.

The line taken by the MOM president shows that the organisation's primary concern is the conservation of different species above the economic survival of the island. Fishermen's interests come after seals and seagulls. MOM is not concerned with the increase in fishery resources either. When asked if fishery resources had increased in the area since the creation of the park, they replied, 'We know nothing about fishing stocks, and we have never done evaluation of fishing stocks'.

The Island's Fishing Community

We will now examine the fishing community's point of view. The president of the fishing co-operative explained how the park had been presented:

> Someone came from Athens to tell us that they wanted to create a marine park around our island. He told us that fishing would be forbidden within 500 metres of the Piperi islet [the core protection zone] for a period of three months. They promised us money as compensation for the loss of profits resulting from the ban. Apparently, there are caves around there that seals use to mate in. We thought that the loss of 500 metres of fishing territory wasn't too bad – it wasn't a very productive fishing area. But the three-month ban quickly became a two-year ban and eventually turned into a total ban by presidential decree.

Fishermen understood that the ban would offer them long-term benefits. First, it would encourage stock reproduction, and second, the compensation money would allow them to buy new nets. But the greatest benefit would be the exclusion of trawlers and seines from the park area: "We gave this gentleman our agreement because the exclusion of the daytime seines offers us better fishing without any competition." The fishermen of Alonisos did not take kindly to the presence of trawlers and seines from other ports around their islands. Possibilities offered by the park were very attractive. Within the national park, only coastal fishermen using fix gears have the right to work.

Disputed Restrictions on Fishing Territory

The ban on fishing around the island of Piperi is now being disputed, as it is no longer the only ban with which the fishermen are confronted. Fishermen say the expected benefits never materialized. They are not finding more fish in the area, and they are therefore obliged to go a lot further out in order to fish. In addition, there is an ever-increasing number of total bans in order to protect species such as the silver gull.

If fishermen are caught fishing illegally within the high protection area, they are subject to a fine of 730 euros. What the fishermen find most objectionable is that MOM representatives issue this fine. In addition, the scientists who disembark onto the island of Piperi to see the seal colony are scientists linked to environmental NGOs, because Greek research institutes have not been involved in the procedure. The fishermen doubt that such bans aid seal reproduction. As one Alonisos fisherman said,

> Before the creation of the park, we had seen seven seals, whereas now we never see any. They seem to have disappeared, but you must remember that we have never hit a seal and have never caught one in our nets. It's actually the seals who come to steal fish from our nets. They don't damage the nets like dolphins do. They simply eat the fish they find there.

According to MOM, seal births have increased from three in 1990 to twelve in 2002.

Other Parties' Positions

For the head of the island's maritime authorities, the park's creation provoked negative reactions from people working in tourism and from the fishing community. However, he saw an advantage, because the park banned tourists who practiced dive fishing not only for their own consumption but also to sell to local restaurants. According to a local maritime officer, they were "Italian tourists who paid for their holidays by selling their illegally caught fish and people who rented out rooms to them were against the park". The officer said, "The park protects the marine environment, which has improved greatly since the park's creation, as the seals are reproducing". For the fisheries inspector responsible for the area, the park has had a positive impact on the region. It has helped to reduce over-fishing in the area because it bars trawlers and seines. The creation of the park has also helped to reduce, or virtually stop, illegal deep-sea fishing.

The Park Management System is Called into Question

Everyone who was interviewed challenged MOM's management of the park. Most people felt that the organisation has been looking after its own interests and excluding the interest of other groups. The fact that the organisation monopolises power within the park lends weight to this feeling.

The creation of a management body is necessary and urgent. New management should serve to reduce the predominant role played by the environmentalists by including the other park users. A local maritime officer said, 'Park management should now be performed by a body which includes the local community. All the groups involved should be included in the management body, as well as the local authorities'. An advisor at the Ministry of Agriculture added, 'The implementation of national parks should be a concerted decision and not left to a dominant group to control others. It was not difficult to persuade coastal fishermen to accept the idea of the park once we offered to ban other fishermen'.

Cap de Creus Natural Park (Catalonia, Spain)

In 1998, Cap de Creus Natural Park was declared a 'natural reserve between the sea and the land'. The maritime area of the park starts at the Cala Tamariu beach in Port de la Selva territory and ends in front of the town of Roses on Falconera Point. The maritime surface of the park is about 138 km². The protected land area is composed of no more than 90 hectares. Fauna and flora are protected. Most of the area, 40 hectares, is located in Port de la Selva municipal area.

This example will only be examined from the fisheries sector point of view and through interviews of the different parties in the fishing sector. The interviews were carried out in the spring of 2000. Some of those interviewed no longer hold the positions they held at the time.

We look now at how the former Director of Fisheries of Catalonia presented the issue of the Cap de Creus Natural Park. For him, the park constituted the sole means of saving and preserving a part of the marine environment which had been greatly damaged by highly developed local tourism. He said, 'We have few areas where we can create parks or reserves; just the Northern Cap de Creus and the Elbo Delta in Catalonia'. In 1985, the government of Catalonia declared the Medes Islands to be a reserve, claiming that Cap de Creus constituted an ideal site to create a park, as it is an exceptional place for preservation. The decision to create a marine and terrestrial park aimed to cover this objective.

However, for the former Director of Fisheries, the classification of some areas does not go far enough for the protection of the marine environment in the region. He said that fishing should also be banned within a distance of fifty metres from the coast, using an artificial reef to block the access. According to him, this is the only way to stop the trawlers. For him, lessening the effects of fishing represents a means of preserving the ecosystem. In spite of the interest shown by the director in limiting the effects of the fishing industry by the creation of parks or marine reserves, his department holds no authority in environmental protection.

Originally, the Fisheries Department did have some influence in this field, but this authority was quickly ceded to the Ministry of the Environment. The Fisheries Department did not play a direct or major role during the park creation process, yet the park includes zones where fishing is reduced or completely forbidden. There is a total ban on all forms of fishing in zone A. In zone B, seasonal fishing is permitted, and in zone C, small boats may operate year-round. Trawlers are completely forbidden throughout the park because it is not permissible for trawlers in Catalonia to operate in depths less than 65 metres.

The Catalan park was created very quickly: only four years were necessary for informing the relevant parties and consulting with them. In contrast to the Greek park, the Catalan park has a management body where, theoretically, the following parties are brought together: the relevant town councils, the regional authorities, tourism representatives, and fishing organisations (*cofradías*).

We turn now to the question of how the fishing community and the scientists perceive this park and the Medes Islands. Quotations from interviews will illustrate their perception.

In principle, the president of the Palamos *cofradía* agrees with the ban on fishing within the parks, as a halt to activities can only benefit fish stock levels. But experience with the reserve shows that this kind of project serves tourism more than it does the fishing stock. In addition to this, the creation of the reserve is considered to be a decision that satisfies political and administrative interests, and this is why the *cofradias* did not want to be involved. According to him, 'Exactly what a reserve is and above all its goals should be defined. That is how the fishing community will come to accept it'. The fishermen in this *cofradia* believe that such protections are aimed more at tourism, as the number of tourism vessels and the number of observation divers is constantly on the increase.

The secretary of the Laça *cofradía*, who also runs the town's nautical club, attended the park's preparatory meetings. He said, "It was essential to follow the proceedings in order to avoid a big reduction in the fishing territories, as we have already seen with the reserve". Yet fishermen's organisations were not in attendance at these meetings. Consequently, they did not defend their interests. The secretary added further, 'I told them what the stakes were with the creation of this park, but as per usual if there isn't a law against it, they disregard the issue'. We are not sure which role the *cofradía* secretary was playing during these meetings.

However, the secretary regrets that the information dissemination and consultation period prior to the creation of the park was not long enough. He noted,

> One day they turned round and said: 'We've discussed this for long enough, now we'll vote in the law for the creation of the park.' The discussion was over just like that... the ecologists attended all the meetings and defended their interests well. They were listened to, as their proposals were included in planning the park... The absent fishermen were not heard...

That the parks were designed foremost to satisfy tourist interests is not an opinion coming exclusively from the side of the fishing community. It is also shared by scientists working in the sector.

> These measures are useful (...) but they can serve other interests, as is the case in the Medes Islands, which have a very rich seabed. Since the creation of the reserve in 1985, the number of observation divers has continued to increase, and nobody seems worried about the negative impact this could have on the area. Pleasure boats mooring in the area destroy the seabed, even if people are only there to swim.

Parks and reserves attract tourists who are looking for untouched places where they can admire the seabed, untamed landscapes, and other such attractions. Fishing might be regulated in these zones, but tourism certainly is not. The tourists' freedom does not impress the fishermen, who have witnessed their business shrink. This is in spite of the fact that fishing communities in coastal towns also directly benefit from tourism, through room or apartment rental and sales of fish to restaurants. The secretary of the Laça association says that tourists want to eat good fish.

The National Park in the *Mer d'Iroise* in Brittany (France)

Concerns for the protection of the natural heritage of the Mer d'Iroise led to the proposal of creating a national park there. Although the ruling to study the project of a national marine park in the Mer d'Iroise happened recently (September 2001), the notion of such a park is relatively old. Since it was first proposed at end of the 1980s, the marine park project (initiated at the request of the inhabitants of Finistère themselves) has seen four Environment Ministers enter and leave office.

On September 25, 2001, the Prime Minister gave a ruling to study the project of creating a National Marine Park in the Mer d'Iroise (PNMI). In its first article, it states that

> the national marine park project in the Mer d'Iroise shall allow for the permanent protection of the area's outstanding natural beauty; the development of human activities compatible with this preservation will be taken into consideration (Sabourin and Pennanguer 2003).

The core zone for the PNMI would be 2000 km², and the buffer zone 2800 km² (Mission PNMI 2003). However, the government took into account reservations expressed during the previous consultation process, and it set three strong conditions: the preservation of fishing activities, the preservation of maritime and island tourism, and the development of the islands of Ouessant, Molène, and Sein. Under these conditions, the park will not be a sanctuary, but rather a vast area that will have to reconcile the protection of the environment with the development of human activities.

No marine parks currently exist in France. The Port-Cros National Park, while it resembles a marine park is, in fact, a mere extension of the inland park in a marine environment. If the project comes to fruition, the PNMI will therefore be the first marine park.

The Mer d'Iroise, classified as a biosphere reserve by UNESCO in 1989, is a remarkably well-preserved area, providing habitat for many sensitive species on fragile sites of national and even international significance for nature conservation. The area has been put under great strain by the fishing industry and by the influx of tourists during the summer months. It is also a coastal area where water quality is threatened by heavy usage of the catchment areas and extremely heavy maritime traffic.

The Fishing Community: In Favour of the Implementation of a National Park

As for the fishing community of the Mer d'Iroise, professional fishermen from the area have adopted a largely positive attitude towards the project of a national park in Iroise. Their involvement in the consultation and decision process was gradual, but not without difficulties.

At the beginning of the 1990s, these professional fishermen felt excluded from the feasibility study (carried out by the Armorique Regional Nature Park). Invited to steering committee meetings, the local fishing council for North Finistère voiced its dissatisfaction with this. They also expressed their hope that the fishing community would be actively associated with the park's creation. They wanted to see IFREMER (a scientific institute) better represented on the scientific board. Kelp farmers (seaweed fishermen) from the Molène archipelago were the first to express their concerns regarding the area envisaged for the future park. They wanted to be better informed about the project's progress. They were afraid the project would become an obstacle to their business' economic development, through the banning of fishing and seaweed activities.

In 1995, they were followed by fishermen from the port of Conquet, who feared the national park project would lead to overly protective measures for seals. The future of kelp gathering grew more worrying, as the adopted plan aimed to impose constraints on habitats, but not on species. Seaweed is both a used resource and a habitat for many species.

The implementation of the Mission, the administrative body in charge of managing the park project, permitted a review of the working methods and allowed for the more active involvement of professional fishermen. Thus, since 1996, professional sea-fishermen's organisations have become a more important part of the decision-making process. Two explanations allow us to understand their role. First, the four local fishing committees have for some years been thinking about new, long-lasting management mechanisms for fishing in the coastal area. Some view the national park project as a way of facilitating the implementation of these mechanisms, such as an improvement in the selectivity of devices, closed seasons, co-management or diversified activity, with the help of public authorities. Second, because they distrust aspects of the project and because they want to be able to balance excessive pressure from environmental agencies, fishermen have preferred to place themselves within the park implementation procedure in order to influence its direction.

During the advisory consultation stage in 2000, the four local fishing committees (North Finistère, Douarnenez, Audierne, and Guilvinec) and the Regional Committee of Brittany assumed a common position concerning the project. They expressed their opposition to a project that would be centred on the islands and linked to the Armorique National Park, fearing the implementation of additional regulations. They demanded that their decision-making powers be upheld in regard to fisheries management in the future park. They wanted therefore to be represented in decisive meetings and also within a fisheries commission. Finally, they came out in favour of an enlargement of the future park area, requesting the extension of the outer limit of the zone to the edge of French territorial waters (a 12 mile strip).

Like the islanders, professional fishermen talked about the appropriation of space. They claim exclusive territorial rights for the zone, in order to "protect" themselves against other uses or against fishermen from other areas.

Fishermen local committees now demand that coastal fishing activities continue within the confines of the park, and they refuse to entertain the idea that the park should mean a total control over the marine environment of the Mer d'Iroise. They request the guarantee that no area will be classified as a full-scale reserve. They also request the recognition of the part coastal fishing plays in the local economy. They want the park to guarantee the continuation of a sustainable fishing industry: economic viability for fishing companies, a defence of coastal fishing interests, and the preservation of fisheries heritage.

Regarding the surface area put forward during the consultation process, the fishing community would like a larger area that is more relevant for the management of fishing.

The fishing community is committing itself to the concept of an experimental management area. They want to make the Mer d'Iroise a pilot scheme for sustainable management of fishing in the coastal strip, and to try out new practices (device selectivity, artificial barrier reefs, et cetera). They are looking for financial compensation for closed seasons for certain areas, in order to rebuild stock levels, and they are thinking in terms of financial incentives to develop fishing methods that respect the environment (Anon 2003). Lastly, they are examining different ways of promoting fish products (labelling et cetera).

Representatives of professional fishermen believe that the park could help fishing overcome some of the difficulties attributed to the European Union Common Fisheries Policy (CFP), particularly plans for fleet reductions. Their willingness to actively involve themselves in the park's creation demonstrates that they are searching for an alternative to the CFP (Alban 2003). Water quality also represents a major stake for professional fishermen. Indeed, they believe that stock levels are not only a result of over-fishing, but also of telluric pollution. The park must therefore bring the financial means to improve the quality of the water.

However, the current involvement of fishermen is not unanimously supported and is still weak. The number of fishermen supporting the project differs according to maritime area and according to the trade in question. Fishermen using lines, from southern Brittany, are more likely to support the project than fishermen who use nets, or trawlers, who benefit from a special dispensation to fish in forbidden areas. Fishermen from Glénans support the project in the hope that the extraction of aggregate from banks of 'maërl' sediment will be outlawed. An opposition movement coming from Conquet fishermen (both professional and recreation) grew during the summer of 2002, casting doubt on the legitimacy of their representatives to the CLPM (Local Maritime Fishing Committee) and the CRPM (Regional Maritime Fishing Committee). The president of the Douarnenez CLPM, who has been openly opposed to the park project since the beginning, believes that the presidents of the other CLPMs (particularly North Finistère CLPM) do not represent the interests of the 'main parties', i.e.: the Conquet fishing community. His rejection of the park is shown through his strong distrust of the environmental lobby, referring to the European Union's ban on fishing with drift gillnets. The park project became a campaign topic during local fishing committee elections in January 2003. The *Syndicat National des Chefs d'Entreprise de la Pêche Maritime* (National Union of Maritime Fishing Company Executives, SCEP) has voiced its categorical opposition to the project (Sabourin and Pennanguer 2003).

Conclusions

The three cases presented here raise several issues. One is the impact of the creation of parks on fishermen's income. In the Greek and Spanish cases, where fishing activities have been reduced or even banned, the fishing community views the parks rather negatively. In terms of fisheries management, to outlaw particular categories of fisherman may bring temporary benefits to those who remain in the activity, but it makes no sense over the long term when restrictions continue to increase and tend to affect all categories. Another issue is that opportunities to generate new sources of income have not emerged. The 'fishing and tourism' business that exists elsewhere in Europe has not been able to develop in these places. That the Greek and Spanish parks have had no influence on their revenue turned the fishermen against the parks. Breton fishermen, in the third example, intend to use the park in order to improve the image of their products and to diversify if necessary. The fisheries law of 1997 provides the legal opportunity for the transportation of passengers once certain administrative procedures have been completed. This could open up the development of new activities, but it is very difficult to say if the opportunity will result in an overall increase of incomes in the fishing community.

The aims and procedures for the creation of parks also pose important questions. In Greece, an environmental organisation was key to the foundation of the park. This organisation created the park in order to protect and save a species of seal. The authorities were not involved in the process. Funding obtained by the NGO easily allowed it to convince the other parties (the fishermen), who received some of the money. The Greek fishermen allowed themselves to be seduced by MOM's promises without being capable of weighing up the impact of the park's creation over the long term. It should be noted that they did not receive advice from either the fisheries administration or from the relevant local authorities. This example highlights the

CHAPTER SEVEN

weakness of the Greek state, which allowed private interests to govern environmental issues.

In the Catalan case, the approach came from a region that also, in record time, established a natural park without taking the time either to inform users or to allow them to express themselves. It appears that the creation of such a park was aimed at saving an area before it became subject to a tourist invasion. The fishing community, despite warnings given by several people, neither participated in the implementation procedure of the park nor recognised the impact of such a park on its business. Thus, although they were well organised, fishermen did not benefit from advice from their relevant local authorities.

In the case of the Mer d'Iroise, the fishing community, which has long-standing experience with stock management in the area, felt that the park could benefit them if they used it well. They tried, first of all, to include themselves in the decision-making process in order to defend their ideas and put them to good use. They relied on scientists to promote their position.

Unlike their Greek and Spanish counterparts, the Breton fishermen had the advantage of being advised by people who understood the impact such a park would have on their business. The fact that the French procedure is very long, although too centralised, gives all parties the possibility of expressing themselves and of taking a position on the park.

Timing appears to be an essential element. Adequate time allows for democratic debate between the different parties, if the political will exists. The level of decision-making is another important factor. It is unfortunate that the process of creation of these parks is often a centralised one in which local authorities have little or no place. As a result, they tend to oppose the process as a way to reassert their control.

References

Alban, F.
2003   *Contribution à l'analyse économique des aires marines protégées: applications à la rade de Brest et à la Mer d'Iroise*, Thèse de doctorat en Sciences Economiques. Brest: UBO. P. 291.

Anon.
2003   *Groupe de travail 'gestion halieutique'. Document de synthèse (point d'étape)*.Mission pour un parc national marin en Iroise, Brest. P. 16.

Mission Parc Marin de la Mer d'Iroise – MPMI
2003   *Projet de territoire. Projet d'organisation du parc*, Documents de travail de
        la Mission. Brest. P. 68.

Sabourin, A. and S. Pennanguer
2003   *Le parc national en mer d'Iroise: un territoire, un projet et des hommes.* Brest:
        Programme de recherche 'Espaces protégés'. CEDEM – UBO, IFREMER,
        Portances Conseils, C3ED, P. 165.

8

An Assessment of the Potential Interest of Fishermen to Engage in Boat-Chartering in the Context of a Marine Park: The Case of the Iroise Sea, Western Brittany, France

Frédérique Alban and Jean Boncoeur

Introduction

Even if favourable in the long run, standard methods designed to curb overcapacity in the fishing industry have immediate consequences that are either harmful to fishermen or costly to taxpayers. In response to overexploitation, the strategies of individual fishermen can be very different. Some decide to harvest different stocks elsewhere in order to maximise their catches, and so undertake the necessary modifications to their boats and gears. Other fishermen adopt the alternative strategy of controlling their investment and fishing costs by harvesting an inshore zone, like a small bay that is more protected from bad weather. This attempt to minimise their costs requires the adaptation of their gears to the access regulation of the coastal zone. As suggested by the case of agriculture (Disez 1999), an alternative solution could consist of developing pluri-activity in the fishing industry through combining commercial fishing with boat chartering for recreational fishing and/or ecotourism (Le Sann 1997; Cheong 2003). In other words, fishermen try to diversify their activities. Testing the relevance of this idea has been the starting point of the research presented in this paper.

In some countries, this type of diversification is already a significant source of income for inshore fishermen (Kusakawa 1992). In France, this is not yet the case. The relationship between commercial and recreational fishing is dominated by competition for the access to scarce fish stocks. Until now, the well-known appeal of fishing harbours for tourists has mainly been considered by professional fishermen as an opportunity to develop the market for their traditional activity.

The Iroise Sea adjacent to western Brittany in France is a good case for investigating the opportunities to develop pluriactivity in the fishing industry, combining commercial fishing and boat chartering. Due to the richness and variety of its ecosystem, the Iroise Sea is an attractive site for human activities including tourism in particular, and a national marine park is planned. After presenting this zone and the project of a marine protected area, the paper tests the degree to which the pluriactivity approach is realistic. For that purpose, it investigates first the potential demand for ecotourism and boat chartering, and then the interest of fishermen and their economic incentives to develop such a part-time activity.

The Case for Developing Pluriactivity Combining Commercial Fishing and Boat Chartering in the Iroise Sea

This first section is devoted to a brief presentation of the survey area, and to the ongoing project of creating a marine protected area.

Activities in the Iroise Area

Due to its richness, the Iroise Sea shelters a high diversity of small-scale activities.

Richness of the Iroise Ecosystem

Located at the western extremity of Brittany, the Iroise Sea is a coastal sea located on the frontier between the English Channel and the Atlantic Ocean. It is bounded to the north by the Isle of Ouessant and the Molene Archipelago and, to the south, by the Isle of Sein. In the east, the Iroise Sea is connected to the Bay of Brest and the Bay of Douarnenez. In the west, the limit between the Iroise Sea and the Celtic Sea is the 100 meters isobath. The whole area is included within the 12 nautical mile line of French coastal waters. Several small islands, only three of which are inhabited, are located in the area.

The shallowness of the area, the diversity of its sea beds and its specific hydrodynamism produce a high diversity of habitats, and explain the presence of an important number of remarkable animal and plant species (Le Duff *et al.* 1999). The Iroise Sea shelters a high variety of fish of commercial interest (monkfish, pollack, rays, conger, turbot, pilchard, mackerel, edible crab, spider-crab, lobster, spiny lobster, scallop, and donax). Moreover, the Iroise Sea shelters some species considered remarkable by scientists and/or by the public. Some of these species have received special media coverage, such as marine mammals (dolphins, seals, otters) and seabirds.

Due to the richness and variety of its ecosystem, the Iroise Sea was labelled by UNESCO in 1989 as a 'MAB reserve' (Man and Biosphere). This biological richness is an attractive element for human activities. Thus, the Iroise Sea faces high anthropogenic pressure (Anon. 1999).

The High Diversity of Activities in the Iroise Sea
Traditionally, the Iroise area was the site of a range of small-scale activities on the sea and in the coastal zone including commercial fishing, seaweed harvesting (by boat or on the beach), *maerl*[1] extraction for local agriculture, and seafood processing. Traditionally, these activities were family-based. Another characteristic of the Iroise Sea until now has been the absence of trawling.

A historical cultural difference between the south Iroise area and the north should be stressed. In the north, it was common to combine fishing and farming activities. Since the 19th century people have dredged shellfish in the Bay of Brest during the winter season and engaged in cultivation in the summer.[2] On the north coast of the Iroise Sea, people were simultaneously farmers and seaweed harvesters. Seaweed harvesting is a speciality of the Iroise area.[3] In the south Iroise area, fishermen and farmers were two different groups. The targeted species varied by fishing harbour. Inside the Bay of Douarnenez, pilchards were very abundant until the beginning of the 20th century. After the decline of the pilchard fishery, the fishermen of Douarnenez tried to diversify into the offshore fishery. Nowadays, this harbour has preserved the pilchard tradition, by the way of canning factories, but it is in decline. Camaret, which was a very small fishing harbour, became a prosperous harbour during the 1950s and 1960s due to Mauritanian lobsters. This harbour has deeply declined since the 1970s, in parallel with the decline of that stock. In the Bay of Brest, shellfish dredging has long been a tradition, particularly for oysters, a fishery that has existed since the 18th century. Scallops became the main targeted species at the beginning of the 20th century. Several innovations explain the development of this fishery in the Bay of Brest (Boncoeur *et al.* 1995). This fishery was the last important commercial fishery in Western Europe operated by sailing boats. Motorisation developed only during the 1950s. It was followed by the collapse of the scallop fishery in the 1960s. In response, fishermen diversified the targeted shellfish in the bay by creating oyster farms. Since the early 1980s, a scallop-restocking program has been developed in order to sustain the shellfish fishery in the Bay of Brest.

This rapid history of the Iroise fisheries shows the diversity of traditional activities. Today, the Iroise area is still characterised by diversity. However, traditional activities are matched by the development of recreational activities.

Commercial fishing is still economically important in the area. It is mainly a small-scale, multi-species, and multi-gear fishery, largely within the 12 nautical miles zone. Landings are geographically scattered, and only partly marketed through fish auctions. Nowadays, some 900 fishermen frequent the Iroise Sea and operate relatively small boats of under 16 metres.[4] The total number of commercial fishing boats operating in the Iroise Sea has been estimated at 350 units (Boncoeur *et al.* 2000b). Most of them are registered in fishing harbours bordering the Iroise Sea. Less than one-third of the boats come from other districts that do not border the Iroise Sea. The Iroise fleet practises generally two types of capture, or *métiers*, per boat (Boncoeur *et al.* 2000b).[5] A total number of 25 *métiers* have been identified, among which 12 are considered as main *métiers*. Fixed nets with large mesh or small mesh target finfish (monkfish, bass, pollack, hake, et cetera) or crustaceans (spider crab and spiny lobster); handlines target mainly bass and seabream; longlines target bass, seabream, and conger; dredges target common scallop and other shellfish; and pots target crustaceans and cuttlefish.

Seaweed harvesting represents the bulk of the regional and national output of kelps.[6] The resource (mainly *Laminaria digitata*) is sedentary, the fleet purely local, and all landings are directly sold to two processing plants (Arzel 1998).[7] This activity is operated seasonally by a specialised fleet of around 40 seaweed-harvesting boats, which often complement their summer activities by scallop dredging in the Bay of Brest during the winter season.

Commercial fishing and seaweed harvesting in the Iroise Sea are also practised by fishers and harvesters operating on foot on the beach or in shallow coastal waters. These activities include dredging for donax along the sandy beaches of the Bay of Douarnenez and harvesting various types of edible seaweed (*Laminaria, Condrus*, and *Fucus*) on the rocky coast of the northern Iroise area. There are seasonal or occasional activities for some fishermen, unemployed or retired persons, and students.

The quality of ecosystems in the Iroise Sea is also an attractive element for recreational activities such as yachting, recreational fishing, and tourism (Anon. 1999). Before the middle of the 1970s, few places were devoted to tourism in the Iroise area. The exceptions were *Morgat*, which is a tourist resort devoted to sailing and sunbathing, and the *Pointe du Raz*, which is a headland famous for its seascape. Tourism is nowadays an important activity in Brittany (ORTB 1998), and the creation of a marine national park in the nearby Iroise Sea might encourage tourists to visit the area (Hoyt 2000; Hvenegaard 1997; Mazaudier and Michaud 2000). Family members meeting relatives constitute an important part of this tourist flow. Visiting the inhabited islands of the Iroise Sea (Ouessant, Molène, and Sein) represents an important activity and is highly concentrated during the summer season, but only a minority of tourists stay overnight.[8] The main declared motivations of tourists from outside Brittany who visit the Iroise area for leisure are its natural and cultural heritage and the possibility of undertaking sea related activities. Yachting and sailing are widespread hobbies. The total number of resident leisure boats in the Iroise Sea is estimated at around 10,000 units, most of which are small boats (Boncoeur *et al.* 2000b).[9] Recreational fishing includes fishing on board leisure boats, underwater fishing (snorkelling), and picking shellfish and small crustaceans on the beach at low tide.[10] Recreational fishermen using boats are in most cases resident males who are fairly old (with a mean age of 53) and often retired. They usually fish on small boats (5.5 meters long on average), and stay close to the shore (within 3 nautical miles). Handlines, small nets, and pots are the main gears used during these recreational fishing trips (Véron 1999). Five species are usually targeted: mackerel (targeted by 59 percent of fishermen), pollack, spider crab, bass, and seabream. Recreational underwater fishing is authorised only for snorkelling and represents approximately 7,500 divers in the Iroise Sea; a significant figure considering the relatively cold water temperature. It is essentially practised by males who are younger than recreational fishers fishing from boats (34 against 53 years old on the average). Five species are targeted: spider crab in priority, wrasse (sea-wife), bass, flat fish, and pollack. Picking shellfish and small crustaceans at low tide is a popular recreational activity in Brittany, involving the resident population all the year round and tourists during their holidays. The variety of targeted species is high, but 4 species account for the most effort: carpet shells, oysters, winkles, and shrimps (Véron 1999). In contrast to other types of recreational fishing, picking shellfish and small crustaceans at low tide is well balanced as regards the participation of both genders. The age of participants and their social origins are highly varied, including students, retired people, and unemployed persons (Appéré 2002). The share of recreational fishing in the Iroise Sea has been estimated at 6 percent of the overall landings of the commercial Iroise fishery (Alban 1998; Boncoeur *et al.* 2002).

Interactions between Fisheries and Recreational Activities in the Context of the Iroise Ecosystem
The ecosystem can mediate interactions between fisheries and recreational activities, or interactions can occur directly between different users of the same space.

The development of various human activities may become a threat for the equilibrium of ecosystems. For instance, attempts to develop the harvesting of *Laminaria hyperborea* to complement the extraction of *Laminaria digitata* raises the issue of the protection of fish habitat. At the same time, the use of gears with low selectivity by some recreational fishermen is a cause of environmental damage, whereas the development of tourism generates increasing pollution and sometimes gives incentives to harvest juveniles and undersized organisms (King 1997).

Use conflicts are frequently reported (Alban 1998). There are sometimes congestion problems between traditional activities and the growth of yachting as, for example, in the construction of marinas to the detriment of fishing harbours. Some competition problems between commercial and recreational fishing for access to scarce fish stocks are mentioned. It appears to be more frequently related to space interactions (competition for the use of space when using fixed gears) than to stock interactions (competition for the same targeted species). Few problems of cohabitation related to non-compliance with regulations are recorded. Underwater fishers are sometimes charged with illegal actions such as the 'plundering' of pots.

The main issue between commercial and recreational fishermen relates to the question of the illegal selling of catches (Alban 1998; Véron 1999). Underwater fishers mentioned negative interactions with fishing boats, whether commercial or recreational, because of non-compliance with safety rules. This subject of concern is also mentioned about sailboards. However, in contrast to other coastal zones, there is no significant interaction between 'picking' recreational fishing and commercial fishing in the Iroise area, since the main targeted species and fishing places are different (Véron 1999).

However, there are also positive interactions between fishermen and recreational activities. The well-known appeal of fishing harbours for tourists has mainly been considered by professional fishermen as an opportunity to develop the market for their traditional activity. The development of boat chartering could be another positive interaction (Alban 1998). Moreover, the project to implement a national park in the Iroise Sea could contribute to creating other favourable relations.

The Project of a Marine National Park and the Conditional Support of Fishermen

The concern for protecting the natural environment has led to the proposal for the creation of a national marine park in the Iroise Sea (PNRA 1993). The process of creating a national marine park in the Iroise Sea, which was launched in the early 1990s, is still ongoing. If, according to French law,[11] environmental preoccupations are the *raison d'être* of national parks, business considerations are also present because of the tourist use which parks are liable to stimulate and which may be a cause of contradictions in the process of park management.[12] Because of the cultural, social, and economic importance of fishing in Brittany, fishing is also an important issue. After a first consultation in 2000, a prime ministerial order in September 2001 stressed that the marine park should promote both the protection of the natural heritage and the sustainable development of human activities. Scientists, conservationists associations, tourist businesses, and representatives of local fishermen are involved in the decision-making process. Stakeholders are still debating the size, the borders of the parks, and restricted or prohibited activities (Anon. 2000).[13] Despite the implementation of thematic working groups on the themes of conservation, tourism, and sustainable fisheries, nothing precise has been decided concerning the management of human activities inside the park. Concerning fisheries management, only the principle of a fisheries management plan for the park area has been decided.

However, the final decision will be taken at the national level by the government, following a legal procedure based on public consultation with the different stakeholders (residents of the Iroise area, local authorities, and local administrations) about the final project. Regional and local inter-professional organisations of fishermen (*Comité Régional des Pêches Maritimes et des Elevages Marins [CRPM]* and *Comité Local des Pêches Maritimes et des Elvages Marins [CLPM]*) have backed the project,[14] because representatives of local fishermen regard it as an opportunity to improve the management of the Iroise fishery.[15] Indeed, professional fishermen have started thinking of new management mechanisms for inshore fisheries of the area. They consider the project of a national marine park as an opportunity to implement these mechanisms (like co-management) with the help of the government. The reasons for the growing concern of local fishermen for management mechanisms are institutional, especially in response to the prospect of the Common Fisheries Policy reform in 2002, but also economic: increasing signs of overfishing have brought the executives of local organisations of fishermen to the conclusion that limiting the fishing effort in the area has become a priority. However, the commitment of fishermen is liable to turn to hostility if they feel that they might be deprived of these expected benefits by phenomena such as a proliferation of seals in the protected area. They also prefer to be insiders rather than opponents of a project liable to receive an important degree of public support. A possible way of preventing future conflicts is to make fishermen aware of the benefits generated by the development of ecotourism in the area where the marine park is implemented. This hypothesis comes directly from observing the strategy of some fishermen who are trying to take advantage of the tourist presence to develop a pluriactivity that combines commercial fishing and boat chartering.

Finally, the interest in diversification provides an opportunity to reach both goals: limiting the fishing effort in the inshore area and avoiding conflicts (e.g. Agardy 1993; Bohnsack 1993; Badalamenti *et al.* 2000).

CHAPTER EIGHT

The Potential Demand for Recreational Boat Trips on Commercial Fishing Boats

This section is devoted to a brief presentation of the potential demand for ecotourism and boat chartering. Hardly any business firm is proposing ecotourism and/or boat chartering activities in the Iroise area. Despite the permanent presence of remarkable marine mammals such as seals, dolphins, and marine birds, only one ecotourism business currently takes tourists aboard a glass-bottomed boat in order to view the underwater ecosystem.[16] Only one commercial fisherman (in the south Iroise area) provides tourists with the opportunity to undertake onboard recreational fishing, although not on his own commercial fishing boat. A few maritime transport businesses in the southern Iroise Sea offer site-seeing tours, which is sometimes combined with the possibility of recreational fishing. Until now, no fisherman has offered tourists the opportunity of going aboard a commercial fishing boat, in order to discover the richness of the Iroise ecosystem or to try recreational fishing.

In order to assess the potential interest of tourists visiting the Iroise Sea for boat chartering tours on small-scale commercial fishing boats devoted to recreational fishing and/or ecotourism in the Iroise Sea, a sample survey was undertaken around Brest during the summer of 1998 (Alban 1998).[17] This survey provides evidence of an actual demand for boat chartering devoted to ecotourism and/or recreational fishing on small commercial fishing boats.

A high percentage of people (75 percent) declared a general interest in onboard tours with a guide. The attractive marine environment and the traditional and natural heritage included in this type of activity can explain this great interest.[18] If we try to isolate the demand for tours on commercial inshore fishing boats, we can observe that a relatively high percentage (41 percent of the whole sample) declared that they are interested in tours on commercial fishing boats. Among this subset of the sample, people are more interested in visiting the area (73 percent of the subset) than in fishing (54 percent), but these two types of activities do not necessarily exclude each other (27 percent of the subset are interested in both). Thirty-eight percent of the sample agree to pay a realistic price (around €33) for a half-day guided tour on a commercial fishing boat dedicated to the viewing of the natural environment and traditional fishing activities or recreational fishing.[19] Females express a relatively great enthusiasm (39 percent of the subset sample), and the interested population is younger than that of the recreational fishermen (85 percent are between 20 and 55 years old). They are mostly tourists, that is they spend their vacations in the Iroise area (69 percent don't live in the Iroise area). Their social origin is mainly senior and white-collar workers (51 percent of the subset sample). Their attitudes vary according to the type of trip (ecotourism or fishing). Most of people interested by ecotourism tours (71 percent) declared they would come 'with their family'. In contrast, persons declaring their interest for recreational fishing boat chartering prefer mainly to come 'alone' (65 percent declared they would come without their family).

Assessing the potential demand for guided tours on commercial fishing boats in the Iroise Sea raises the question of the possibility of extrapolating the results of the survey.[20] When taking the yearly flow of summer visitors as a minimum basis of extrapolation, this leads to an estimation of yearly 37,000 persons potentially interested in this type of activity in the Iroise area. However, for various reasons (Alban and Boncoeur 1999), this result should be interpreted as an indicator more than as the existence of a substantial amount of economically realistic interest in ecotourism onboard commercial fishing boats in the Iroise Sea. This interest should logically grow in the future with the creation of a marine national park in the Iroise Sea (Agardy 1993; Kenchington 1991).

The Interest of Fishermen in Pluriactivity and the Issue of Economic Incentives

The likely existence of significant demand for guided tours on commercial fishing boats in the Iroise Sea does not imply by itself that a corresponding supply will meet this demand. Fishermen may be unwilling to diversify their activities, for various reasons, among which economists are prone to emphasise the lack of economic incentives.

In order to investigate the attitude of professional fishermen of the Iroise Sea in developing pluriactivity, several indications may be derived from two sample economic surveys of the commercial fishing fleet in Brittany, restricted to boats under 25 metres in length, undertaken in 1999-2000 (Alban *et al.* 2001a, 2001b; Boncoeur *et al.* 2000a).[21] However, despite the potential interest of fishermen, the institutional context and the profitability of diversification must be analysed to assess whether pluriactivity is realistic.

The Potential Interest of Fishermen in Diversification

Both surveys included a question related to the potential interest of skippers in the potential diversification of their activity towards boat chartering for recreational activity. The question did not mention any price consideration. Its purpose was just to test the *a priori* attitude of artisanal fishermen towards an activity which is commonly said to be quite far from their own culture.

Slightly over one-fourth of the skippers (27 percent of the whole sample) mentioned a potential interest (Boncoeur *et al.* 2002).[22] But this ratio varied significantly according to various characteristics. There is little difference in interest between South Brittany skippers and Iroise Sea skippers. The difference in interest is possibly due to differences in average boat length, the main *métiers* practised, and the proportion of time operated inside the 12 nautical miles zone.[23] Unsurprisingly, the size of the boat plays a major role in this variability: skippers of smaller boats, whose activity is mainly inshore and who return to harbour every day, are more interested than skippers of larger boats, whose activity is mainly offshore and relies on trips lasting several days. While the percentage of positive answers is only 5 percent for boats between 16 and 25 metres, it rises up to more than one third for boats under 10 metres. A second key differentiating factor is the type of activity of the boat: the proportion of positive answers is much lower among skippers of boats using mainly towed gears and purse seines (11 percent) than among skippers mainly using lines, nets, and pots (41 percent). This factor is partly correlated to the former one, since the class of boats between 16 and 25 metres is largely dominated by trawlers, a type of boat almost non-existent in the class under 10 metres. However, within each class, a distinction exists according to the type of activity. If only for technical and safety reasons, boats using towed gears are generally much less adapted to boat chartering than boats using fixed gears, and the answers of skippers probably reflect this reality. Moreover, interest depends on the *métiers* practised by the fishermen, because of the strong link between season and some *métiers*.[24] In fact, seaweed is harvested during the summer (from May to October for *Laminaria digitata*, which is the main seaweed in this area). Scallops and clams are dredged during the winter (from October to March in the Bay of Brest). So, the interests of seaweed harvesters differ from the interests of the dredgers, because their main activity overlaps the tourist season. This can be confirmed by the distribution of turnover by *métier* and fleet. Skipper's net income is also highly correlated to the size of the boat. However, the rate of positive answers to the question of interest in diversification does not vary solely according to this variable. The rate is almost 40 percent in the class of income between €15,000 and €23,000 per year, while it is only 30 percent for skippers earning less than €15,000 per year. This result suggests that interest in diversification is not simply regarded as a possible solution to the problem of low incomes. Such a conclusion is strengthened by the variance in answers according to skippers' ages. The trend here is clearly linear, with a sharp differentiation between young skippers and older ones: while only 11 percent of the skippers over 50 years old declare that they are interested by diversification, the rate of positive answers rises to 57 percent among skippers under 30 years old. It would be useful here to be able to distinguish the relative importance of two effects. The most obvious one is the effect of age, which is due to the fact that fishermen, as other people, are probably less prone to change their habits when they grow older. But the answers might also reflect a generation difference, consisting of a change of attitude towards ecotourism and recreational activities among younger generations of professional fishermen. There seems to be a potential here for integrating fishermen in the process of marine protected area management.

Institutional Obstacles

Despite the positive attitude of some fishermen toward pluriactivity, other considerations are likely to act as powerful brakes to diversification. The present state of French administrative and fiscal rules makes it difficult for a commercial fisherman to combine boat chartering (on his own fishing boat) with his basic activity (Alban 1998). In fact, the laws applicable to commercial fishing boats and to chartering are not the same. The various regulations include those controlling the sale of catches, safety standards, the number of passengers, and the number and the type of gears aboard. Another difficulty concerns the tax system related to boat chartering.

The law of 1942 strictly defines the conditions of boat use according to the boat category. Commercial fishing boats must not embark passengers without special dispensation. This system of special dispensation is actually not propitious to the development of boat chartering on commercial fishing boats. Nevertheless, the French Fish

Law of 1997 has considered the possibility of commercial fishermen engaging in pluriactivity on their own commercial fishing boats. Article 32 stipulates that the embarkation of passengers like tourists on commercial fishing boats is conditional on the purchase of civil responsibility insurance and on the respect of some safety rules. But the decree that should describe the specific safety rules has not yet been drafted. While waiting for this decree, regional maritime administrations are applying different rules, depending on the regions. Some regional maritime administrations agree to allow embarkation of passengers in return for payment during the summer season. Other regional maritime administrations do not give these kinds of authorisations.

Interviewed about their interest in pluriactivity, fishermen themselves emphasised the difficulties in diversifying their activities from the legal viewpoint. Dredgers, who seem to be the most interested by pluriactivity, are the most conscious of the administrative obstacles. Some of the reasons given by fishermen to explain their lack of interest in this kind of activity related to difficulties with regulations. Other reasons were the unsuitability of commercial fishing boats for this activity, the insecurity for passengers, and the length of a fishing day. But the most common reason was the difference of culture between fishing and tourism.

Moreover, it could be necessary to adapt the regulation of fishing efforts and the fisheries to the constraints of the pluriactivity in terms of time and season in order to give fishermen the opportunity to diversify their activities (Berthou 1995).

The Lack of Economic Incentives for Fishermen

The likelihood of diversification is related to its expected profitability. To assess this profitability, a diversification towards boat chartering scenario has been conceived (Alban and Boncoeur 1999; Boncoeur et al., 2002). It is based on an assessment of the direct costs incurred by a commercial fisherman who would supply this type of activity and an estimation of the opportunity cost of this diversification.[25] These costs were then balanced against the average revenues provided by boat chartering. This simulation has been applied to the subset Iroise fleet which mentions the most interest in diversification, that is the group of netters/potters/liners under 10 metres long (Boncoeur et al. 2002). The simulation makes economic profitability dependent on the average occupancy rate and on the intra-annual distribution of commercial fishing benefits. The results suggest that pluriactivity is not economically profitable because of the high opportunity cost. Diversification may be profitable only if commercial fishing is low during the summer season.

The poor economic performance of diversification should be balanced by two considerations.

1. The results presented here concern an average boat and a median fisherman. But the statistical dispersion of individual values of fishing activity is high, so it is quite possible that diversification towards boat chartering is a profitable alternative for a limited number of fishermen operating in the Iroise Sea.

2. The opportunity cost considered in assessing the profitability of diversification is purely private, that is it does not account for externalities due to the common pool character of the fish stock. If some of the boats operating the fishery were seasonally decommissioned, this would create a positive externality for other fishermen, which would make the social opportunity cost of diversification lower than its private cost. Therefore, accounting for the positive externality due to part of the fleet reducing its fishing effort could improve the overall economic balance of diversification, especially if commercial fishing is high during the summer season. So, a system internalising this positive externality could be set up in order to translate it into private profit for fishermen practising pluriactivity.

Conclusions

In this paper, pluriactivity combining commercial fishing and boat chartering was considered as a possible solution to overfishing and to the potential hostility of some fishermen to the project of a national marine park in the Iroise Sea. The relevance of this solution is conditioned by several factors, including demand for chartering on commercial fishing boats, interest of fishermen, costs of diversification, and the institutional context. These factors were investigated subsequently in the case of the Iroise Sea fishery.

Due to the characteristics of the area, potential demand seems fairly important according to the results of a sample survey realised in the summer of 1998. However, two major impediments have to be stressed despite the potential interest of fishermen in pluriactivity that combines commercial fishing with boat chartering for recreational fishing and/or ecotourism.

The most obvious impediment to diversification relates to the administrative and fiscal framework. According to French law, it is difficult for a commercial fisherman to combine boat chartering with his basic activity on the same boat. However, if the institutions in charge of fisheries management regard diversification as a possible answer to overfishing, they will have to tackle this problem first and implement more flexible regulations.

The second obstacle is the lack of economic stimulus. In fact, with the exception of some specific cases, diversification towards boat chartering does not seem to be profitable. However, the implementation of a system internalising the positive externality of diversification (that is, lowering the fishing effort) could improve economic profitability. In fact, some compensation in favour of fishermen practising pluriactivity (for example, monetary compensation provided by permanent commercial fishermen) could be set up to improve their private profit.

Even if the Iroise Sea does not seem the most pertinent place to develop boat chartering on commercial fishing boats, pluriactivity may be considered as an alternative solution in other fisheries.

Notes

1. Maerl is a collective term for several species of calcified red seaweed. For more details see http://www.ukbap.org.uk.
2. During the 1950s, some of them became sea-farmers and dredgers.
3. The tradition of seaweed harvesting is very old in Brittany and can be considered as a cultural activity (Arzel 1984). This traditional activity constitutes a cultural heritage.
4. Seventy percent of boats are under 12 metres in length, and 75 percent of the fishermen operate on boats under 12 metres in length (Boncoeur et al. 2000b).
5. Basically, this expression represents the combination of a type of gear and a targeted species (or group of targeted species). For a more detailed definition, see (Tétard et al. 1995).
6. Kelps are industrially processed in order to extract alginates. Seaweed yield in the Iroise Sea represents 89 percent of the French yield (Arzel 1998).
7. The yield of Laminaria digitata varies between 50,000 tonnes and 65,000 tonnes per year in the Iroise Sea (Arzel 1998).
8. Two-thirds of the tourist visits, which are estimated at 800,000 persons in the Iroise area, is concentrated during July and August (Boncoeur et al. 2000b).

9. Fifty-seven percent of leisure boats are under 6 meters long, and only 3 percent over 10 meters.
10. French law prohibits selling catches by non-professional fishers.
11. French law on National Park of the 22th July 1960, article L241-1.
12. In the case of the Iroise Sea, the potential development of "ecotourism" is often regarded as high for several reasons, including the presence of marine mammals in the area and the importance of tourist visits in western Brittany.
13. Commercial fishermen ask for a larger park on the scale of the Iroise fishery. They conceive of the park as a means to exclude other fishermen from the Iroise Sea. However, they are opposed to the idea of a complete interdiction of fishing.
14. Since the 1991 French law, commercial fishermen's organisations participate in the management of marine resources and in the enforcement of rules. All commercial fishermen are automatically members of these organisations. They elect representatives at local, regional, and national levels.
15. One should avoid drawing exaggeratedly optimistic conclusions from this relative consensus, since precise questions concerning the management of fishing and other human activities within the limits of the park have not yet been addressed. It is noticeable that expressions such as 'marine reserve' or 'no-take zone' are at present generally avoided by stakeholders. Among recreational and commercial fishermen and other users, some dissenting voices appear, which are not always represented. Thus, a lobby opposed to the project has been created (*Association de défense et de valorisation des îles et du littoral* – Advil). But this dissident association is not yet involved inside the working groups.
16. It is located at *Conquet*, which is a fishing harbour on the north Iroise Sea.
17. One hundred and fifty-nine direct interviews have been completed, representing approximately 70 percent of the total number of persons who were asked to answer the questionnaire. Residents of the Iroise area were also interviewed.
18. Most people have a limited knowledge of marine ecosystems and of traditional marine activities like fishing. The idea of going on board a traditional wooden fishing boat is very attractive.
19. However, it is important to underline that the acceptance of payment is only virtual, since no actual transaction was, of course, proposed during the survey (Alban and Boncoeur 1999).
20. Several reasons make this type of operation hazardous, the first one being due to the fact that, as often in this type of survey, it is difficult to quantify the main population of the sample (Alban and Boncoeur 1999).
21. One survey was conducted in southern Brittany in 1999-2000 by Pascal Le Floc'h, the other in the Bay of Brest and the Iroise Sea by Frédérique Alban in November and December 2000.
22. The sample is composed of 222 skippers-owners of commercial fishing boats, operating in South Brittany or the Iroise sea.
23. In the first sample survey conducted in southern Brittany, fishermen operated inside the 12 nautical miles boundary 42 percent of the time and had an average boat length of 12.4 metres. In the other sample in the Bay of Brest and Iroise Sea areas, fishermen operated inside the 12 nautical mile boundary 100 percent of their time and had an average boat length of 9.65 metres.

24. The highly seasonal character of tourism in the Iroise area as well as weather conditions imply that most chartered trips are likely to take place during July and August.
25. Diversification generates not only direct costs, but also an opportunity cost. This cost is due to the fact that when fishermen are busy with chartering, they do not get money from commercial fishing (the scenario assumes that both activities cannot be conducted in the same period, and that catches due to sport fishing are not sold). The opportunity cost of diversification is therefore equal to the gross margin usually realised by commercial fishing during the period dedicated to chartering according to the scenario.

References

Agardy, M. T.
1993   Accommodating Ecotourism in Multiple Use Planning of Coastal and Marine Protected Areas. *Ocean and Coastal Management* 20:219-239.

Alban, F.
1998   *Pêche Professionnelle et Activités Récréatives. Examen des Potentialités de Développement d'une Pluri-activité: le Cas de la Mer d'Iroise.* Mémoire de DEA (UBO/ENSAR).

Alban, F. and J. Boncoeur
1999   *Commercial Fishing, Recreational Fishing and Tourism: Investing the Potential for Developing a Pluri-activity: The case of the Iroise sea, Western Brittany, France.* XIth annual conference of the EAFE, Dublin, 7-10 April 1999.

Alban, F. *et al.*
2001a   *Contraintes socio-économiques de l'activité des navires goémoniers de la région Bretagne.* Etude réalisée pour le CRPM de Bretagne dans le cadre du programme PESCA, Rapport final. UBO-CEDEM, Brest.
2001b   *L'impact socio-économique du programme de production artificielle de coquilles St-Jacques de la rade de Brest.* Etude réalisée pour le CLPM du Nord-Finistère dans le cadre du programme PESCA, Rapport final. UBO-CEDEM, Brest.

Anon.
1999   *Etude économique des activités liées à la mer d'Iroise.* ADEUPa de Brest/Portances Conseils/SAFI (3 volumes), Brest.
2000   *Consultation pour avis sur le principe de la création d'un parc national en mer d'Iroise.* Document d'intention. Préfecture maritime de l'Atlantique/Préfecture du Finistère. Mission PNMI, Brest.

Appéré, G.
2002   *Analyse économique des comportements face à un risque sanitaire. Le cas de la pêche récréative des coquillages.* Ph.D. Thesis, UBO, Brest.

Arzel, P.
1984   *Etude sur l'aménagement traditionnel de l'exploitation des algues dans le Léon.* FAO Document Technique sur les Pêches n°249, FAO, Rome.

1998   *Les laminaires sur les côtes bretonnes. Evaluation de l'exploitation et de la flottille de pêche, état actuel et perspectives.* Plouzané: Editions Ifremer.

Badalamenti, F. *et al.*
2000   Cultural and Socio-Economic Impacts of Meditarranean Marine Protected Areas. *Environmantal Conservation* 27 (2):110-125.

Berthou, P.
1995   *Quelques questions sur la régulation de la pêche en rade de Brest.* Rade Inf'Eaux 6:43-46.

Bohnsack, J. A.
1993   Marine Reserves: They Enhance Fisheries, Reduce Conflicts and Protect Resources. *Oceanus* 36(3): 63-71.

Boncoeur, J. *et al.*
1995   *L'économie de la rade de Brest. Evaluation du poids économique des activités liées à la rade de Brest.* UBO-CES-CEDEM, Brest.
2000a   *Les aides publiques à la flotte de pêche de la région Bretagne et leurs effets économiques.* Etude réalisée dans le cadre du Contrat de Plan Etat-Région. Rapport final. UBO-CEDEM, Brest.
2000b   *Activités halieutiques et activités récréatives dans le cadre d'un espace à protéger : le cas du Parc National Marin de la Mer d'Iroise.* Projet de recherche cofinancé par le programme national « Environnement Côtier » (PNEC). Rapport 1ère année. UBO, CEDEM/IFREMER, 213 p.
2002   *Activités halieutiques et activités récréatives dans le cadre d'un espace à protéger: le cas du Parc National de la Mer d'Iroise.* Projet de recherche cofinancé par le programme « Espaces protégés » du Ministère de l'Ecologie et du Développement Durable, Rapport 1ère Année. UBO-CEDEM/ IFREMER/UVSQ-C3ED, Brest.

Cheong, S.M.
2003   Privatising Tendencies: Fishing Communities and Tourism in Korea. *Marine Policy* 27(1):23-29.

Disez, N.
1999   Agritourisme: logiques d'acteurs ou logiques de territoires? *Economie Rurale* 250:40-46.

Hoyt, E.
2000   *Whale-Watching 2000. Worldwide Tourism Numbers, Expenditures, and Expanding Economic Impacts.* Crowborough (UK): International Fund for Animal Welfare.

Hvenegaard, G.T.
1997   *The Social and Economic Aspects of Ecotourism.* A View Relevant to Whale Watching. Workshop on the Socioeconomics of Whale Watching, Kaikoura, New Zealand.

Kenchington, R.
1991   Tourism Development in the Great Barrier Reef Marine Park. *Ocean and Shoreline Management* 15:57-78.

King, T.
1997   Folk Management and Local Knowledge: Lobster Fishing and Tourism at Caye Caulker, Belize. *Coastal Management* 25:455-469.

Kusakawa, T.
1992   Commercial Fisheries and Sport Fishing: Conflict and Cooperation. In: M. Antona, J. Catanzano, and J.G. Sutinen (Eds.), *Proceedings of the 6th Biennal Conference of the International Institute of Fisheries Economics and Trade.* Paris: Ifremer. Pp.1201-1211.

Le Duff, M. *et al.*
1999   *Environnement naturel de l'Iroise. Bilan des connaissances et intérêt patrimonial.* MATE/UBO, Brest.

Le Sann, A.
1997   De la gestion de la pêche à la gestion du littoral. *Aménagement et Nature* 125:75-85.

Mazaudier, L. and J. C. Michaud
2000   Gestion des activités d'observation des mammifères marins: quelques études de cas. *Revue de l'Université de Moncton* Numéro Hors Série: 55-80.

Office Régional du Tourisme de Bretagne (ORTB)
1998   *Fréquentation touristique extra-régionale en Bretagne : premiers résultats de l'enquête cordon réalisée d'avril à septembre 1997.* Rennes.

Parc Naturel Régional d'Armorique (PNRA)
1993   *Un parc national marin en mer d'Iroise. Eléments de réflexion et d'orientation.* Hanvec: Ménez Meur.

Tétard, A. *et al.*
1995   *Catalogue international des activités des flottilles de la Manche, approche des interactions techniques.* Plouzané: Editions Ifremer.

Véron, G.
1999   *Pêche à pied professionnelle et pêches récréatives en Bretagne.* Rapport d'étape du 11ème contrat de Plan Etat-Région Bretagne. Brest: Ifremer.

9

Marine and Coastal Issues in Local Environmental Conflict: Greece, Spain, and Portugal[I]

Maria Kousis

Introduction

The most serious problems facing marine and coastal resources in regions around the globe are environmental ones (Huber *et al.* 2003). In European Mediterranean regions the main factors affecting coastal and marine areas are urban development, tourism, fisheries and aquaculture, agriculture, population change, industry, energy, and transport growth (EEA 1999). Southern European Union coastal regions host large metropolitan areas such as Athens, Barcelona, or Lisbon. In the mid-1980s almost 90 percent of urbanised land in the Mediterranean was found in the coastal zones of Spain, France, Greece, Italy, and the former Yugoslavia (EEA 1999). Socio-economic groups often compete for the use and control of coastal resources, such as coastal wetlands or forests, which are usually threatened by a wide variety of land uses.

Tourism, a major industry in Italy, France, Spain, Greece, and lately in Portugal, is an important source of negative environmental impacts (Lozato-Giotart 1990). Thus, in comparison to other European tourist regions, southern European coastal areas, especially the islands, have experienced drastic changes due to the development of tourism in the past few decades (Boissevain 1979, 1996; Gonzalez and Moral 1996; Konsolas and Zacharatos 1992). The Mediterranean region is the world's prime tourist destination, with the French, Spanish, and Italian coasts accounting for 90 percent of the tourists travelling to this region (Plan Blue and UNEP 1998a).

The European Union Mediterranean coasts, where agriculture and urbanisation grew simultaneously at the expense of natural areas, are specialised in monocultures, with significant impacts of chemically intensive agriculture on the local ecosystems. The Mediterranean fisheries and aquaculture are in great need of sustainable management, as the latter increased sharply in their number – 185 percent – within a decade (EEA 1999).

Oil, which is transported across the Mediterranean Sea and is processed within its coastal zones, remains the dominant energy source used in European Union countries. The environmental impacts of the extraction, transportation, refining, and use of oil have been extensive (EEA 1999). Although Greece, Italy, and Portugal do not have nuclear power stations, Spain has four stations with more than 2500 MW maximum output capacity and three stations with a lower capacity (Eurostat 1997:392). The threats to coastal and marine ecosystems imposed by the nuclear industry are serious during normal operations (as from, for example, nuclear waste) or especially in the case of an accident.

In the Mediterranean, the main commercial mode of transportation across countries is by sea, mostly by cargo vessels. About 220,000 trips by vessels of more than 100 tons cargo capacity are estimated to cross its waters annually. This amounts to an estimate of 30 percent of the total merchant shipping in the world and twenty percent of oil shipping, which comes mainly from the Middle-East (EEA 1999).

Overall, especially since the 1960s, there has been an extension of economic growth in southern European coastal and marine areas. This growth has altered the dynamics of natural resource use and has led to local conflicts. In their drive for profitable capital accumulation, powerful economic actors often manage to attain direct or indirect control over natural resources that leads to 'ecological disorganisation'. The loss of the natural resource base and the generation of a wide range of socio-economic, political, and public health risks are inevitable products of this process. In response, citizens, on the basis of their organisational resources and their perceptions of the world as well as the economic and political opportunity structures open to them, either protest the erosion of their ecological base and their health, in environmental conflicts, or remain passive. A group of studies of environmental activism point out that it is related, in part, to exposure effects with immediate health impacts (e.g. Szasz 1994; Gould et al. 1993; Kousis 1999a).

Environmental conflicts often interfere significantly with the management of coastal and marine resources. Environmental conflict data are necessary (Salmona 2002) for both researchers of resource conflicts and responsible resource management agencies. Unfortunately, efforts in this direction are hardly visible.

Questions that deserve particular consideration include: Which are the outstanding sources of coastal ecosystem offences, and what types of local protest have taken place? More specifically, what has been the focus of rural and urban local protest over the use and exploitation of coastal and marine resources in coastal regions of Greece, Spain, and Portugal? What have been the major features of longer and shorter-term conflicts?

This chapter sets out the theoretical premises for analysing social conflicts around coastal resources and the research method that was followed. For illustrative purposes it proceeds by presenting short case studies of such conflicts in Greece, Spain, and Portugal over a period of 20 years, between 1974 and 1994. This is followed by the quantitative analysis of coastal zone-related environmental protest cases. The presentation of data begins by identifying environmentally damaging sources or activities by type of region, and by outlining the spatial and national distribution of conflicts concerning coastal and marine ecosystems across regions and metropolitan areas. The characteristics of local environmental protest related to their time duration are also portrayed in terms of activist type, protest form, the sources/activities of ecosystem intervention, and resolutions proposed by the activists. Finally, conclusions are offered on the basis of the evidence provided and in view of current discussions concerning coastal environmental issues.

Review of the Literature

For contemporary societies of the 21st century, the study of social conflict related to coastal natural resources has become even more important than it was in the past (e.g. Suman 2001). Most studies focus mainly on economic interest issues, involving claims made by different socio-economic groups at the local or regional level. Some of these deal with fisheries (e.g. Kurien and Achari 1988; Bavinck 2001), others with tourism (Salmona and Verardi 2002). Nevertheless, embedded in the latest works, which appear as case studies at the local or regional level, are the underlying environmental dimensions of contemporary modernisation efforts.

The examples of such works, which follow, clearly delineate the indisputable need to bring to the surface conflicts referring exclusively to negative environmental impacts on coastal natural resources. Rodríguez and Carlos (2001) analyse the impacts of an accidental spill of toxic substances from the mining dam of Aznalcóllar on the coastal ecosystems and the related activities, i.e. fishing, mariculture, tourism, and marine protected areas, as well as the involvement of a variety of local groups, including environmental groups. Boissevain and Theuma (1996) examine how local environmentally based opposition succeeded in halting the construction of a large tourism complex on Malta's Munxar point. Boissevain (this volume) investigates the key groups which contest Malta's coastline and are related to tourism and fishing/fish-culture activities. Emphasis is placed on the complexity of the socio-economic, political, and environmental issues, and on the importance of local environmental protest.

As elsewhere within and outside of the European Union, ecosystem degradation does not necessarily lead to grassroots environmental activism. Thus, for example, in agricultural or tourism-intensive regions, protest against these activities as sources of ecosystem damage is limited (Figuereido *et al.* 2001; Kousis 1999a, 2000; Kousis and Eder 2001). This limited social demand for environmental protection is in part related to being economically dependent on these activities while simultaneously having no other financial or organisational resources with which to confront the environmental issue (Kousis 2001).

When local environmental protesters do organise, their actions and claims are directed at the users[2] of the ecosystem, the environmentally damaging sources or (in)activities controlled by these users, the offences created thereby, and the impacts resulting from these offences. Consequently, locals may blame a source and its operator (a factory owner) or inactivity (the failure of implementation of environmental measures), or alternatively, they may only make claims about ecosystem offences (marine pollution) without necessarily relating the problem directly to specific environmental offenders (Kousis 1998, 1999b).

Environmentally damaging sources or activities appearing in the claims of local protesters tend to differ among rural and urban regions. A cross-national examination shows that overall while rural activists are more affected by waste disposal, as well as construction and extraction-related activities in undeveloped areas, urban environmental protesters mobilise more often about land transport, traffic, and construction-related projects in already developed areas

CHAPTER NINE

(Kousis 1999b). Rural environmental activists are found to be more homogeneous, less likely to be linked to political parties, and less numerous compared with their urban counterparts. Urban activists are more representative of groups, such as political parties and formal organisations that are rich in resources e.g. media connections, funding, and effective organisation. Autonomous environmental networks that extend beyond the immediate community level characterise a minority of environmental protest cases (Freudenberg and Steinsapir 1991; Taylor 1995; Kousis et al. 2001) and are visible after the mid-1980s in Greece, Spain and Portugal. When such networks arise, environmental activism is strengthened (Gould et al. 1996, 1993). Cross-regional environmentalists are expected to surpass urban or rural ones in terms of heterogeneity, numbers, and political ties. Extensive network building appears significant in such mobilisations (Weinberg 1997).

State and economic actors are frequently, directly or indirectly, involved in the decisions and policies that lead to or intensify the process of 'ecological marginalisation' (Kousis 1998; Schnaiberg 1994; Broadbent 1998). The institutional apparatus of the contemporary competitive world economy leads to a continued demand for ecosystem utilisation due to growth in production. The most intrusive and persistent environmental offenders are state bodies like state-owned enterprises and state run infrastructural projects, suprastate organisations, and corporations aiming at greater profits and increased competitiveness by externalising environmental costs (Perrow 1997). In local environmental conflicts the state is challenged more often than any other group, followed by producers and sub-state groups such as provincial or regional agencies in Greece or autonomous communities in Spain (Kousis 2001). Research on the responses of the state to environmental protest in southern European countries is limited (Eder and Kousis 2001). Usually, studies remain at a case study level (Aguilar-Fernandez 2001, Aguilar-Fernandez et al. 1995). Recent work (Kousis 2001) shows that challenges to the state and, even more so, the producers, are rarely answered in a positive manner.

Of the resolutions proposed by the environmental activists, one that rarely receive positive responses are as follows: those that focus on halting the source or activities that damage the ecosystem, those that propose the creation or implementation of environmental regulations, those that advocate the preservation of the local ecosystem, and those that call for the application of the latest ecological technologies. As far as making claims is concerned, health impacts are of special importance to residents and local government (Kousis 2001).

Sustained environmental activism, which is community-based, has been found to depend on network extension, intensive protest activity, and exposure to more pervasive impacts (Kousis 1999a). Although during the past 30 years increases have been noted in the number of environmental groups and organisations in the three countries, environmental activism patterns vary, with Greece and Spain showing more similarities to each other than to Portugal (Kousis 1999a). Participants in local environmental mobilisations usually represent a wide variety of community-based or popular groups such as residents, neighbours, citizens, workers, local environmental associations, or school-affiliated groups (Freudenberg and Steinsapir 1991) and, to a lesser extent, local government, local professionals, and local political party representatives (Kousis 1999a). The majority of local environmental protests tend to be non-violent (Taylor 1995; Freudenberg and Steinsapir 1991; Kousis *et al.* 1996).

Systematic examination of the sources of coastal environmental degradation that stimulate local environmental protest is missing. At the same time, no works have provided a mapping of *local environmental* contention related to coastal and marine natural resources at the national, regional, or metropolitan level. This paper aims to fill a gap in the aforementioned literature. Specifically, to examine the differential character of the resistance between shorter and longer duration cases, as regards the type of environmentally damaging sources, the protesters involved, the actions they propose, and the resolutions they demand.

Research Design and Method

The research method rests on protest-event analysis, a specific form of content analysis of printed media reports established in social movement research during the last 20 years (see Rucht *et al.* 1997). The undertaken protest-case analysis (Kousis 1999b) is applied here to grassroots environmental activism in Greece, Spain, and Portugal from the end of their dictatorial periods to 1994. The data are extracted from articles located by reading every issue of the major national newspapers *Eleftherotypia* (GR), *El Pais* (ES), *Jornal de Noticias* (PT), and *Publico* (PT), as well as the ecology magazines, *Oikologia* and *Perivallon* (GR), *Nea Oikologia* (GR), *Integral* (ES), *Quercus* (ES), and *AAVV-Forum Ambiente* (PT)[3] for the same period. In addition to all sections of the main (including Sunday) editions, all supplements to the main edition of the newspapers were also read.[4]

About 80 percent of the mentions of local environmental activism come from national newspapers. Once copies of all mentions of local environmental activism were gathered, they were collated into location files and subsequently into cases.[5] From a pool of 15,032 mentions, 1,322 protest cases were identified for Greece, 2,447 for Spain, and 550 for Portugal (Kousis 1998).[6] This work uses a sample of 856 Spanish cases, which includes all large cases, and a selection of small and medium cases. These 856 cases were selected from the 2,447 Spanish cases according to their size (in terms of numbers of participants), salience of environmental issues, and action repertoires – the wide spectrum of action types, such as petitions, demonstrations, rallies, et cetera.[7]

Out of the above pool of 2,728 cases, a total of 396 cases were selected for the purposes of this paper. They all make reference to negative environmental offences and/or impacts on islands, coastal zones, and/or marine areas. Each case represents collective incidents in which five[8] or more persons from a specific geographic area – excluding members of the national government – express criticism, protest, or resistance, and make a visible claim for their health, for the physical environment, or for their economic status. If realised, these claims would affect the interests of some person(s) or group(s) outside their own numbers during a given time period.

In each case, the coded claims of the environmental activists mentioned in the media reports focus on: a) the single or multiple sources or (in)activities causing damage to the ecosystem, usually associated with the state or an economic actor; b) the ecosystem offences produced by the source/s or (in)activity/ies, which usually appear in the form of noise, atmospheric, fresh water, coastal, marine, and land pollution, or the destruction of natural ecosystems; c) the variety of impacts of the ecosystem offenses as are manifested in negative impacts on public health and the human environment; and d) the resolutions proposed by the protesters for the amelioration of the environmental problem (Kousis 1999b).

Protest-case analysis combines elements from both the qualitative and the quantitative approaches to environmental activism, and, having the *protest case* as its unit of analysis, rests on four main features: a) concentration on community-based environmental mobilisations; b) possible extension of claim repertoire (i.e. the extension of demands) or time period (the diachronic view of protest); and c) possible change in action repertoire and network ties (relationships with other groups) (Kousis 1999b).

To make the issues at hand more comprehensible, the section that follows furnishes sample accounts of the types of coastal resource conflicts encountered in the form of short case studies of such conflicts, preceding the presentation of the analysed data.

Selected Case Studies

Greece: Against the Siting of a Municipal Waste Water Treatment Plant

Between 1987 and 1989 more than 3,000 citizens from a variety of local groups in Corfu mounted intense protests against the planned operation of a biological wastewater treatment facility to serve the municipality of Ioannina in the regions of Epirus. Protestors included residents, farmers, tradesmen, students, professionals, and members of local government and the local cultural association, along with local representatives of a mix of leftist, right, and centre parties, supported by Corfu emigrants living in Athens.

All of the above groups were collaborating with locals from many Thesprotian rural communities who were running the major campaign against the siting of the project, arguing that the treated effluents would pollute their river, Kalamas, which ends in the Ionian Sea, on the other side of the island of Corfu. The action forms taken included procedural complaints to authorities, demonstrations, occupation of the local airport and port, strikes and closing of all shops and civil services, as well as road blockades. Some violence did occur in these actions. The participants demanded the annulment of the planned project in order to stop the expected river, sea, and coastal pollution and the subsequent negative economic impact of decreasing incomes expected from an affected tourism industry.

The state and the municipal authority of Ioannina were viewed as the groups responsible for the project. At first, government representatives refused to hold talks with the protesters, arguing that ecosystem protection already exists with biological treatment technology. After the intense protests, negotiations began, and eventually additional measures to protect the environment were promised. Those promises did materialise, but only to some extent.

Spain: For and Against a Tourism-Related Project

Between 1992 and 1994, a conflict arose in Palamos of the Cataluna region over the use of local coastal resources. Local environmental groups, representatives of different political parties (PSC, PP, CUI), and a neighbourhood action committee, 'Salvem Castell', protested against a planned tourism-related project at the untouched Beach 'El Castell'. They argued that the project, which was supported by the state, regional, and local government and by private interests, would lead to negative aesthetic, cultural/historical, and ecosystem impacts on the coastal zone, including threatening its flora and fauna. The aim of the protest groups was the conservation of the wildlife area through proper regional planning and through the creation of environmental policy to protect the coastal zone. As many as 13,000 participants collected signatures, made public announcements, held a public protest assembly, and blockaded roads.

The companies El Castell S.A. and CAMO S.A., the project sponsors, as well as the landowners involved and their 4,200 supporters argued that the relevant urban plan, which was reformulated in 1992, had characterised the beach as urban, and not as a wildlife area. They viewed the project positively, noting its high economic expectations and arguing that environmental protection already existed. They took actions such as public announcements, procedural complaints to the authorities, land occupation, damage to property, and a public referendum. They were strongly supported by the regional government. In August 1993, *the Departamento de Politica Territorial Y Obras Publicas* accepted an appeal from El Castell S.A. requesting an increase in the number of units to be built per square metre.

Following pressure by the groups protesting against the project, in January 1993 the local government requested a public referendum in order to decide its fate. On June 16, 1994 those against the project were victorious. In October 1994, the regional court rejected an appeal from El Castell S.A. requesting the annulment of the referendum. As promised, in November 1994 the local government declared the 'El Castell' beach as a wildlife area not to be developed, and took legal and technical measures against CAMO S.A. for damage to the path to the beach – which the company occupied. At the same time, however, the regional government and the *Comision de Politica Territorial Y Obras Publicas* did not take the major steps needed to assure the protection of El Castell beach since this would mean that they had to purchase the land – which they had no interest in doing. Nevertheless, after intense protests, the referendum did succeed in halting the project.

Portugal: Against a Fossil Fuel Power Plant

During the early 1980s (1981-83), 18 rural and urban *freguesias* (i.e. the lowest administrative unit in Portugal, at the community level), led by that of Vila Nova de Anhã, from the municipality of Viana do Castello (Norte) mounted intense protest actions against the siting of a fossil fuel power plant in their area. More than 6,000 estimated participants included local groups such as the residents' action committee (Comissão de Luta Contra a Central Térmica), tradesmen's co-operatives (Associação Comercial de Viana), environmental groups (Associação Regional de Protecção ao Ambiente – ARDA), and the local development association Comissao Regional do Turismo do Alto Minho. They were supported by local governments from adjacent areas (the mayor of Caminha, Esposende) and the Socialist Party (PS).

Protests included procedural complaints to authorities, debates, signatures, public letters, demonstrations, and one incident of damage to property. The mobilised groups demanded that the plans to site the power plant should be cancelled, that they should have equal say and participation in the decision-making affecting their area and, finally, that in order to be protected, the concerned land should be given to the municipalities. If the project materialised, they argued, the area would suffer from atmospheric, coastal, and soil pollution and, more generally, the destruction of the local ecosystem.

When the mobilisers approached the *Governador Civil*, the central state representative at the local level, its response was one of indifference. The initial responses of the state government, the promoter of the project, and the semi-private semi-public companies (EDP) were similar. The protesters challenged both of these groups as being responsible for the expected environmental damage. Nevertheless, the state groups – i.e. the *Ministro da Industria e Energia*, the *Ministro da Qualidade de Vida*, the *Secretaria de Estado da Industria e do Turismo*, the Prime Minister, the *Presidente da Assembleia da Republica*, and the *Secretário de Estado da Administração Regional* – opened negotiations with the protesters and did temporarily halt the continuation of the project.

Conflicts over Maritime Resources: The Evidence

What Are They Mobilising About?

Urban and Rural Protests against Sources of Environmental Degradation
Environmental protesters usually make reference to specific sources of pollution or other activities affecting their environment, the damage to the ecosystem (e.g. coastal pollution), and/or the impacts which result from the offences (e.g. health or economic). Table 9.1 illustrates the sources of coastal and marine pollution by region.

Table 9.1. Cases of Protest Against Environmental Degradation by Region and by Source of Environmental Damage

Sources or (in)activities	Urban % (protest cases)		Rural % (protest cases)		Rural & Urban % (protest cases)		Total % (protest cases)	
Nature protection	26.1	(47)	31.5	(53)	17.4	(8)	27.4	(108)
Agric/animal husbandry	3.9	(7)	6.5	(11)	13.0	(6)	6.1	(24)
Fishing	10.0	(18)	7.7	(13)	4.3	(2)	8.4	(33)
Resource extraction	5.0	(9)	5.4	(9)	6.5	(3)	5.3	(21)
Tourism/recreation	13.9	(25)	10.7	(18)	13.0	(6)	12.4	(49)
Manufacturing	21.7	(39)	20.8	(35)	41.3	(19)	23.6	(93)
Transp/commun/ storage	8.4	(15)	8.9	(15)	4.3	(2)	8.2	(32)
Toxic/nuclear/haz waste	11.2	(20)	8.9	(15)	32.6	(15)	12.7	(50)
Domestic/non toxic waste	35.0	(63)	26.8	(45)	36.9	(17)	31.7	(125)
Energy	4.4	(8)	4.2	(7)	28.3	(13)	7.1	(28)
Weapons/ military activities	7.2	(13)	3.6	(6)	4.3	(2)	5.3	(21)
Environ. policy related	37.2	(67)	21.4	(36)	54.3	(25)	32.6	(128)
Total No. of protest cases		(180)		(168)		(46)		(394)

The sources of damage to ecosystems involved in urban and rural environmental protest are usually different, as shown in Boxes 9.1 and 9.2, respectively.

Box 9.1. Portugal: Agucadoura e Estela – Porto against sand extraction/ destruction of Masseiras

In 1990, a conflict arose in Agucadoura e Estela, *freguesias* of the Povoa do Varzim municipality in the city of Porto (Norte) over the extraction of sand and the subsequent destruction of the 'masseiras' (type of land field). The local government (junta e camarã; type of local government) and the local environmental group *Fundo Para A Protecção dos Animais Selvagens* (FAPAS) in their public accusations and through a press conference argued that sand extraction activities should be permanently stopped in order to prevent the loss of cultivated land and to protect the related coastal zone from soil erosion and from the destruction of associated flora and fauna. They also argued that sand mining threatened the farmers' economic viability and thus had a negative social impact.

The mobilised groups sought help from the *Comissão de Coord. Região Norte* (CCR-N), a representative of the central state at the local level. They accused the *Ministério da Agricultura* and the Secretary of the Environment Ministry of being fully responsible for the ecosystem-damaging activities, and demanded an environmental impact assessment as well as a permanent stop to sand extraction.

However, the outstanding causes of urban and rural protest are, in order of importance, domestic and non-toxic waste, environmental policy improvement, countryside protection, and manufacturing activities.

Box 9.2. Portugal: Sines – industrial incinerator

The environmental conflict over the siting of an incinerator for toxic industrial waste in the municipality of Sines (Setúbal, Alentejo) which began in May 1988 and lasted over six years mobilised an estimated number of 6,000 plus participants. Local participating groups included residents and their action committee (*Comissão de Luta Contra a Instalação da CIRTP*), the International Department of Fauna Conservation and Wetland Migratory Birds Protection (LUC Hfram), local government, trade unions, a local environmental group (*Grupo Lontra*), students, church groups (*Associacao Projecto Jovem do Centro Pastoral Joao Paulo II de Santiago do Cacém – Procris*), a mix of left- and right-wing local politicians opposing their party's views (i.e. PS, PSD, and CDU – *Partido Socialista, Partido Social Democrata*, and *Coligação Democrática Unitaria*), civil and health protection services, firemen, and a local radio station. They were supported by local governments from adjacent areas (Grandola, Santiago de Cacem) as well as other nonlocal groups including the environmental organization QUERCUS, Portuguese and foreign celebrities, and a mix of leftist and green political party representatives – such as José Socrates e José Reis (PS), Mario Tomé (*União Democrática Popular*), André Martins (*Verde*) and José Manuel Maria (*Partido Comunista Português*).

They publicised their demands via procedural complaints to the appropriate agencies, press conferences, debates, public letters, signatures, and source/site blockage. They claimed that the siting of such an incinerator along with improper regional planning and the lack of participation opportunities in decision-making concerning the environment will lead to serious environmental offenses. These would include atmospheric, coastal, freshwater, and soil pollution. In their attempt to stop the siting of the incinerator, they sought assistance from the large environmental organisations Greenpeace International-Holland, *Liga de Protecção de Natureza* (LPN) and GEOTA, as well as scientists like Jacques Cousteau and Paul Connett. These groups and individuals responded positively, offering them technical and organisational aid.

The groups challenged by the mobilisers as being responsible for the project and its consequences on the environment varied in their reactions. Although initially state units such as the *Secretário de Estado dos Receursos Naturais* and the *Ministerio do Ambiente e dos Receursos Naturais* asked the protesters to stop their actions, requesting evidence to substantiate accusations about the problem, they eventually promised to consider alternative measures. Local government agencies only went as far as formally recognizing the protesters. 'Ecopredi', the private company involved, at first asked for evidence of the problem, arguing that ecosystem protection existed, but later they promised compensation.

In cases of protest which involve a mix of both urban and rural protesters, this order changes. Environmental policy improvement ranks first, followed by manufacturing activities, domestic/non-toxic waste, and toxic/nuclear/hazardous waste and energy installations. It is worth noting that, the above causes of protest outrank the more often mentioned fishing and tourism interventions in coastal and marine ecosystems.

Where Are Mobilisations Taking Place?

National Distribution Across Region, Province, Metropolitan Area, and Number of Communities Involved

The regional distribution of cases of environmental protest in Greece, Spain, and Portugal appears in Table 9.2. Cases of environmental protest occurred in all Greek regions with the exception of Thrace, one of the poorest regions. These cases tend to concentrate in the eastern Sterea and Kyklades region, which includes the metropolitan area of Athens and a large industrial zone, as well as the Peloponese and western Sterea, both of which have pockets of industrial development. The lower protest frequencies in other such regions, like central and western Macedonia, are probably due to the coverage of the newspaper. All regions are coastal.

Table 9.2. Cases of Environmental Protest by Country and Region

Greece			Spain			Portugal		
Region	%	(protest cases)	Region	%	(protest cases)	Region	%	(protest cases)
E Sterea & Kyclades	50.8	(121)	Andalucia	35.6	(36)	Norte	43.9	(25)
C & W Macedonia	3.8	(9)	Aragon	1.0	(1)	Centro	12.3	(7)
Pelopon & W Sterea	20.6	(49)	Asturias	4.0	(4)	Lisboa & Vale do Tejo	33.3	(19)
Thessalia	3.8	(9)	Baleares Islas	3.0	(3)	Alentejo	3.5	(2)
E Macedonia	3.4	(8)	Canarias	4.0	(4)	Algarve	7.0	(4)
Kriti	5.0	(12)	Cantabria	2.0	(2)			
Epiros	5.0	(12)	Cataluna	13.9	(14)			
E Aegean Islands	7.6	(18)	Com Valenciana	13.9	(14)			
			Galicia	8.9	(9)			
			Com Madrid	5.0	(5)			
			Murcia	5.0	(5)			
			Pais Vasco	4.0	(4)			
Total	100	(238)		100	(101)		100	(57)

Twelve of the 17 regions of Spain show environmental protest activity that concerns coastal and marine resources. With the exception of Madrid and Aragon, ten are coastal regions. The highest frequencies appear in the regions of Andalusia, Catalonia, Valencia, and Galicia. Andalusia, Spain's most populous region, is one of the largest coastal regions in the European Union, containing, among a huge variety of ecosystems, the last great European wetlands reserve of Donana (province of Huelva). Pressures for economic development and mass tourism have led to conflicts over the protection of Andalusia's rich natural heritage. Whereas in 1980 only 6 percent of the surface area of Andalusia was protected, by the early 1990s, 81 protected areas represented 17 percent of the region's surface area (Eurostat 1993).

Most of the environmental problems in Valencia – mainly relating to the water cycle – occur in its coastal areas, which host the majority of the region's population and industry. In these areas agricultural irrigation is extensive, and in some localities the number of tourists is four times that of the locals. The water supply is subject to contamination and infiltration of seawater (Eurostat 1993). In

Catalonia, intensive urbanisation and the expansion of industry and tourism during the 1960s and 1970s led to riverine, atmospheric, and coastal pollution. In Galicia, pockets of environmental degradation in estuaries and beaches are usually the products of uncontrolled industrial effluents. Galicia's major industries are agriculture, shipbuilding, and automotive engineering (Eurostat 1993).

Portugal's reported environmental conflicts appear for five of its seven regions; no such protest occurred in the Açores and in Madeira, island regions with populations of less than 300,000 each. With contributions of less than 5 percent to national GDP, Alentejo and Algarve remain less active than Norte, Centro, and Lisboa and Vale do Tejo (Eurostat 1993). As environmental quality is related to the development of a region, the latter three regions show the highest frequencies of environmental protests.

An examination of the sub-regional distribution of environmental conflict reveals that for Greece, with the exception of Attica County, there is more or less an even country-level distribution of conflict. The Almeria and Huelva districts of Andalucia, as well as that of Valencia show higher concentrations of environmental protest than most Spanish provinces. For Portugal, the districts with the highest frequencies belong to the more developed regions of the country.

Table 9.3. Frequency of Environmental Protest Cases by Country

Greece			Spain			Portugal		
Metro Area	%	(protest cases)	Metro Area	%	(protest cases)	Metro Area	%	(protest cases)
Athens	51.7	(31)	Barcelona	12.9	(4)	Lisboa	60.9	(14)
Thes/niki	11.7	(7)	Bilbao	16.1	(5)	Do Porto	39.1	(9)
Patra	5.0	(3)	Candiz	9.7	(3)			
Irakleio	3.3	(2)	Huelva	16.1	(5)			
Volos	5.0	(3)	Madrid	16.1	(5)			
Chania	5.0	(3)	Pontevedra	6.5	(2)			
Agrinio	5.0	(3)	Sevilla	9.7	(3)			
Kalamata	3.3	(2)	Valencia	9.7	(3)			
Katerini	1.7	(1)	Zaragoza	3.2	(1)			
Chios	8.3	(5)						
Aigio	1.7	(1)						
Sparta	1.7	(1)						
Total	100.0	(60)		100.0	(31)		100.0	(23)

Table 9.3 shows the distribution of conflict by metropolitan area for the three countries of focus. Athens accounts for half of all cases occurring in metropolitan areas, followed by Thessaloniki. A more even distribution is noted for the remaining cases. The greater Athens area has changed dramatically since the 1960s, due to high rates of urbanisation based on industrial and tourism development. The county of Attica is the largest industrial centre in Greece. The tertiary sector contributes 33 percent to the region's GDP. Athens and Piraeus are the largest commercial centres in Greece. In addition to the above developments, Athens has become one of the most polluted capitals in Europe. Areas especially affected are the Elefsina plain and the Saronicos Gulf which host a number of petrochemical and other industries.

The metropolitan areas of Spain with higher frequencies of environmental conflict are major industrial and port areas. Barcelona is Spain's major Mediterranean port and commercial centre. Bilbao is Spain's most important port and the centre of many of the country's banking, shipping, shipbuilding, and steel industries. Huelva is an important commercial port city and centre for the export of pyrite ores and other minerals. It also hosts the headquarters for sardine, tuna, and bonito fisheries. Madrid has a strong concentration of economic activity and population, and is the political and administrative centre of the country. Sevilla is an inland port of the Guadalquivir estuary and capital of Andalusia province.

In Portugal, Lisboa and Do Porto, the two main urban centres and ports, host all cases of local environmental protest in the country.

Data presented in Table 9.4 indicate the number of communities involved in these environmental conflicts at the lowest administrative level of each country. For Greece and Spain, with more similar administrative divisions than Portugal, in approximately three-quarters of cases protesters come from one community, while the rest come from no more than 20 communities. In very occasional and mostly Spanish cases do protesters come from more than 20 communities. For Portugal, 40 percent of the communities cannot be identified at the *freguesia* level but only at the municipality level.[9] Protests with participants from more than two communities are only 9 percent in Portugal, compared with 26.3 and 24.0 for Greece and Spain, respectively.

CHAPTER NINE

Table 9.4. Cases of Environmental Protest by Country and Number of Communities Involved

No. of Municipalities, villages or freguesias (PT):	Greece Frequency % (protest cases)		Spain Frequency % (protest cases)		Portugal Frequency % (protest cases)		Total Frequency % (protest cases)	
Not identified					40.4	(23)	5.8	(23)
1	73.2	(174)	71.3	(72)	50.9	(29)	69.5	(276)
2-20	26.3	(63)	24.0	(24)	8.9	(5)	23.3	(63)
21-100	0.4	(1)	3.0	(3)			1.1	(4)
101-400			1.0	(1)			0.3	(1)
401+			1.0	(1)			0.3	(1)
No. of metropolitan areas:								
None	74.9	(179)	67.3	(68)	59.6	(34)	70.8	(281)
1	24.3	(58)	21.8	(22)	40.4	(23)	25.9	(103)
2	0.8	(2)	5.0	(5)			1.8	(7)
3-18			5.0	(5)			1.4	(5)
90			1.0	(1)			0.3	(1)
		(238)		(101)		(57)		(396)

The row labelled 'None' in Table 9.4 above also shows that a majority of cases of environmental conflict occur outside of metropolitan areas. In Greece, such cases amount to about three-quarters of all cases, while in Spain they comprise 67 percent of all cases, and in Portugal about 60 percent of all cases. On rare occasions protesters originated from a number of metropolitan areas.

The national distribution of the types of groups challenged by the activists is shown in Table 9.5. Although some national differences are apparent, the two major groups challenged by the protesters are common in all three countries: state groups and economic entrepreneurs. Local government is also an important group in Portugal, while regional government is important in Spain. State producers are a smaller but also important focus of protest in Spain and Greece.

Table 9.5. Cases of Environmental Protest by Country and Main Groups Challenged

Main groups challenged	Greece % (protest cases)	Spain % (protest cases)	Portugal % (protest cases)
State	47.3	57.4	40.4
Central state repr (local level)	15.1	15.8	31.6
Regional government	-	42.6	-
Local government	14.3	39.6	45.6
State producers	10.1	9.9	1.8
Semipriv-semipublic producers	-	5.0	8.8
Private producers	56.7	43.6	36.8
Farmers	0.4	5.9	3.5
Fishermen	2.9	5.9	-
Total no. of cases	100 (238)	100 (101)	100 (57)

*Each category was coded as a dichotomous, yes/no variable, thus percentages do not add up to 100.

Table 9.6. Cases of Environmental Protest by Duration and Types of Resolutions Proposed by Activists

Resolutions proposed by activists	<1year % (protest cases)		>1 year % (protest cases)		Total % (protest cases)	
Preservation/conservation	21.2	(50)	32.0	(51)	25.6	(101)
Policy related	50.0	(118)	62.1	(99)	55.0	(217)
Technology related	10.6	(25)	21.4	(34)	15.0	(59)
Radical/Eco centered	69.1	(163)	81.1	(129)	73.9	(292)
Total no. of cases		(236)		(159)		(395)

*Each category was coded as a dichotomous, yes/no variable, thus percentages do not add up to 100.

How Enduring Are the Conflicts?

Case Duration by Activists' Resolutions, Environmentally Intrusive Sources, Protest Groups, and Action Forms

Through their actions, the protesters propose a wide set of resolutions in order to address the environmental problem they are confronting. Table 9.6 above presents the general types of resolutions proposed. Once more, although policy-related options are proposed

CHAPTER NINE

in more than half of the cases – being somewhat more important for the longer cases – radical proposals, such as the annulment of planned projects, or the closure of existing facilities, are also proposed quite often regardless of case duration.

In 69 percent of short cases and 81 percent of longer ones, protesters demand the removal/relocation, discontinuation, or decrease of the environmentally destructive activities, or the total restoration of the affected area. Through these actions they demonstrate that they do not trust technological solutions. Table 9.7 reveals the sources of coastal and marine pollution by duration of each case of environmental protest. Compared with those of a shorter duration, sustained cases of resistance are usually network-extensive and bring together urban and rural activists. These cases tend to focus on environmental policy improvement, manufacturing activities, and domestic or toxic waste-related sources.

Table 9.7. Cases of Environmental Protest by Duration and Sources of Environmental Degradation

Sources/(in)activities	<1year		>1 year		Total	
	% (protest cases)		% (protest cases)		% (protest cases)	
Countryside protection	28.7	(68)	25.8	(41)	27.5	(109)
Agric/animal husbandry	3.8	(9)	9.4	(15)	6.1	(24)
Fishing	8.4	(20)	8.8	(14)	8.6	(34)
Resource extraction	5.1	(12)	5.7	(9)	5.3	(21)
Tourism/recreation	11.0	(26)	14.5	(23)	12.4	(49)
Manufacturing	16.9	(40)	34.0	(54)	23.7	(94)
Transport/commun/storage	8.0	(19)	8.2	(13)	8.1	(32)
Toxic/nuclear/haz waste	7.6	(18)	20.8	(33)	12.9	(51)
Domestic/non-toxic waste	28.7	(68)	35.2	(56)	31.3	(124)
Energy	3.0	(7)	13.2	(21)	7.1	(28)
Weapons/military activities	3.4	(8)	8.2	(13)	5.3	(21)
Environ. policy related	22.8	(54)	47.2	(75)	32.6	(129)
Total no. of cases	(237)		(159)		(396)	

*Each category was coded as a dichotomous, yes/no variable, thus percentages do not add up to 100.

An example of a short duration case focused on manufacturing activities appears in Box 9.3.

Protesters active around issues of coastal resources come from a
wide variety of local groups, as shown in Table 9.8. If we compare
those involved in cases lasting for less than a year and those for one
year or more, some changes are notable, even though the general pattern appears similar.

Table 9.8. Cases of Environmental Protest by Duration and Types of Local Protesters

Type of local participating or initiating groups	<1year % (protest cases)		>1 year % (protest cases)		Total % (protest cases)	
Residents	57.6	(136)	74.8	(119)	64.6	(255)
Local government	24.6	(58)	41.5	(66)	31.4	(124)
Labour and trade unions	15.7	(37)	36.5	(58)	24.1	(95)
Cooperatives	2.5	(6)	8.2	(13)	4.8	(19)
Employers	2.1	(5)	3.1	(5)	2.5	(10)
Hunters	7.2	(17)	4.4	(7)	6.1	(24)
Activities clubs	14.4	(34)	22.0	(35)	17.5	(69)
Environmental groups	27.5	(65)	45.9	(73)	34.9	(138)
Physicians	1.7	(4)	11.9	(19)	5.8	(23)
Other professionals	6.4	(15)	18.9	(30)	11.4	(45)
Courts	1.9	(3)	0.8	(3)		
Parents/teachers associations	0.8	(2)	4.4	(7)	2.3	(9)
Students/pupils	2.5	(6)	9.4	(15)	5.3	(21)
Women's groups	2.1	(5)	5.7	(9)	3.5	(14)

Type of local participating or initiating groups	<1year % (protest cases)		>1 year % (protest cases)		Total % (protest cases)	
Religious/church groups	0.8	(2)	4.4	(7)	2.3	(9)
Political party representatives	6.8	(16)	34.0	(54)	17.7	(70)
State affiliated local agencies	3.8	(9)	6.9	(11)	5.0	(20)
Development associations	1.9	(3)	0.8	(3)		
artists	0.8	(2)	3.8	(6)	2.0	(8)
Total no. of env. protest cases	(237)	(159)	(396)			

*Each category was coded as a dichotomous, yes/no variable, thus percentages do not add up to 100.

In the majority of cases local participants include residents or neighbours. Local environmental groups, local government, and labour and trade unions follow in importance. For cases of sustained resistance, networks are more extensive, and group participation is more intensive. In addition, political parties also play an important role.

Box 9.4. Portugal: Aveiro-Murtoza dike project

Between 1973 and 1992 *Núcleo Português de Estudo e Protecção da Vida Selvagem*, a local environmental group of the Baixo Vouga *freguesia* in the municipality of Aveiro (Centro), mobilised against the planned Aveiro-Murtoza dike project. Through public letters and announcements it claimed that the construction of a dike-infrastructure project in the area as well as the lack of wetland protection would lead to the destruction of the related local ecosystem, including negative impacts on the involved wetland and marine ecosystems, as well as negative aesthetic and cultural/historical impacts. In this endeavour, the local group had the support of a non-local environmental group. It also approached WWF-UK, the European Commission, and UN organisations, seeking their assistance in the preservation of the above wildlife area and the related cultural heritage area via the annulment of the planned project and the adoption of an environmentally sound alternative project.

Those challenged by the actions of the environmental groups were essentially state bodies in support of the project, such as the *Secretário de Estado das Vias de Communicação* and the *Ministro do Ambiente e dos Receursos Naturais*, and at the local level, Zita Seabra (the Deputy of the APU). Although the central state agencies did respond to the demands of the mobilised groups by formally recognising them, opening negotiations and seeing the need for more studies as well as a more appropriate alternative, no change was noted in this case by 1992.

As in most instances of environmental protest, the data in Table 9.9 also indicate that the great majority of actions taken come in the form of appeals. For an example of this, see Box 9.4.

Table 9.9. Cases of Environmental Protest by Duration and Types of Action Taken

Actions taken	<1year		>1 year		Total	
	% (protest cases)		% (protest cases)		% (protest cases)	
Appeal	95.3	(225)	99.4	(158)	97.0	(383)
Demonstrative	0.4	(1)	2.5	(4)	1.3	(5)
Confrontational	8.5	(20)	36.5	(58)	19.7	(78)
Violent	3.4	(8)	16.4	(26)	8.6	(34)

*Each category was coded as a dichotomous, yes/no variable, thus percentages do not add up to 100.

Note: *Appeal*: demanding/general claiming, complaints to authority, press conference, signatures.

Demonstrative: court route, public referendum, demonstration/public protest, hunger strike.

Confrontational: occupation of public buildings, strikes and closing of shops, activity/ source blockage, road blockades/sit-ins.

Violent: threats to use arms, damage to property, throwing things at those responsible, unintended injuries, intended injuries, deaths.

Interestingly enough, although demonstrations are rare, confrontational tactics are used in about 8.5 percent of short duration cases but 36.5 percent of sustained resistance cases. The increase in action intensity of the latter is also shown in the higher occurrence of violent cases (16.4 percent). Grassroots environmental activists are in general more radical in their actions than are environmental organisations.

Conclusions

This chapter provided systematic cross-national evidence concerning local environmental conflicts over coastal and marine resources in southern Europe from 1974 to 1994, pointing to their major characteristics while depicting them spatially. By highlighting the roles of protest and target entities involved in these conflicts as socio-economic groups competing for the use and control of coastal resources, the present work aims to enhance our understanding of the social-political dynamics related to environmental conflict.

The present analysis offers a mapping of coastal-related environmental conflicts, pointing to the importance of ecosystem-damaging activities which have been recently recognised in related discussions (e.g. Huber *et al.* 2003). However, the analysis undertaken enriches and extends these discussions by showing for the first time trends in environmental conflicts with cross-national data. Community level claims related to coastal and marine resources do not focus primarily on tourism, but on waste, manufacturing, energy installations, and the lack of effective environmental policy, or its implementation. The persistence of environmental protests in rural and urban communities of Greece, Spain and Portugal demonstrate the significance for local groups of the associated risks to their health and the economic impacts of the deterioration of their natural resources. Given the intensification of growth under neo-liberalism policies at a global level and the expected increase in Mediterranean tourism development, such protest levels are likely to intensify.

At the same time, the evidence provided in this chapter fills in an additional gap in the prevailing literature, which does not provide a systematic examination of environmental protesters demanding coastal environmental amelioration. For example, attention is centred on the deterioration of marine and coastal resources, on environmental education policies by media, governments, special interest groups, and scientific organisations, and on economic incentive policies aimed at stimulating private sector involvement and investment (e.g. Huber *et al.* 2003). Such analyses tend to ignore the cumulative experience of community-based environmental protesters living with affected marine and coastal resources at the local level, but more importantly, they overlook the importance of the powerful groups that are being challenged in environmental conflicts.

The analysis undertaken contributes to the filling in of this gap in two ways. First, it provides cross-national evidence showing that at the community level, southern European environmental protest groups have been requesting (at least since the 1970s) the creation, improvement, and/or implementation of environmental policy affecting coastal and marine resources as well as radical and ecocentric measures to stop or decrease a wide variety of ecosystem-intrusive activities. They have done so not only in 'ad hoc' protests but also through sustained resistance. The later is characterised by time durability, more intensive actions, a wider representation of participating groups, and more demanding resolutions.

Secondly, for the first time at the cross-national level and over a 20-year period, the data presented in this chapter expose the crucial role of the national, regional, and entrepreneurial groups in the use and abuse of coastal and marine resources, something which current works recently bring up for discussion at a more abstract level (e.g. Huber *et al.* 2003). State, regional, and local government groups and strong entrepreneurial groups (appearing as private or state economic 'producers') are shown to be challenged by protest in more or less similar patterns across the three countries. Such evidence points to the vital importance of addressing deeper issues involving the politics of sustainable development and the sustainability of production, rather than that of consumption raised in prevailing discussions of ecological modernization. In this way, the approach taken in this chapter cautions that one-dimensional economic incentive-oriented policies aiming at diverting powerful economic actors from coastal and marine resource abuse must be accompanied by comprehensive sustainable development policies (especially concerning the production sector) that ensure the amelioration of environmental and socio-economic conditions as well as the associated public health risks.

Notes

1. An earlier version of this paper was presented at the Inaugural Conference "People and the Sea: Maritime Research in the Social Sciences – an agenda for the 21st century", August 29-Sept.1, 2001. The data originate from project EV5V-CT94-0393 funded by the European Commission, DG XII for Science, Research & Development. Collaboration with project partners Susana Aguilar and Teresa Fidelis as well as with all research assistants is gratefully acknowledged. I wish to thank Jeremy Boissevain and Tom Selwyn for their helpful comments.
2. Meaning 'developer, exploiter, destroyer', et cetera, and not 'consumer, resident', or 'guest'.
3. The Portuguese environmental magazine first appeared in 1994.
4. For Spain, the 'Valencia,' 'Andalusia,' 'Catalonia' and 'Ciudades' supplements begin in 1986. For Catalonia only the years 1982-85 were excluded due to lack of time and funding. For Portugal, Publico's two regional supplements were also read.
5. The following selection criteria were applied in the three countries uniformly, leading to the exclusion of 1,813 mentions. 1. Local groups of more than five persons (or their representative/s) mobilising for local problems. 2. Local problems dealing with economic or health issues that were related to environmental issues, or just environmental issues. 3. Initiatives taken by local groups who are not directly involved in conventional politics but may collaborate with political parties. 4. Action forms ranging from the minimum: making general demands or public accusations towards the challenged group on the problem, to the maximum: violent episodes. 5. Local groups collaborating with various non-local groups on local problems. 6. Local groups collaborating with local authorities on local problems. 7. Local

CHAPTER NINE

and/or national group/s mobilising for national problems that affect them directly at the local level.

6. Case listing underwent repeated revisions as cases were collated. The same assistants were employed during the different phases (locating, collating, and coding of the articles) in the three countries and therefore were able to use the accumulated knowledge they acquired about their country's cases from consecutive readings of the articles. The final 'code sheet' was tested in more than 30 trials across the three national teams.

7. This selection procedure was applied systematically by Ilse Borchard, head of the coders' team in Spain, by examining all cases that were traced for every month of the whole period.

8. If the number was not mentioned explicitly in the articles, the coders applied rules estimating the number of participants.

9. Not appearing here for Portugal. The category 'Municipality' (based on population size) applies only to Greece.

References

Aguilar-Fernandez, S.
2001   Is Spanish Environmental Policy Becoming More Participatory? In: K. Eder and M. Kousis (Eds.), *Environmental Politics in Southern Europe: Actors, Institutions and Discourses in a Europeanizing Society*. Dordrecht: Kluwer. Pp. 255-276.

Aguilar-Fernandez, S., T. Fidelis-Nogueira, and M. Kousis
1995   Encounters between Social Movements and the State: Examples from Waste Facility Siting in Greece, Portugal and Spain. *Proceedings of the International Conference: Alternative Futures and Popular Protest*, Manchester Metropolitan University. April 4-6.

Bavinck, M.
2001   *Marine Resource Management: Conflict and Regulation in the Fisheries of the Coromandel Coast*. London: Sage.

Boissevain, J.
1979   Tourism and the European Periphery: The Mediterranean Case. In: D. Seers, B. Schaffer, and M-L. Kiljunen (Eds.), *Underdeveloped Europe: Studies in Core-Periphery Relations*. Sussex: The Harvester Press Limited. Pp. 125-138.
1996   *Coping with Tourists: European Reactions to Mass Tourism*. London: Bergham Books.
2004   (this volume)

Boissevain, J. and N. Theuma
1996   Contested Space: Tourism, Heritage and Identity in Malta. Biennial EASA Conference, Barcelona. July.

Broadbent, J.
1998   *Environmental Politics in Japan: Networks of Power and Protest*. New York: Cambridge University Press.

Chekki, D. A. (Ed.)

1997 *Research in Community Sociology: Environment and Community Empower-ment*, Vol.7. London: JAI Press Inc.

Eder, K. and M. Kousis

2001 Is There a Mediterranean Syndrome? In: K. Eder and M. Kousis (Eds.), *Environmental Politics in Southern Europe: Actors, Institutions and Discourses in a Europeanizing Society*. Dordrecht: Kluwer.

European Environmental Agency (EEA)

1999 Environment in the European Union at the Turn of the Century: Environmental Assessment Report No.2. Brussels.

Eurostat

1993 *Portrait of the Regions. Vol.3 Portugal, Spain, Italy and Greece*. Luxembourg: Office for Official Publications of the European Communities.

1997 *Environment Statistics 1996 8A*. Luxembourg: Office for Official Publications of the European Communities.

Figueiredo, E., T. Fidelis, and A. da R. Pirez

2001 Grassroots Environmental Action in Portugal (1974-1994). In: K. Eder and M. Kousis (Eds.), *Environmental Politics in Southern Europe: Actors, Institutions and Discourses in a Europeanizing Society*. Dordrecht: Kluwer.

Freudenberg, N. and C. Steinsapir

1991 Not in Our Backyards: The Grassroots Environmental Movement. In: R.E. Dunlap and A. Mertig (Eds.), *American Environmentalism*. Washington: Taylor and Francis. Pp. 27-35.

Gil Nave, J.

2001 Environmental Politics in Portugal. In: K. Eder and M. Kousis (Eds.), *Environmental Politics in Southern Europe: Actors, Institutions and Discourses in a Europeanizing Society*. Dordrecht: Kluwer.

Gonzalez, P. and P. Moral

1996 Analysis of Tourism Trends in Spain. *Annals of Tourism Research* 23(4): 739-754.

Gould, K. A., A.S. Weinberg, and A. Schnaiberg

1993 Legitimating Impotence: Pyrrhic Victories of the Modern Environmental Movement. *Qualitative Sociology* 16(3):207-246.

Gould. K. A., A. Schnaiberg and A. S.Weinberg

1996 *Local Environmental Struggles: Citizen Activism in the Treadmill of Production*. Cambridge: Cambridge University Press.

Huber, M.E., R.A. Duce, J.M. Bewers, D. Insull, L. Jeftic, and S. Keckes, on behalf of GESAMP and ACOPS

2003 Priority Problems Facing the Global Marine and Coastal Environment and Recommended Approaches to their Solution. *Ocean and Coastal Management* 46(5):479-485.

Jimenez, M.
2001   National Policies and Local Struggles in Spain: Environmental Politics over Industrial Waste Policy in the 1990s. Paper presented at the 29th Joint Sessions of the European Consortium for Political Research, Grenoble, 6–11 April (Local Environmental Politics).

Konsolas, N. and G. Zacharatos
1992   Regionalization of Tourism Activity in Greece: Problems and Policies. In: H. Briassoulis and J. van der Straaten (Eds.), *Tourism and the Environment*. Dordrecht: Kluwer Academic Publishers.

Kousis, M.
1998   Ecological Marginalization: Actors, Impacts, Responses. *Sociologia Ruralis* 38(1):86-108.
1999a Sustaining Local Environmental Mobilizations: Groups, Actions and Claims in Southern Europe. *Environmental Politics* special issue on *Environmental Movements: Local, National, and Global* 8(1):172-198.
1999b Environmental Protest Cases: the City, the Countryside and the Grassroots in Southern Europe. *Mobilization* special issue on *Protest Event Analysis* 4(2):223-238.
2000   Tourism and the Environment: A Social Movements Perspective. *Annals of Tourism Research* 27(2):468-489.
2001   Competing Claims in Local Environmental Conflict in Southern Europe. In: K. Eder and M. Kousis (Eds.), *Environmental Politics in Southern Europe: Actors, Institutions and Discourses in a Europeanizing Society*. Dordrecht: Kluwer.

Kousis, M., S. Aguilar-Fernandez and Teresa Fidelis
1996   *Final Report: Grassroots Environmental Action and Sustainable Development in Southern European Union*. European Commission, DGXII, contract no. EV5V-CT94-0393.

Kousis, M., E. Petropoulou, and E. Dimopoulou
2001   *Local Environmental Politics in Urban and Rural Greece: A Study of North-Eastern Athens and the County of Chanea*. Paper presented at the 29th Joint Sessions of the European Consortium for Political Research, Grenoble, 6–11 April ('Local Environmental Politics' Session).

Kousis, M. and K. Eder
2001   EU policy making, local action and the emergence of institutions of collective action: a theoretical perspective on Southern Europe. In: K. Eder and M. Kousis (Eds.), *Environmental Politics in Southern Europe: Actors, Institutions and Discourses in a Europeanizing Society*. Dordrecht: Kluwer.

Kurien, J. and T. R. T. Achari
1988   Fisheries Development Policy and the fishermen's struggle in Kerala. *Social Action* 38 (January-March):15-36.

Lozato-Giotart, J-P.
1990   *Mediterranee et tourisme*. Paris: Masson.
       Mediterranean Commission for Sustainable Development (MCSD), Plan.

Perrow, C.

1997   Organizing for Environmental Destruction. *Organization and the Environment* 10(1):66-72.

Plan Bleu and UNEP

1998a *Synthesis Report of the Working Group: Tourism and Sustainable Development in the Mediterranean Region.* Mediterranean Action Plan, Monaco, 20-22 October.

1998b *A Blue Plan for the Mediterranean Peoples: From Ideas to Action.* Sophia Antipolis: Blue Plan Regional Activity Centre.

Rodriguez M. and J. Carlos

2001   The case of the Aznarcollar mine and its impacts on coastal activities in Southern Spain. *Ocean and Coastal Management* 44(1-2):105-118.

Rucht,D., R. Koopmans and F. Neidhardt

1997   *Acts of Dissent: New Developments in the Study of Protest.* Berlin: Edition Sigma.

Salmona, P.

2002   The Regional Seas in the 21st Century: the Need for Data. *Ocean and Coastal Management* 45(11-12):935-964.

Schnaiberg, A.

1994   The Political Economy of Environmental Problems and Policies: Consciousness, Conflict, and Control Capacity. *Advances in Human Ecology* 3:23-64.

Suman, D.

2001   Case Studies of Coastal Conflicts: Comparative US/European Experiences. *Ocean and Coastal Management* 44:1-13.

Szasz, A.

1994   *Ecopopulism: Toxic Waste and the Movement of Environmental Justice.* Minneapolis, MI: University of Minnesota Press.

Taylor, B. R. (Ed.)

1995   *Ecological Resistance Movements: the global emergence of radical and popular environmentalism.* Albany: State University of New York Press.

Weinberg, A.

1997   Local Organizing for Environmental Conflict: Explaining Differences between Case of Participation and Nonparticipation. *Organization and Environment* 10(2):194-216.

10

Hotels, Tuna Pens, and Civil Society: Contesting the Foreshore in Malta

Jeremy Boissevain

> The environment ... is a collective good that serves as a new
> medium for rearranging social relations between groups, thus
> rearranging relations of power and restructuring forms of social
> inequality in an emerging European society.
>
> (Kousis and Eder 2001:16)

Introduction

This chapter discusses the struggle between the traditional stakeholders in the Maltese foreshore, such as fishermen and locals enjoying the seaside in their free time, and new stakeholders associated
with the tourist, building, and aquaculture industries. National and
local authorities, intent on earning foreign exchange, creating jobs
and appeasing the powerful building and tourism lobbies, generally
favour the new stakeholders. Although the power balance between
these rival stakeholder coalitions is grossly unequal, the position of
the traditional stakeholders defending the foreshore is not completely hopeless. To protect their interests, they occasionally mount ad
hoc campaigns against specific developments. They are usually supported by local and, occasionally, international non-governmental
organisations (NGOs), which often take the initiative. This paper explores three such confrontations: the extension of the Hilton Hotel,
the construction of a tourist complex on an undeveloped bay, and the
establishment of a tuna farming operation. How effective have the
campaigns been in combating these specific developments? Have
their efforts had any significant impact on Maltese society? Before
looking more closely at these cases, a few words about Malta, its political climate, and the environmental lobby are useful to establish the
context.

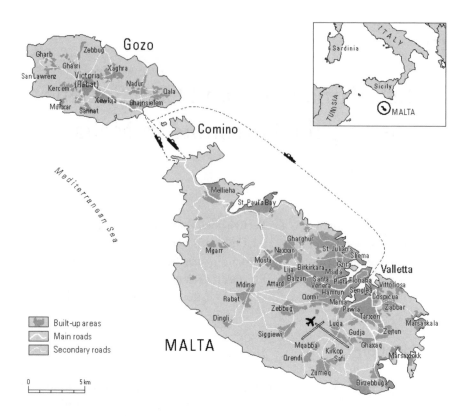

Fig. 10.1. Map of Malta.

Malta

The Maltese archipelago is minute, covering only 315 square kilometres. Malta, the largest island, is 27 kilometres long and just over 14 wide, roughly the size of the Channel Island of Jersey or the Dutch island of Schouwen-Duiveland. Gozo is only 14 by 8 kilometres. Finally, Comino, which lies in the channel separating the two larger islands, covers less than two square kilometres. The islands are oriented along a northwest-southeast axis. From 250-meter cliffs on the southwest coast, Malta's hilly terrain descends to an accessible foreshore on the eastern side. Most of the tourist and industrial development has taken place along this foreshore. With a population of 380,000, Malta is the most densely populated state in Europe. Awareness of this density and the small geographic scale is basic to understanding the environmental problems facing the Maltese.

CHAPTER TEN

The Context: Parties, Environmentalists, and the Planning Authority

Parties

Malta became independent from Britain in 1964, and since then it has been an extremely lively democracy. Much of Maltese social life is dominated by the intense, corrosive rivalry between the two long established parties, the Nationalist Party (PN) and the Malta Labour Party (MLP). The political culture is characterised by intense party loyalty, patronage, nepotism, and clientelism. The country is almost equally divided between the two parties. The newer and smaller Green Party, *Alternattiva Demokratika*, is not represented in Parliament because of the peculiarities of the Maltese electoral system.[1] The PN, traditionally the party of the clergy, professional classes, and farmers, is similar to Christian Democratic parties elsewhere. Generally, it has been more tolerant of the voice of civil society and NGOs. It strongly supports Malta's forthcoming membership of the European Union. The Labour Party has traditionally favoured industrial workers and the less well-off and has been more closed to the voice of civil society, and environmental NGOs in particular. It is strongly opposed to Malta joining the European Union. During its first tenure of government (1971-1987) the MLP became increasingly autocratic and dealt harshly with grassroots and NGO criticism. Both parties favour industrial development, foreign investment, and tourism. While paying lip service to the environment since the mid-1980s, neither party has systematically undertaken firm action to enforce existing laws designed to protect the country's monumental heritage and landscape (Boissevain 2001). The intricate networks of nepotism, patronage and political clientelism, the pervasiveness and intensity of which are a function of the country's small scale, population density, and strong family ties, are largely responsible for this failure (Baldacchino 1997; Boissevain 1974, 2001:292-293).

Environmentalism

Environmental sensitivity in Malta evolved slowly. Until quite recently, there was little interest in the countryside or nature. Concern for environmental heritage only acquired an organised form after

Malta's independence (Mallia 1994; Boissevain and Theuma 1998). The Malta Ornithological Society was founded in 1962 and *Din l-Art Helwa* ('This Fair Land') in 1965. The latter promptly began a successful campaign to reduce the height of a luxury hotel being built against Valletta's bastions. Its members, at least initially, were educated bourgeois concerned with protecting the country's monumental landscape. During the 1970s environmentalists were concerned mainly with protecting monuments and the flora and fauna. They rarely demonstrated in public. By the mid-1980s targets and tactics changed. Younger and more radical activists, some of whom had worked with environmental groups abroad, began to engage in physical action. *Moviment ghall-Ambient* [Movement for the Environment, which later became Friends of the Earth (Malta)], *Zghazagh ghall-Ambjent* (Youths for the Environment), Din l-Art Helwa and the Society for the Study and Conservation of Nature (SSCN) demonstrated to protest the general neglect of the environment. They targeted the rampant development of beach concessions, uncontrolled building activity, illegally built tarmac plants and the massive allocation of government building plots in spite of much vacant property.

The increasing activity of environmental NGOs and growing public criticism of rampant building finally placed environmental issues on the agenda of the 1987 general election. In 1989, one of the radical NGOs, *Alternattiva Demokratika*, became a fully fledged green political party. It developed close links with other European green parties via the European Federation of Green Parties. Henceforth, local environmental issues were assured of a wider European audience, an important resource given the Nationalist government's eagerness to join the EU. In the 30 years following independence, environmentalism has become established, and the government, the two dominant political parties and civil society have become somewhat more sensitive to environmental issues and tolerant of the NGO campaigns.

Planning

By 1992 Malta finally had a Structure Plan (1990), an Environment Protection Act (1991), and a Development Planning Act (1992) that provided for a Planning Authority to administer and enforce the relevant legislation (Boissevain and Theuma 1996). Under the terms of the 1990 Structure Plan, the Planning Authority (PA) must approve all applications for external building work. Minor and intermediate works are delegated to the Directorate's officers or the Development Control Commission. Major applications and those requiring an Environmental Impact Assessment (EIA), such as those discussed below, are decided by the full Planning Authority Board.

The members of the PA Board are appointed by the President on the recommendation of the Prime Minister. The Board consists of 15 members: eight independent members, including the chairman; a representative of each of the two parliamentary parties; and five civil servants.[2] Applications for major projects are decided in two steps: an Outline Application and, if that is approved, a Full Application. Meetings regarding applications and appeals are public, but those wishing to make interventions must arrange this with the PA's secretary. These public hearings often become very acrimonious. Though the PA Board is not a homogeneous body, the government's interests are the most strongly represented and thus prevail. Members representing environmental NGOs, in spite of their requests, are not permitted to sit on the Board.

Growing Pressures on the Foreshore

After independence, tourism began to be promoted in earnest as an alternative source of income. Between 1960 and 1970 annual tourist arrivals increased from 28,000 to almost 236,000. By 1980 they had reached 789,000 and by 2000 over 1.1 million. The advent of mass tourism has had a severe impact on the landscape. Hotels and cheap apartment complexes mushroomed in disorderly fashion along the northeastern shore, in Mellieha, St. Paul's Bay, Bugibba, St. Julian's, Sliema, and Marsascala. Malta's once economically marginal coastal zone has been transformed into a prime economic resource. This transformation has precipitated social conflict and seriously affected the environment. Tourist developments have taken up most of Malta's accessible coast. The mass tourist influx, together with an expanding population and rising affluence, aggravated existing water supply, energy and waste disposal problems, necessitating the construction of desalination units, a new power station, and a giant landfill, nicknamed 'Mount Maghtab'. All are located on the coast. Desalination consumes almost one-fifth of the island's electricity output; the power station emits toxic fumes; the noxious smoke from Mount Maghtab affects four down-wind villages and an adjacent hotel, and it leaches toxic effluent into both the island's aquifer and its fore-shore. Eighty-six percent of sewage is discharged untreated into the sea. The drive in the 1990s to attract 'quality tourists', via the construction of luxury hotels and marinas, and the recent expansion of fish farming appreciably increased the existing pressure on the environment and thus provoked conflict with the environmental lobby (Moviment ghall-Ambjent 1997; Mallia 2000).

Conflict

The Hilton Extension[3]

In 1995 the Spinola Development Co. Ltd. submitted its Outline Application and Environmental Impact Statement (EIS) to the Planning Authority to redevelop the Hilton Hotel in St Julian's.[4] This $122 million project involved a new 300 bed hotel, 250 luxury apartments, a 16-story business centre, the excavation of a marina to accommodate 100 yachts and the construction of a breakwater. The NGOs united to argue in well documented briefs that the marina excavation would destroy a unique fortification built by the Knights of Malta; that pollution caused by excavating the marina and its subsequent effluent would damage nearby sea grass meadows and pollute several popular swimming beaches; that the EIS failed to examine the project's socio-economic consequences; that the public would be denied access to sections of the foreshore; and that the project's excavation, blasting, and building would subject residents in this densely populated neighbourhood to five years of extreme inconvenience. The NGOs organised a press campaign and numerous demonstrations to little avail.

The public hearing on the Full Application and the final vote were held on May 23, 1996. The application was approved after a four-hour, acrimonious hearing. Admission was tightly controlled and limited. There was a list of persons permitted to enter, and police searched those who were admitted. The NGOs and the public had not been informed of this tighter procedure.

Employees of the developer arrived hours before the meeting and were thus able to occupy virtually all the limited number of seats reserved for the public. For the most part they were weather beaten and roughly dressed workmen. Only NGO members intending to speak had notified the PA Secretary and so appeared on the list. Others, arriving later and unaware of the stricter admittance rules, were not on the list and were not admitted. Most of the Moviment Ghall-Ambjent members and the entire delegation of the radical NGO *Graffitti* were consequently left standing at the entrance. One of the NGO speakers, noting that there were still three unoccupied chairs at the back of the room, tried to gain admittance for three of those waiting outside. This was refused because they were "not on the list". He commented on this anomalous situation to the developer's principal consultant, who replied: 'Last time you caught us on the wrong foot. This time we were prepared'. This referred to the public hearing on the Outline Plan held the year before when NGO members had packed the meeting and suddenly displayed anti-Hilton banners and placards.

The Director of Planning opened the meeting. He outlined the reasons the PA Directorate supported the project: it conformed to government's policy to develop luxury tourist accommodation; the Environmental Impact Statement was favourable; and the developer had met the technical stipulations imposed during the discussions on the Outline Plan the previous June (which included provisions to dispose of rubble and excavated cuttings and protect the surroundings from dust and disturbance, measures to control pollution from the marina, the handling of resident's complaints, and so on). The developers and the NGOs repeated most of the arguments used the previous year at the hearings on the EIS and the Outline Application. The Friends of the Earth spokesperson, a lawyer, pointed out that there was an appeal pending, thus no decision could be taken before its outcome. After all parties had spoken, the Director of Planning replied to queries and objections: there would be daytime access to the foreshore, the site would be landscaped and thus be good for residents, blasting would be controlled, the EIS was well done, the Lands Department had done its work well. Regarding the appeal, he maintained that it was all right to proceed pending its outcome because third-party appeals in the past had all been turned down by the Appeal Board.

The Friends of the Earth spokesperson rose and protested that the Director had not given correct information on the pending appeal. The chairman first ruled him out of order but later allowed him to speak. The lawyer's point was that the court had not yet ruled on the constitutionality of an appeal by a third party against the ruling of the PA. Hence, he argued, it was not possible to proceed with the project.

At this point, the developer, a rough, imposing bulk of a man, roared his disapproval. He lurched at the lawyer and began grossly to insult him and his family. Security guards separated the parties and quieted the developer's noisy supporters, some of whom had begun to move threateningly towards the lawyer. Order was restored.

After ten minutes of lackadaisical questions by Board members, during which the developer was obliged, finally, to grant 24-hour access to the foreshore, the project was put to the vote. As expected, 13 Board members voted in favour and one against. The sole dissenter, the University Professor of Classics and Archaeology, again opposed the development, among other reasons on aesthetic grounds: the planned eight story apartment blocks reminded him of a collection of airport hangers.

After the vote most of the public stormed out as a number of the developer's employees surged forward to congratulate him, patting his shoulder in a show of solidarity. Work on the redevelopment of the hotel began almost immediately (Boissevain and Theuma 1998: 106-108).

The NGOs were far from satisfied, and continued protesting. They wrote letters to the papers, publicised the confidential negative report on the project by the Planning Authority's own Environmental Management Unit, lobbied the European Greens, and called for a public inquiry to investigate the irregular transfer of public land to the Spinola Development Company. The newly formed *Front Kontra l-Hilton* (the Front), composed chiefly of *Graffitti* members and a few others, mostly from *Moviment ghall-Ambjent*, began a campaign of passive resistance, which included some chaining themselves to earth-moving equipment used to excavate the marina.

Four months later there was a change of government. The newly elected Labour Party gave the NGOs some hope that their allegations would be looked into. When this did not occur, they acted again. Following a week-long hunger strike in January 1998 by Front activists camped in front of the Prime Minister's Office, the national Ombudsman agreed to examine the alleged illegal land transfer. The new Labour Party Prime Minister also authorised the Front to examine the Planning Authority's files relating to the favourable Hilton decision reached under the previous (Nationalist) administration. Though most of the public did not agree with the objectives of the Front or its tactics, some admired its young activists for their courageous and, for Malta, innovative action in challenging established authority.

The Ombudsman concluded that while the original land grant conditions were not illegal, they clearly constituted "a case of bad administration without due consideration to the national interest" (Ombudsman 1997:13). The Front's report on the Planning Authority files concluded that the project went against Structure Plan policies; the Environmental Impact Assessment was not correctly conducted; the Planning Authority ignored a highly critical internal report; there were many extraordinary and suspicious circumstances; the rushed decision precluded proper study of all its consequences; and no evidence was provided to support its claimed economic benefits (*Front Kontra l-Hilton* 1997a, 1997b).

Particularly piquant in the Front's analysis (*Front Kontra l-Hilton* 1997a) was the degree of co-operation, even intimacy, between the PA experts and the developer. This was perhaps not surprising since they had been working together on the project for years, but it was still instructive to read the Front's report. The Front found that the Director of Planning had asked his staff to check the draft text of a letter to be sent by the developer's architect to the PA on the Outline Application and that the developer's legal advisor was also the legal advisor of the Planning Authority [although the PA maintained it had not consulted him on the Hilton project (Planning Authority 1997:32)]. Furthermore, the report revealed that the Director of Planning persuaded the Director of Museums to overrule a previous Museum Department 'strong objection' to breaching the listed monumental entrenchment so that the Marina could be built and that the developer had added a personal note to a fax (on January 22, 1996, thus well after approval of the Outline Application) sent to the PA case officer handling the project (who at the time was Chairman of the Fund Raising Committee of the Malta Hospice Movement): 'Dear Chris, I gladly (sic) enclose a donation of LM 2,000 for the Hospice movement which is so close to your heart. George' (Boissevain and Theuma 1998:111).

The Planning Authority branded the report as simplistic (Planning Authority 1997); the developers dismissed the Front as a handful of undemocratic fundamentalists (cit., 1997).

Although the efforts of the NGOs were defeated and the Hilton reopened in 2000 (with a 21-storey tower), and the extension and marina were being marketed as Portomaso, they did achieve something. They assured the public access to the foreshore surrounding the hotel. Their robust, multi-pronged campaign exposed the way powerful developers operated and displayed the laxity of government in deal-

Fig.10.2. Some of the 250 luxury apartments that enclose the newly excavated marina of the contested Hilton Extension (photo: Lietje Bonello).

ing with such developers. The NGOs also showed the importance of extreme vigilance and demonstrated what could be achieved by determined non-violent action. Finally, they put both Planning Authority and future developers on notice that their actions would be monitored and that irregularities would be attacked.

It is obvious that both Nationalist and Labour interests supported the project. Their representatives on the PA had both voted for the project. Although there is no actual evidence, *Alternattiva, Moviment ghall-Ambjent*, and *Graffitti* suggested that there were additional reasons influencing a decision in favour of the project. They particularly stressed the personal links between politicians and administrators. In Malta, because it is so small, ties linking people to each other are frequent and unavoidable. Hidden networks of influence permeate Maltese society. As already noted, the legal consultant of the Planning Authority was also the legal advisor to the Hilton developer. Opponents of the project cited other ties: the sister of the Nationalist Minister of Finance (at the time of the Hilton decisions) was married to the developer's brother; two daughters of the shadow Labour Finance Minister worked for the developer's company; the developer and both ministers came from the same rural town (Qormi) – and parochialism in Malta is very strong; the developer's architect looked after clients of the former Nationalist Minister of Public Works when the latter was appointed to the cabinet (later he became Minister of Education); and the developer's chief consultant was also financial advisor to the Labour Party. After Labour's 1996 electoral victory he was appointed chairman of the government controlled Mid-Med Bank. In sum, *Alternattiva*, *Moviment ghall-Ambjent*, and *Graffitti* believed these personal links must also have influenced the decision that favoured the Hilton project. They consequently accused the Labour and Nationalist parties of collusion.

The Munxar Project[5]

Around the same time, another confrontation concerned an Italian-Maltese project to develop a leisure complex at Munxar point (Boissevain and Theuma 1996). In contrast to the Hilton case, opposition to this project was successful.

In November 1995 the St.Thomas Bay Development Co. Ltd filed an application with the PA to develop a large tourist complex on Munxar point. Located southeast of Valletta, Munxar is an unspoiled area on the Delemara peninsula facing St. Thomas Bay. It is an area of terraced fields and spectacular views. Munxar point and the bay are popular with the residents of Zejtun and several other inland southern villages for swimming, hunting, and bird trapping. The developers, a consortium of Maltese landowners backed by Italian financiers, proposed building 143 luxury residential units, a two-storey five-star hotel with 120 rooms, swimming pools, underground parking, sporting and leisure facilities. The development would cover some 14 hectares and cost some Lm30 million (US$81.9 million/ €62 million).

The developers in 1993 had informally discussed the project with tourism officials and with the Marsascala local council, in whose territory Munxar and St.Thomas Bay were located. Generally, they were sympathetic to the project. But with the filing of the application, sympathy became a rare commodity. On Sunday, November 26, 1995, *The Malta Independent* published an article headlined 'Tourist village plans for Marsascala beauty spot'. The paper's reporter had been briefed and taken to the site by the coordinator of *Moviment ghall-Ambjent* and one of the two Marsascala councillors opposed to the project. His article alerted the public. A week later, Father Angelo Seychell, *Dun Ang*, a charismatic Zejtun priest, wrote an emotional letter to the press pleading for the preservation of the Munxar area.

Fig.10.3. The Munxar peninsula and St. Thomas Bay form one of the few popular seaside areas still free of the extensive tourist developments that have scarred most of Malta's northern coastline (photo: Lino Bonello).

He urged the district's representatives in Parliament (two National-ist and three Labour) and the Marsascala and Zejtun local councils to see that the Structure Plan was not violated and that the issue was not politicised. His letter was carried in all papers and immediately pro-voked many sympathetic responses.

The same day the Zejtun local council formally protested to the Planning Authority that the project contravened several policies of the Structure Plan: the site lay outside the development zone and, furthermore, it been identified in the Structure Plan as an 'Area of Ecological Importance'. A fortnight later, *Alternattiva Demokratika* protested to the Planning Authority along similar lines.

On December 17 the Marsascala local council organised a public hearing. Some curious locals, NGO representatives, four MPs, Mar-sascala councillors and representatives of the consortium backing the project attended. No more than 50 participated. A lawyer pre-sented the case for the developers. The two Labour MPs asked critical questions, while the Marsascala mayor and the two Nationalist MPs refused to be drawn out. The latter explicitly stated that the govern-ment was 'not involved in the project and that it was a private initia-tive' (*In-Nazzjon*, December 18, 1995). The project was subsequently widely discussed in the press. In all, some 105 items and a poem,

'Munxar's Anguished Groan' (*Il-Karba tal-Munxar*), were published between November 1996 and April 1997.

The campaign against the project developed rapidly. On December 29 the newly formed Action Committee for the Protection of Munxar held its first meeting. The committee was non-partisan, and all members were from Zejtun. Initially, the Labour Party was reluctant to get involved because the Labour mayor of Marsascala, who was commercially involved with the tourist industry, supported the project. It was said that MLP openly began to oppose the project only after the St.Thomas Bay boathouse owners put the prominent Labour MP from Zejtun under pressure. On January 6, *Alternattiva Demokratika* held a protest meeting at Munxar and called for the PN and MLP members of the Planning Authority to take a clear stand against the project. The following day the action committee collected more than 1000 signatures in Zejtun. Some of those who signed remarked that the petition was a good idea, but that it would not do any good against 'the people with money'.

Dun Ang complained of the big parties' 'conspiracy of silence'. The Society for the Study and Conservation of Nature (SSCN) submitted a well-documented brief against the project to the Planning Authority. On January 17 the district's three Labour MPs came out openly against the project and promised their support.

A week later, the action committee held a press conference at Munxar. It detailed its objections to the project and announced that it would collect signatures from the district, the Grand Harbour area and Valletta. It also planned to distribute 1000 protest postcards to be sent to the chairman of the Planning Authority. On February 2, Dun Ang was interviewed on television about the project and the campaign. The following week the Marsascala Local Council unanimously voted to oppose the project but noted that it was willing to consider other development projects in the area. Three days later, on February 11, the Labour Party district committee held a protest meeting at St. Thomas Bay against the planned project.

The next week the action committee met with the developers to discuss certain revisions to the project. The committee rejected these. The representative of the project's Italian backers branded the committee as 'communist', blaming political motives for the new rejection. "It is difficult to understand why they do not want the project when it will be good for everyone, for the area and for the economy," he said (*The Malta Independent*, 25 February 1996). The campaign was speeding to its climax. On Tuesday, March 12, the action committee presented a petition with 10,700 signatures to the Planning Authority chairman. Two days later, the committee held a protest picnic for children at Munxar.

Then, suddenly, on Saturday, March 16, the newspapers announced that the developers had withdrawn their application. The battle had been won. Not surprisingly, the withdrawal touched off another flux of press reports, letters, and announcements. The Sunday papers featured the withdrawal, attributing it to the successful campaign waged against the project. Dun Ang claimed it as 'a victory for the democratic process, because this showed that when a group of citizens unite, they could be as powerful as big speculators and major economic interests' (*The Sunday Times*, 17 March 1996). The project's representative, on the other hand, complained that 'Our project would have rehabilitated the environment, not damaged it' (*The Malta Independent*, 17 March 1996). He maintained that the withdrawal '... was definitely not conditioned by the protest of the action committee set up to lobby against the project' (*The Sunday Times* 24 March 1996).

All the parties attempted to harvest political hay. The Labour press and *Alternattiva Demokratika* welcomed the withdrawal of the application as a victory for public opinion. AD warned that the project was only suspended. It accused the Parliamentary Secretary for Tourism of having initially favoured the project. The Secretary then denied this, while AD stood by its accusation. A Nationalist Party columnist wrote that the project was not withdrawn because of the efforts of the action committee, the Labour Party or *Alternattiva Demokratika*, as was being claimed. Its withdrawal, she argued, was due to the transparent system the Nationalist government had introduced for issuing building permits. This is what made protest campaigns and petitions possible (*In-Nazzjon*, 26 March 1996). Officials at the Planning Authority and the Tourism Secretariat were shaken by the effect of the protest. It was evident that environmentalists had scored a decisive victory against developers. It was the first time they had succeeded in mobilizing the public at large on such a scale. Was this a sign, an official asked us, of the way future development applications would be treated?

The Munxar case provides an interesting contrast with that of the Hilton. Why, if the application was patently inadequate, did the PA patiently wait while the public debate raged on? No question here of unseemly haste that had characterised PA actions during the Hilton confrontation. The campaign swiftly gained public support because the Labour party quickly began to defend the leisure interests of its constituents in Munxar's hinterland. Hunters, bird trappers, nature lovers, and environmentalists united to fight the issue. Moreover, the PN Members of Parliament present at the December hearing in Marsascala had explicitly stated that, 'government had no interest' in the project. In fact, given the project's proposed infringements of the Structure Plan and the widespread opposition to it, the PA Board might well have voted against it. In view of Labour's strong opposition and the Nationalist Party's fence-sitting, had the project been formally presented to the Board, the PA's rejection of it would have been viewed as a victory for the Labour Party and thus left the PN with egg on its face. It was thus politically less costly to let the debate rage in public until the developers withdrew the application. Perhaps this explains why the public debate was permitted to continue for so long.

The Tuna Penning Project[6]

Aquaculture was introduced to Malta in the 1980s. Initially, it involved the production and export of sea bream and sea bass raised in pens in shallow bays along Malta's eastern coast and, later, off Comino. In 1998 Azzopardi Fisheries proposed a tuna-farming project to the Planning Authority. The company commissioned a team of independent consultants chaired by a former Nationalist Party Minster of Agriculture and Fisheries to prepare the Environmental Impact Study required by the Planning Authority.

The project promised an investment of Lm 1 million ($2,230,000) and the creation of 35 jobs. Eight tuna pens would be constructed in the sea below Gozo's Ta'Cenc cliffs. Each pen would have a diameter of 40 meters and a depth of 15 meters. Each would hold approximately 300 fish, which would be fattened for several months and then flown by Air Malta to Japan. Eventually, some 500 tons of tuna would be exported annually. Young tuna for fattening, weighing at least 50 kilos each, would be purchased from foreign fleets operating beyond Malta's territorial waters. The six tons of food required daily would be imported and/or purchased from Maltese fishermen. It was estimated that ten per cent of the food would remain uneaten and the fish would excrete some six tons of faecal matter a month. The EIS claimed that this waste would not threaten the marine environment. The operation would be monitored from a 550-ton boat moored nearby.

Four days before the first hearing on the proposal, Malta's leading environmental journalist, a founding member of AD, vigorously criticised the scheme (*The Malta Independent on Sunday*, 25 April 1999), thereby opening a heated debate. He warned that the project would endanger Malta's prime wildlife site. The Ta'Cenc cliffs housed the largest colony of Cory shearwaters in the Mediterranean. It was internationally regarded as one of Europe's most important seabird sites. The EIS had failed to mention the huge bird colonies. Contrary to the EIS claim that the marine environment would be unharmed, divers had reported seabeds burnt out by concentrations of food rests and excrement under other fish pens.

At the public hearing, environmental NGOs deplored the threat to the bird colony and seabed. The National Fisheries Cooperative claimed the application was illegal because the Planning Authority had not consulted directly interested parties. No study had been made of the impact on the local fishing industry. The expected 400 tons of tuna that the farm would produce threatened the welfare of local fisherman. Moreover, the small tuna to be penned would be caught in purse seines, which Malta had agreed to ban in an international protocol. The Planning Authority instructed the investors to deal with the criticism in the final application, to be examined the following year.

After the hearing, Azzopardi Fisheries and their independent experts furiously crossed swords with NGOs and the National Fisheries Cooperative in the press. Contributors from the public generally opposed the project. Supporters defended the project's promised contribution to the economy, its benefit to local fishermen – who could sell baitfish to feed the tuna – and the fact that it would reduce pressure on wild tuna stocks. The developers' consultants also slammed critics, one of whom was a university lecturer in marine biology, for daring to question internationally recognised experts and government policy. Unless Malta started penning tuna, they argued, others would take this natural resource from under its nose. Opponents repeated their warnings of the threat to the bird colony, damage to the seabed, depletion of tuna stocks, dependence on the use of proscribed purse seines, and the welfare of the local fishing community. Sub-aqua clubs warned of the threat that burnt out seabeds posed to the fiercely competitive diving-tourism market. Others questioned the wisdom of locating pens of live tuna near popular swimming locations, given that Great White sharks breed in Maltese waters.

The final hearing was held the following spring. Apart from situating the pens two kilometres northeast of Malta, thus well away from the disputed birds, there were few changes. The NGOs and the Fishermen's co-operative repeated their criticism via formal submissions. Nonetheless, the plan was approved by the PA on May 18, 2000, with a license for one year only and with four cages instead of the eight originally requested.

The following year tension increased sharply with the advent of the tuna-fishing season (May through July). The Fishermen's Co-operative withdrew from the committee planning Malta's EU membership negotiating strategy because the prime minister refused to discuss fish export problems with it. Furthermore, the co-operative deplored the government's decision, against all advice, to approve the tuna project. Azzopardi Fisheries' independent consultants vigorously denied any lasting damage to the seabed.

Three weeks after the season began there were reports that Italian planes operating out of Malta's international airport were being used to spot tuna. From Brussels, the Secretary General of the European Federation of Green Parties, a leading member of *Alternattiva Demokratika*, reminded the Maltese public that EU regulations prohibited the use of spotter planes for tuna fishing in the Mediterranean during June and that purse seining was forbidden from 16 July to 15 August.

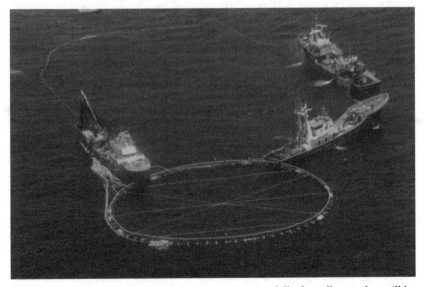

Fig. 10.4. A Spanish trawler hauling in a purse seine full of small tuna that will be transferred to the cage in the foreground and then towed to a tuna pen in Malta for fattening (photo: Steven Vella).

A week later shots were fired at one of the planes acting for Spanish interests. These latter blamed the attack on Maltese fisherman whose long lines were damaged by tugs towing cages of young tuna to Malta.

The Maltese claimed the tugs steered straight at them when they went to free their lines. Maltese and Italian fishermen sheltering in Malta scuffled and threw crates at each other near the Fisheries Department in Valletta. Forty Maltese fishing boats blockaded Marsaxlokk harbour to protest the threat to their livelihood. Sicilian, Spanish, Maltese, and Korean interests involved in the towing operations agreed to pay Lm20,500 compensation to the Maltese for the damage to their equipment.

Then, late Thursday, June 28, the tension became white hot. Maltese fisherman Joe Bugeja discovered a shoal of tuna in Maltese waters. An Italian boat observed this and subsequently encircled the tuna, almost ramming him when he refused to give way. The Italians subsequently manoeuvred the shoal into international waters and enclosed it in a Spanish-owned cage. Bugeja radioed for help. Some thirty Maltese boats cut their long lines and rushed to his assistance, thereby losing their equipment and catch. The Maltese, many allegedly brandishing firearms, then seized the cage. It contained some 400 tuna worth Lm 150,000 ($223,000), which they claimed as compensation for their lost equipment and catch. They began to manoeuvre the cage towards Maltese waters. An Armed Forces of Malta (AFM) patrol boat, alerted by the call for help, arrived on the scene at dawn and ordered the Maltese to return the cage to the Italians. They refused. Masked soldiers in dinghies tried to approach the cage, but Maltese trawlers closed in on them and blocked their way. At that point the soldiers fired warning shots, unfortunately hitting at least one Maltese boat. Not surprisingly the Maltese fishermen were furious. After heated discussions, the parties agreed to continue the talks in Malta. The cage, escorted by AFM patrol boats and the Maltese tuna fishing fleet, was then towed to Malta and anchored at sea, where it was guarded by the AFM.

During the next few days, meetings took place between the Maltese Minister for Fisheries and his officials, the Italian Ambassador, the Maltese National Fishermen Cooperative, and lawyers representing the Maltese and Italian fishermen. Maltese fishermen and their families demonstrated in Valletta. Their placards proclaimed that Maltese soldiers had shot at them and that the government was supporting the Italian fishermen because it was eager to join the European Union. Maltese also attacked Italian fishermen whose boats were moored in Malta over the weekend.

The rather surprising result of all the talks, protests, and violence was that the fishermen's co-operative told the Minister to dispose of the tuna as he saw fit. They wanted peace. He immediately returned the cage and catch to the Italians. The furious fishermen denied agreeing that the fish should be returned immediately. Thirty-six co-operative members stated under oath that the AFM had fired at Maltese fishing boats. AFM denied this, claiming that the 9 mm bullets found on board the mv Rosario did not match bullets fired as warning shots! Earlier a fisherman had caustically observed, 'They either fired at us, or they were damned poor shots'. The fishermen then boycotted the governing Nationalist Party's annual fish festival to which they normally donated Lm 1000 worth of fish. The Nationalists subsequently cancelled their festival. The opposition Labour Party hailed the cancellation as confirmation that the Nationalists had lost the support of the fishing sector. The fishermen then organised their own fish barbecue in Marsaxlokk, where they staged a skit and used numerous placards to lampoon the AFM attack and denounce the government for betraying them and stealing their fish.

Two weeks later, on July 26, 2001, the Planning Authority Board met to decide on Azzopardi Fisheries' new application to increase the number of its tuna pens from four to eight. The NGOs [*Din L-Art Helwa*, Nature Trust/Marine Life Care Group (MLCG), ECO Foundation, *Moviment ghall-Ambient* – Friends of the Earth (Malta), and The Biological Conservation Research Foundation] had prepared a joint submission opposing the Azzopardi extension and the establishment of new tuna farms. The fishermen's co-operative filed a separate objection. After a long debate, the Board voted seven to six to reject the application on the grounds that Azzopardi Fisheries had violated the conditions of the previous permit regulating the size and location of the pens and the environmental monitoring procedures. Azzopardi Fisheries was shocked. In anticipation of approval, it had purchased four cages of tuna, which were now waiting just offshore.

Yet a month later, on August 30, the PA Board met again at the instigation of the Nationalist Party's representative. Against the very strong advice of the PA's own experts and its chairman, it now voted by 9-4 to reverse its previous decision. Azzopardi Fisheries' request was approved. Strings had obviously been pulled. Both Nationalist and Labour Party representatives on the Board supported the extension. The Board gave no explanation for its erratic behaviour. Azzopardi's four cages waiting offshore could now be accommodated. The PA chairman was outraged, as were the NGOs. It was the first time that the Board had reversed a previous decision against the urgent advice of both its legal and technical advisors and its chairman. The NGOs lashed out at the Board members in the press and called for an investigation of the decision. The PA chairman demanded a meeting with the Prime Minister. He considered resigning, but instead retired when his term ended a month later. Editorial comment in all the English-language papers strongly condemned the PA Board's behaviour. The leaders of both parties expressed the utmost confidence in their representatives on the Board. In fact, a few weeks later the Board approved the application by another fish farmer for three tuna pens that he had been operating illegally for months off the Delimara peninsula. Furthermore, the Board granted permission to two other companies which had been raising sea bream and sea bass to open another five tuna pens: in all twelve new tuna pens. When the new PA Board was appointed at the end of October, four NGOs requested that the Prime Minister include an environmentalist. He declined. These decisions further damaged the PA's already tarnished credibility with the public at large, and especially with environmentalists and fishermen.

In October, at the instigation of *Alternattiva Demokratika*, the Italian Greens, *I Verdi*, raised the dispute between Italian and Maltese fishermen in the Italian Parliament. The Italian Foreign Affairs Ministry indicated that the Agriculture and Forestry Ministry was already discussing this with its Maltese counterpart. AD also succeeded in introducing, through the Green Group in the European Parliament, an amendment to protect Maltese fishermen. The amendment, which was approved, called for the provision of adequate quotas of tuna for Maltese fishermen and called for the severe limitations on the use of purse seine nets in the area around Malta.

The following year the two Maltese fishermen's co-operatives signed an agreement with their Italian counterpart that substantially reduced the tension between their members. Henceforth, Maltese fishing boats would be paid to guide Italian tugs towing tuna cages through the Maltese long lines (some of which were 40 km long) and to compensate Maltese fishermen for any damage to their equipment. Perhaps because of that, there were fewer dramatic incidents in 2002. With 120 foreign trawlers operating near Malta from May through July, five or so incidents did occur, though most seemed to have been resolved. One, however, created considerable bad blood between Maltese and Spanish interests. On June 17, 2002, some 60 miles south of Malta, the Spanish tug Pegasus refused to stop when summoned to do so by a Maltese fisherman, thereby severely damaging his long line. Adding insult to injury, the Pegasus's captain had apparently signalled his refusal with obscene gestures. A few days after the incident, *Alternattiva Demokratika* and the Maltese Secretary of the European Federation of Green Parties in Brussels contacted fellow Greens in Spain. Just ten days later the Spanish Green Party (*Iniciativa Catalunya-Verds*) placed the crude behaviour of the Pegasus and its gesticulating captain before the Spanish Parliament demanding compensation for the Maltese fisherman.

Then, on September 6, 2002, the PA announced that it was to survey an area four kilometres off Marsaxlokk with a view to relocating all existing fish farms in one area. At the same time the PA approved an application for a fourth tuna penning operation. This decision, like the one taken the year before, overturned a decision taken in April to reject the application. This application was for three cages to be located off the cliffs of Malta's southern coast. Once more an anomalous decision raised questions about the Planning Authority's independence and integrity. Of the thirteen tuna farms in the Mediterranean, four were now Maltese.

The outlook for Atlantic Blue Fin tuna in the Mediterranean is not good. According to figures of the Central Office of Statistics, catches by Maltese fishermen in 2001 were only 58 per cent of the previous year's catch (down from 324,393 kg to 188,693 kg) and the average weight of the tuna caught dropped from 163.6 kg to 136.7 kg. Fishermen attributed the drop to greater competition from larger numbers of foreign trawlers and their use of purse seines.

The positive news is that the European network of Greens, in which a Maltese plays a leading role, succeeded in placing before their respective parliaments details of the difficulties Maltese fishermen encountered from Italian and Spanish fishermen. This helped highlight Malta's vulnerable international position as a country located in one of the Mediterranean's richest tuna fishing areas, yet legally obliged to use long lines rather than the purse seines employed by its larger rivals. Possibly because of this exposure, Maltese and Italian fishermen's co-operatives were able to reach an agreement, and Malta was able to negotiate with the EU an exceptionally favourable 25 mile exclusion zone around the islands from which foreign fishermen are banned. *Alternattiva Demokratika* and the Italian Greens are launching a campaign to ban the use of purse seine nets in the Mediterranean. Furthermore, Nature Trust (Malta) is to participate in a new World Wildlife Fund research programme on tuna penning in the Mediterranean.

Conclusions

How effective have environmentalists been in combating the specific developments discussed in the three cases? To begin with, the Hilton project was approved and the Munxar consortium defeated because both Nationalist and Labour interests favoured the former project while they were not really concerned with the latter. Moreover, the Hilton developer had also spent several years honing the project with the PA. The Munxar consortium did not have the same political connections. Unlike the Hilton's backers, the financial backers of the Munxar project were foreign. Hence, Maltese financial magnates and their political patrons were not involved to the same extent. The widespread opposition of the inhabitants of the surrounding villages, who depended on the Munxar peninsula's open countryside and beach for their recreation, was also significant. They represented an important reservoir of votes for both parties. The Hilton, in contrast, was located in the midst of a heavy concentration of hotels and tourist amenities. Inhabitants of this zone were resigned to the congestion, and many depended on the tourist industry, therefore they presented no serious political threat.

The lucrative tuna penning industry is clearly stronger than its opponents. While able to protect the Cory shearwaters, the NGOs were unable to halt the steady increase of tuna farms. The National Fishermen's Cooperative, though representing a small but important segment of the labour market, also emerged bruised from the confrontation.

The cases demonstrate that neither detailed planning procedures nor NGO campaigns guarantee protection to the environment. While operating within the legal framework, lease conditions may be altered to benefit developers, government officers can be persuaded to approve the destruction of monuments, and expert opinion can be suppressed. The public hearings of the Planning Authority are a 'theatre of control' (Pearce 1993:20). They are rituals staged to persuade the public that PA Board decisions are based on expert advice, incorporate the voice of civil society, and conform to Planning Authority protocols. The conclusion must be that, despite the efforts of the NGOs and others, the ostensibly independent Planning Authority – now the Malta Environment and Planning Authority (MEPA) – approves projects and condones infringements that are backed by important political/economic interests.

The efforts of contentious environmentalists have clearly had little or no influence on the Planning Authority. They have, however, made a difference. The NGOs have consistently defended the interests of the traditional stakeholders in the foreshore. In each of the above cases environmental activists were the first to alert the public to the environmental threats the projects posed. Without their vigorous campaigns there would have been no access to the Hilton's foreshore, the Munxar project might well have been successful, Azzopardi Fisheries would have started up with eight instead of four pens, and the seabird colony would have been disturbed. Moreover, without the NGOs the public would have remained ignorant of the scale of the new tuna industry and the threats to the environment and the tourist and fishing industries that it posed.

The network of environmental NGOs in Malta has succeeded in sensitising elements of civil society. If environmentalists were dismissed in the 1960s as 'harmless lunatics' (Boissevain and Theuma 1998:114) and more recently as communists and undemocratic fundamentalists, they are now gaining respect and stature in the public eye. Gradually, they are educating the public about both the value and the beauty of the country's environmental heritage. Through campaigns, demonstrations, and their increasing skills in harnessing the local media – composed in 2003 of four dailies, six weeklies, four TV channels, and six radio stations – they have succeeded both in keeping environmental issues before the public and in politicising them.

The activity of the NGOs is helping to create a vocal civil society. Their constant vigilance and documented criticism of opportunistic manipulation by the political and economic elite are emboldening the public to voice its disgust with the visual and physical pollution resulting from 40 years of *laissez-faire* development. Until recently, the public voice had been muted by what might be called 'the hierarchy of infallibility'. This is an attitude that combines fear of established authorities with a passive acceptance of the legitimacy of their decisions and, above all, avoidance of open criticism and, thus, confrontation. It is a world view that was inculcated by the unquestioning obedience demanded by both the Roman Catholic Church and the various colonial regimes which for centuries dominated Malta and, more recently, by the unquestioning loyalty demanded by the two dominant political parties (Boissevain 1990). Through their expanding personal and organisational networks of influence, environmental NGOs are slowly gaining stature and, thereby, access to decision-making at the local, national, and international levels. Many of Malta's leading environmental activists are also members of *Alternattiva Demokratika*. In the 14 years of its existence, Malta's third party has gradually shifted from environmental radicalism to pragmatic green political activism. It is active throughout the year exposing and campaigning against environmental transgressions, corruption, and administrative injustices. Though at present there are no AD members in Parliament, in 2003 AD candidates were elected to three local councils (Lija, Sliema, and Birkirkara) of the eight to which the party fielded candidates. Increasingly, environmental activists work on the greening of Malta from within the establishment. Some have found employment in the Civil Service and the technical and advisory sections of the Planning Authority. Others, though outside government, are consulted by civil servants and politicians. Their expertise, for example, contributed to the exceptionally favourable concessions on fishing Malta obtained during its accession negotiations with the EU.

At the international level, the networks of NGO members keep growing. Internet plays an important role in this, enabling them to maintain direct and frequent contact with counterparts abroad. Maltese environmentalists now have a direct link to the European Union and the European Parliament via the AD member in Brussels who is General Secretary of the European Federation of Green Parties. He transmits environmental and political news that often reaches AD colleagues before it does the government. This connection enhanced AD's status while Malta was negotiating its entry conditions to the European Union. Once Malta actually enters the European Union, its environmentalists will obtain even more political leverage. A recent comparative study of the political role of NGOs concluded that they often discuss local issues more easily with the EU than with their own governments. The EU, in turn, relies on NGOs for information on the adherence and implementation of environmental regulations. In Italy, for example, the *Lega per L'Ambiente* provided the Commission with dossiers on the problems of applying the EU Environmental Impact Assessment directive to public works projects (Pridham 2001: 86; Eder and Kousis 2001:401).

Clearly, the environmental lobby has had only a limited effect on combating specific developments. On the other hand, it is evident that, as Eeva Berglund has argued, '[L]ack of obvious political efficacy does not mean that collective action is not changing society' (1998:73). Environmental contention is changing Maltese society in a number of ways: it has placed the environment firmly on the national political agenda, it has greatly strengthened the voice of civil society, it indirectly influences environmental policy, it is training a new political elite, and it is directly challenging the traditional clientelist system of decision-making.

The future of Malta's foreshore looks more promising than it has for many decades. Unfortunately, the density of the personal networks linking politicians and entrepreneurs ensure that their appropriation of the environment will continue, at least in the short term, though, hopefully, at a somewhat more moderate pace.

Acknowledgements

Fellow participants at the workshop on 'Aquatourism and multiple-use conflicts' at the inaugural conference of the Center for Maritime Research (MARE), Amsterdam (30 August-1 September, 2001) commented on the first version of this chapter, and participants at the Amsterdam School of Social Research workshop on 'Contentious Politics: identity, mobilisation, and transnational politics' (May 6, 2003), discussed a later version. Their comments were most helpful. I particularly wish to thank Godfrey Baldacchino, Mike Briguglio, Saviour Balzan, Franklin Mamo, Julian Manduca, Sarah Muscat, Rosanna Rutten, James Sacco, Tom Selwyn, Dun Ang Seychell, Petra van der Stolpe, Anthon Theuma, Steven Vella, and Anna Zammit for their help in providing newspaper cuttings, press releases, e-mail briefings, encouragement, and especially, constructive criticism. To Nadia Theuma a very special thanks for her comments and generosity in permitting me to quote extensively from our joint work. Errors of fact and interpretation are, of course, my own responsibility.

Notes

1. Malta uses the system of proportional representation with single transferable vote. This requires a candidate to amass around 3,400 personal votes in order to be elected in one of the 13 five-member constituencies. Although *Alternattiva Demokratika* polled 4,186 votes in 1992 and 3,820 votes in 1996

(respectively, 1.7 and 1.5 percent of the total) none of its candidates were elected. In Malta's patronage dominated, winner-take-all system, voters are reluctant to back a party that is perceived as having little chance of entering Parliament and thus of rewarding its supporters.

2. In 1996 the eight independent members consisted of an architect, a businessman, a teacher, an accountant, and four university lecturers (an architect, a chemist, an accountant, and an archaeologist). The five government members represented the Departments of Agriculture, Environment, Environment Protection, Treasury, and Social Policy.

3. For a more detailed account of the Hilton conflict, see Boissevain and Theuma (1998) and Briguglio (1998).

4. The Spinola Development Co. Ltd. is a subsidiary of the Tumas Group of Companies, founded by the late Tumas Fenech from the village of Qormi. Its assets include hotels, construction enterprises, and car sales.

5. The discussion on the Munxar project is based on unpublished sections of a conference paper by Nadia Theuma and myself (Boissevain and Theuma 1996).

6. This section is based on the following documents: *Alternattiva Demokratika* <Alternattiva@yahoogroups.com>: Media Release:
August 2002, 9 September 2002; *Business Times [Malta] Online* [www.businesstimes.com.mt]: 11 July 2001;
Friends of the Earth (Malta): Letter to Director of Planning, 3 May 2000;
Malta Today Online [www.maltatoday.com.mt]: 15 April 2001, 27 May 2001, 19 June 2001, 1 July 2001, 2 September 2001, 17 October 2001;
The Malta Independent Online [www.independent.com.mt]: 8 April 2001, 7 June 2001, 27 June 2001, 8 July 2001, 2 September 2001; 9 September 2001; 14 September 2002; 16 September 2001; 23 September 2001; 23 September 2001; 29 April 2002, 20 June 2002;
Nature Trust <naturetrust@waldonet.mt>: Press release 17 May 2000, Newsletter no. 217, and 12 August 2000;
Nature Trust (Malta) and Marine Life Care Group Press release: 11 July 2001.
L-Orizzont: 11 August 2001, 20 June 2002, and 14 July 2002.
The Times (Malta) Online [www.timesofmalta.com]: 6 April 2001, 30 April 2001, 8 June 2001, 23 June 2001, 1 July 2001, 3 July 2001, 6 July 2001, 11 July 2001, 12 July 2001, 15 July 2001, 21 July 2001, 22 July 2001, 25 July 2001, 27 July 2001, 30 July 2001, 4 August 2001, 11 August 2001, 19 August 2001, 23 August 2001, 26 August 2001, 31 August 2001, 4 September 2001, 14 September 2001; 18 October 2001, 27 April 2002, 21 May 2002, 26 May 2002, 20 June 2002, 26 June 2002, 30 June 2002, 7 July 2002, 7 September 2002, 8 September 2002.

References

Baldacchino, G.
1997   *Global Tourism and Informal Labour Relations: The Small Scale Syndrome at Work.* London and Washington: Mansell.

Berglund, Eeva K.
1998   Knowing Nature, Knowing Science: an Ethnography of Environmental
       Activism. Cambridge: The White Horse Press.

Boissevain, J.
1974   *Friends of Friends: Networks, Manipulators and Coalitions.* Oxford: Basil
       Blackwell.
1990   Why Do the Maltese Ask so Few Questions? *Education* (Malta) 3(4):16-18.
2001   Contesting Maltese Landscapes. *Journal of Mediterranean Studies.* 11
       (2):277-296.

Boissevain, J. and N. Theuma
1996   *Contested Space: Tourism, Heritage and Identity in Malta.* Unpublished
       paper presented at the Biennial EASA Conference, Barcelona, July.
1998   Contested Space. Planners, Tourists, Developers and Environmentalists
       in Malta. In: S. Abram and J. Waldren (Eds.), *Anthropological Perspectives
       on Local Development.* London: Routledge. Pp. 96-119.

Briguglio, M.
1998   *State Power: Hiltonopoly.* Unpublished B.A. Honours Dissertation,
       Department of Sociology, University of Malta.

Development Planning Act, 1992 (Act No. I of 1992). Malta: Department of
       Information.

Eder, K. and M. Kousis
2001   Is There a Mediterranean Syndrome? Beyond the North-South Divide.
       In: K. Eder and M. Kousis (Eds.), *Environmental Politics in Southern
       Europe: Actors, Institutions and Discourses in a Europeanizing Society.*
       Dordrecht/Boston/London: Kluwer Academic Publishers. Pp. 365-391.

Environment Protection Act, 1991 (Act No. V of 1991). Malta: Department of
       Information.

Front Kontra l-Hilton
1997a *Report on the files relating to the granting of Planning Permission to Spinola
       Development Co. Ltd. for the Hilton Project.* Malta: Author. March.
1997b *Reply to the Planning Authority's comments on our report of 23rd March 1997
       regarding planning permission given to Spinola Development Co. Ltd. for the
       Hilton Project.* Malta: Author. March.

Kousis, M. and K. Eder
2001   EU Policy-Making, Local Action and the Emergence of Institutions of
       Collective Action: A Theoretical Perspective on Southern Europe. In: K.
       Eder and M. Kousis (Eds.), *Environmental Politics in Southern Europe:
       Actors, Institutions and Discourses in a Europeanizing Society.* Dordrecht/
       Boston/ London: Kluwer Academic Publishers. Pp. 3-21.

Mallia, E. A.
1994   Land Use. An Account of Environmental Stewardship. In: R.G. Sultana
       and G. Baldachino (Eds.), *Maltese Society. A Sociological Enquiry.* Malta:
       Mireva Publications. Pp. 685-705.
2000   The Environment: Prospects for the Millenium. In: C.C. Vella (Ed.), *The
       Maltese Islands on the Move: A mosaic of contributions marking Malta's
       entry into the 21st century.* Malta: Central office of Statistics. Pp. 15-28.

Moviment ghall-Ambjent – Friends of the Earth (Malta)
1997   *Towards a Sustainable Europe: Sustainable Malta.* Malta: Author.

Ombudsman
1997   *Land Development by Spinola Development Co. Ltd. (The Hilton Project).* Report on Case No. 1398. Malta: Office of the Ombudsman.

Pearce, A.
1993   Environmental protest, bureaucratic closure: The politics of discourse in rural Ireland. In: K. Milton (Ed.), *Environmentalism: The View from Anthropology.* London and New York: Routledge. Pp. 188-204.

Planning Authority
1997   *Hilton Redevelopment Project. Response to Report from 'Front Kontra Hilton'.* Malta: Planning Authority, March 1.

Pridham, G.
2001   Tourism Policy and Sustainability in Italy, Spain and Greece: A Comparative Politics Perspective. In: K. Eder and M. Kousis (Eds.), *Environmental Politics in Southern Europe: Actors, Institutions and Discourses in a Europeanizing Society.* Dordrecht/ Boston/ London: Kluwer Academic Publishers. Pp. 365-391.

Structure Plan for the Maltese Islands
1990   *Structure Plan for the Maltese Islands: Draft Final Written Statement and Key Diagram.* Malta: Ministry for Development and Infrastructure.

11

All Pervading Island Tourism: The Case of Texel, The Netherlands

René van der Duim and Jaap Lengkeek

Introduction

Coastal tourism is immensely popular, and it often includes the most intensive forms of tourism. As a consequence, many coastal areas have been spoilt, or their inhabitants have to deal with serious problems of natural and environmental conservation (Conlin and Baum 1995; Doody 1997; Gómez and Rebollo 1995; Opperman and McKinley 1997; Priestley *et al.* 1996). Islands constitute a particular variation on the theme of coastal tourism, being bounded by coastal areas and separated from the larger spatial context of the mainland (Briguglio *et al.* 1996). Their attraction is not just their coasts, however, as they often have other important natural and cultural heritage qualities. Islands also tend to be socially and culturally inwardly directed, often creating a specific political context for solving problems of sustainability related to coastal tourism. Tourism is all pervasive on islands, as Cornelia Zarkia (1996) once suggested in her report on tourism development on the Greek island of Skyros.

This chapter discusses the relation between all-pervading tourism and liveability in the context of the Dutch island of Texel. First, it portrays the current state of affairs on the island and the way accelerating tourism developments have changed daily life. Second, it analyses the impacts of tourism in terms of liveability. Liveability will be defined in relation to the construction of (tourism) space as a multi-layered reality. Third, it argues that liveability is not primarily encroached on by the perceived impacts of tourism itself, but by the way these perceptions are dealt with in the context of politics, policies, and planning.

The Island of Texel

Texel is an island approximately 160 square kilometres in size, situated in the northwest of the Netherlands, in the so-called *Wadden area*, the Dutch shallows. In physical-geographical terms, the Dutch shallows are part of a more elaborate wetland area, which includes the Wadden islands located north of Germany and west of Denmark. Texel is the westernmost island of this group (Fig. 11.1). The island has a regular population of 13,450 inhabitants (Van der Duim *et al.* 2001). The main village is Den Burg, with a population of approximately 7000. Other villages include Oosterend (1400 inhabitants), Oudeschild (1275), De Cocksdorp (1250), De Koog (1220), Den Hoorn (965), and De Waal (400). Nature and landscape on the island are varied. Much of the dune area in the western part has been designated as a National Park (approximately 4300 hectares). The rest of the island is mainly used for agriculture (dairy cows, sheep, bulbs, and some arable farming of crops).

In writings from the early Middle Ages, the name '*Insula Texel*' appears for the first time. By that time mainly farmers and fishermen had populated the island. Later Texel became an important stop for ships arriving from places like Amsterdam along the former *Zuyder Zee*. The Golden Age, during the 17th century, brought prosperity not only to Holland, but to Texel as well. The ships of the Dutch East-Indies Company (VOC) left from Amsterdam for Asia, stopping in Texel on their way. In this first phase of globalisation (Waters 2001), local places like Texel were incorporated into the space of a global economy, and the global economy was articulated through a series of connected places (Short 2001:28). However, the declaration of bankruptcy of the VOC in 1799 and the construction of the North Sea Canal in the 19th century, connecting Amsterdam directly to the North Sea, marked the end of the Golden Age for Texel. Fishing and agriculture, especially in the *polders* constructed during the middle of the 18th century, became the dominant spatial practice for nearly a century.

In 1907 Texels Steamboat Company took over the services of a shipping company from the mainland. The increasing transport of people and goods, now in the hands of a Texel entrepreneur, facilitated economic growth, especially through tourism. The island became culturally, economically, and politically more and more related to the rest of the Netherlands, and tourism became the main source of income for the island. In 1896 a beach pavilion opened in De Koog,

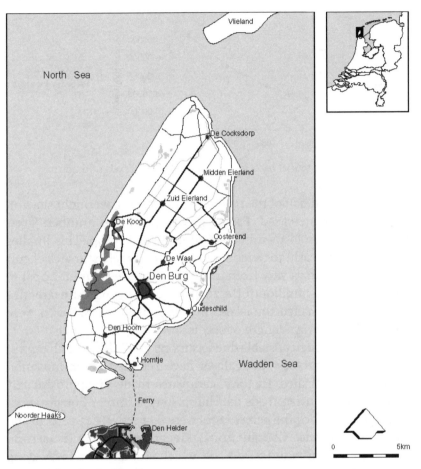

Fig. 11.1. The island of Texel.

and two years later the first *Guide for Texel* was published. In 1908 a beach hotel in De Koog opened, and in the same year locals founded a tourist information office (Barnard and Rommets 1998; Van Ginkel 1995). Since the Second World War, the tourism sector has grown tremendously. This was especially true during the 1960s, when the number of visitors as well as number of tourism beds on the island 'boomed' (Hpart 1990). Between 1960 and 1970, the number of registered beds increased from approximately 14,000 to 33,000 (Hpart 1990:5). An increase in the number of campsites was responsible, for the most part, for this growth. The current number of beds is around 43,000.

The levelling in the growth of tourism beds does not imply stability in tourism development in general. The importance of the sector in terms of turnover rate and employment has continued to grow.

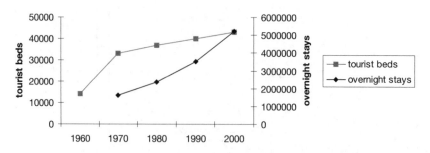

Fig.11.2. Number of tourist beds and overnight stays on Texel 1960-2000.

Since the second half of the 1980s, the number of overnight stays on the island has increased. From 1985 to 1990, the numbers grew from 2.37 million to 3.5 million (Grontmij/BCI 1994). This implies an increase of nearly 50 percent in five years' time. Estimates of current overnight stays vary from 4 million (Texelse Courant 2003) to approximately 5.7 million (EIM 2001). According to EIM nearly 1.14 million people visited the island in 2000, of which 828,000 were tourists. The average length of stay is seven nights.

Growth has been possible due to, among other things, a change in accommodation types: bungalows have replaced accommodation capacity in campsites. In 1987, campsites made up approximately 59 percent of tourism beds and bungalows/summer houses about 30 percent. In 2001 the percentages were respectively 43 percent and 44 percent (Texelse Courant 2003). Geographically, tourist accommodation concentrates in De Koog, which is situated half way along the island on the West Coast, and in De Cocksdorp, located in the north. Smaller bungalow parks, campsites, and hotels are scattered all around the island. Currently, tourism directly employs approximately 25 percent of the total population. However, it is generally acknowledged that the indirect impact and dependency on tourism are much higher. According to some sources, about 75 percent of the population is dependent on tourism (Van der Duim *et al.* 2001; Grontmij/BCI 1994). In terms of gross turnover, tourism accounts for about €90 million, compared with 55 million for agriculture and €32 million for fisheries (WLTO/KAVB 2000).

Agriculture is the second source of income on the island and covers half of its area. By contrast with agriculture in much of the Netherlands, the intensive livestock breeding industry is almost non-existent. In line with developments in the rest of the country, employment in this sector is decreasing, with the number of farms having decreased from 160 in 1985 to 112 in 2000 (WLTO/KAVB

2000). Fisheries have a long history on the island. Just as with agriculture, they are currently under pressure. On the one hand, this is due to restrictions with regard to catch, on the other through increases in scale. The fleet currently consists of 27 North Sea fishing boats, employing nearly 160 people.

The future of agriculture on Texel is highly uncertain. The agricultural sector has economically, culturally, and politically dominated the island for centuries. However, external influences such as climatic change and its consequences for rising sea levels, EU policies, and the possible loss of control over developments due to entrepreneurs from the mainland taking over businesses are causing uncertainty.

As a result of climatic change, a sea level rise is expected between 2000 and 2030 on the order of 25 to 75 centimetres. In combination with an anticipated lowering of the soil level as a result of compaction of clay layers, the most important polders of Texel are projected to become more and more brackish. This would have important consequences for soil fertility and subsequently yield per acre. In addition, agriculture is strongly affected by the opening up of the European market and strong reductions in subsidies. The agricultural sector also faces land claims from housing, nature conservation, and tourism (Gemeente Texel 2002). Parts of the island have already been designated as a National Park; economic activities in other parts are restrained by international policies and regulations on nature conservation. Moreover, tourism has claimed land as well as changed the character of the island.

Tourism Development, Local Identity, and Liveability

Two recent surveys (Lengkeek and Van der Velden 2000; Van der Duim *et al.* 2001, 2002) clearly reflect the (feelings of) uncertainty on the island (see also Philipsen *et al.* 2003). In sum, the following issues were discerned:

- Tourism is considered a 'blight' as well as a 'blessing'. Obviously, tourism leads to more people, traffic, and turmoil on the island, as well as more income, jobs, and (quality of) services;
- Tourism is 'threatening' agriculture as it legitimises the conversion of agricultural land into nature and claims land for the extension of tourism businesses;

– Tourism impinges on local distinctiveness in terms of culture, identity, and architecture, but also reasserts some of the same characteristics;
– Relatively small tourism-related conflicts on policy enforcement illustrate a more general mistrust about the role of the local government and its ability to cope with external influences and changes on the island.

The different opinions on blessings and blights are rooted in a variety of localised forms of knowledge and claims to identity, each based on different notions of attachment to the island and its people. Generally speaking, people from Texel are proud of their island. Green-black flags and stickers on the back of cars symbolise a *Texel-feeling*, just as all kinds of local traditions, museums, and folkways do. More modern ways of expression are used to distinguish Texel from the *Other Side* (mainland). This includes the marketing of products from Texel as *real Texel products*, the founding of a local party called *Texels Belang* (the Interest of Texel), which predominantly represents the interests of the agricultural sector, and of a local action group called *Ten for Texel*, voicing the issue of liveability. All are expressions of the wish to preserve and strengthen local identity.

However, the idea that people from Texel have a homogeneous local cultural identity can also be considered a well-preserved myth (Van Ginkel 1995). To think of communities as homogeneous entities is to assume that everyone in a specific locality will have the same 'sense of place'. However, while some people may have a clear sense of attachment, others may not (Meethan 2001:140-141).

On the one hand, in reference to *Othersiders*,[1] people living on the island of Texel indeed display unity. But at the same time many types of symbolic borders have been created on the island. For example, there are different kinds of farmers: those who intensify their farming, those who combine farming with (subsidised) nature conservation or small tourism services, and those who are phasing out. There are different kinds of entrepreneurs. Most enterprises are still locally owned, others not. Some look for genuine *sustainability*, others just for short-term return on investment. There are many associations representing this variety of interests on the island such as the Texel Association of Entrepreneurs (TVO), the Texel Association for Accommodation Owners (TVL), the Texel Branch of Horeca Nederland, the VVV (Foundation for Texel Promotion), and the Foundation for Sustainable Texel (see Van der Duim *et al.* 2001). There are representatives of various national nature conservation organisations as well as local associations. There are different political parties ranging from the Green Left, the Labour Party, and the Christian Democrats, to the right-wing Liberals and the local party *Texels Belang*. There are *genuine* people of Texel with roots going back several generations, people of Texel living for decades on the island, and new inhabitants or second or weekend house owners. However, this categorisation is continuously contested and used at convenience. There are differences among residents of the various villages. Every village has its own character and mentality. De Koog appeals to the tourists, Oudeschild claims to be a fisherman's village, Den Hoorn considers itself predominantly an agricultural community, Oosterend is considered devout with five churches for 1400 inhabitants, and Den Burg is the administrative and commercial centre. Even within villages, symbolic borders have been created, based on kinship, class, occupation, religion, political party, sex, or place of origin (Van Ginkel 1995). Texel is a blend of people, opinions, and interests. Therefore, on Texel localities are being continuously shaped, and hybrids of the *newly arrived* and the *previously there* are constantly reconfigured through flows of people, values, and ideas (see Short 2001:117). For example, more and more *Othersiders* and/or retired people are coming to live on the island. Although regarded as import people, they share with many islanders the nostalgic feelings of living on an island, while at the same time introducing values, norms, and lifestyles from elsewhere. The result is a cultural fragmentation that becomes at the same time a search for identity. As Van Ginkel (1995:52) states: 'There is unity in variety, but still unity. To outsiders, people from Texel exhibit a harmonious picture of their island society, although it is a façade. Social and symbolic boundaries are always created relative to 'significant others'. Members of a community gain their self-esteem and self-assurance by contrasting themselves with others, especially in a wider context. However, those who are not faithful to the island will never be accepted or feel at home' (authors' translation).

Not surprisingly, there is opposition to as well as support for tourism development on the island. Discussions concentrate on the desired quality of life or *liveability* on the island. Although often used to demarcate the 'quality of life', the concept of liveability is not well defined (see also Spyskma 1996 and Boomars and Hidding 1997). Various options for characterising liveability are viable, for example by means of objective criteria that are affirmed and monitored by policies, or by looking at opinions and perceptions. In the latter approach liveability relates to the feeling of losing control and infringement of values and norms.

The above-mentioned results from recent research show that despite the blessings of tourism on Texel, intrusion in daily life is *perceived*. Some islanders feel as if their individual freedom of action is limited by the presence of around 43,000 beds and almost 1 million tourists against 13,000 local inhabitants, especially in July and August when the occupancy rate is nearly 100 percent. In the last decade growth in tourism primarily has been in low seasons (Texelse Courant 2003). These feelings are reflected in discussions on particular issues. For example, the construction of new bungalow areas for tourism is considered to be out of balance with the regular housing market, which is hardly developing. Many islanders do not think that the new tourist bungalows fit into the local style. Other heavily debated issues include the amount of camping places at farms, the future of the small local airport and local museums, the traffic jams, and crowding on the island. On the other hand, plans such as decreasing auto mobility on the island are also disputed. All these issues are symptomatic of more fundamental issues, however.

First, in the opinion of many tourism offers, a dominant but vulnerable basis for the island's economy. Second, the municipality does not provide an unequivocal framework for tourism policy. As a consequence, feelings of safety are disturbed, and control over developments is considered more restricted (Van der Duim *et al.* 2001; Lengkeek and Van der Velden 2000). Therefore, the *reasons* for some of the dissatisfaction are more noteworthy than the actual percentages found in research projects in which locals were interviewed. An important variable is the so-called *appropriation value* (Lengkeek and Van der Velden 2000). People *appropriate* or *confiscate* and want to become familiar with space, to transform it into *their* place, *their* island. And this transformation process of space into place includes demarcation, exclusion, and containment (Short 2001:15). In other words, tourism is both creating and undermining the construction of place. Tourism constructs space through time-space convergence and processes of homogenisation. But tourism also creates places. In this respect Lengkeek (2002) adapted the concepts of *spatial practice, representations of space,* and *representational spaces* of Lefebvre (1991).

Spatial practices are concerned with production and reproduction and are the realm of the social, cultural, and economic objectives. This dimension of space is created and *lived* in (inter) action. As we have seen, on Texel there is a shift from agriculture to nature conservation and tourism as the principal spatial practices. *Representational spaces* are conceived as *imagined spaces*, which are mental constructions within the realm of the lifeworld (see also Schutz 1975; 1990), which can provide the focus for identity. The increasing dominance of tourism in the production of the place called Texel strengthens processes of commodification on the island. However, in more recent years conceptualisations of the nature of commodities have broadened from a focus on the production and consumption of material goods to encompass non-material or symbolic elements. In the creation of tourism places more intangible qualities of places, are being utilised (Meethan 2001). These intangible qualities are represented in certain forms of narratives, which encapsulate selected readings of the environment, as in tourism promotional literature and brochures. These meanings, narratives and symbols, which are the raw material that are commodified to produce tourist space, are derived from lived experiences. At the level of *imagined spaces*, therefore, struggles over the symbolic construction of space 'are struggles to objectify meanings, to impose upon, or appropriate from the environment a particular order, a dynamic process of contestation and appropriation through which particular interests are maintained and legitimized' (Meethan 2001:37).

Represented spaces are conceptualisations of space in terms of policies and planning and thus the spaces of politicians, planners, and technocrats. This is the realm in which organisations on the island and from the mainland conceptualise, discuss, organise, and plan the future of the island.

Assessing the impacts of tourism on liveability should acknowledge this 'multi-layeredness' of space. At first sight, many discussions on liveability address consequences of particular spatial practices. Tourism facilities are (perceived to be) built in the wrong places, tourism creates crowded places and traffic jams before getting on or off the island, and tourism developments, nature conservation and environmental regulations obstruct agricultural development. However, this realm of *small complaints*, frequently blown up in the local newspaper *Texelse Courant*, reflect more profound struggles over the symbolic production of space. Members of the community of Texel gain their self-esteem and self-assurance from comparison with others, especially in a wider context. Complaints about *Othersiders* or *tourists* have been heard throughout time and divide *us* and *them*, *here* and *there*, the vernacular and the universal. Nevertheless, these complaints need to be acknowledged. More generally, one could even propose tourism not being merely the agent of change, but rather, indicative of other processes (Meethan 2001:169). Perhaps local residues of economic, cultural, and political globalisation processes or the influx of *Othersiders* buying first or second houses on the island equally affects the feelings of loss of control and sense of identity, or in other words, quality of life.

Politics, Policies, and Planning

The feelings of loss of identity and control are directly related to policies and politics of recent decades. From the mid-1970s to the mid-1990s tourism first had to find its niche in local policies at the expense of agricultural interests. The *Texel 2030* project in 1999 accelerated this process (Philipsen *et al.* 2003). In 2002 the results of this project were translated into a new policy vision for the island (Gemeente Texel 2002) and in 2003 into a Policy Document on Recreation and Tourism (Gemeente Texel 2003). These policy documents illustrate that on the one hand the planning horizon is lengthening, but on the other hand aspects of liveability are still insufficiently acknowledged and dealt with.

Against the background of booming tourism, the municipality of Texel issued the first *Recreation Blueprint* [Recreatiebasisplan] in 1974. The plan stipulated the maximum number of tourism beds as 47,000. This figure is still used by all parties on the island as a reasonable *ceiling* for tourism growth. The 2003 Policy Document on Tourism and Recreation on Texel (Gemeente Texel 2003) once again affirmed this upper limit of beds. The number of tourism beds currently amounts to approximately 43,000. However, the maximum is an ambiguous criterion for limiting tourism growth. Many households unofficially offer beds with or without breakfast. Also, the season that visitors come to the island has been expanding. A main reason for this is the growing significance of nature-oriented tourism, which does not depend on warm weather. Official statistics give no decisive answers to the question of volume and growth. The consequence is that the assessment of tourism growth is under permanent debate and exemplifies the importance of the *imagined* state of affairs.

In the 1980s and 1990s, the political climate of Texel did not reflect the need for lengthening the planning horizon and coping with uncertainty. Generally speaking, due to the small scale of the island, municipality and people were and still are closely tied. However, this weave has its disadvantages. First, the interdependence between political parties, local administration, civil servants, and population possibly influences integrity and objectivity. The so-called *Lindeboom Overleg* (a regular meeting, named after a restaurant where this takes place) exemplifies this interlacing of interested parties. In this informal gathering between the mayor, aldermen, and some major stakeholders, particular issues concerning the future of the island are explored and discussed. Meetings, however, are closed, and membership is restricted (Van der Duim *et al.* 2001:59). Remarkably, in the 2003 Policy Document a *Tourism Platform* is proposed between tourism sector, aldermen, and civil servants. For the time being, organisations from other sectors or those opposing tourism developments are excluded. Second, the weave between people and administration on Texel and the specific local culture has another consequence: it promotes a focus on minor issues and overlooks long-term planning. Many locals complain about the lack of vigour from the side of the municipality (Van der Duim *et al.* 2001). The traditional island way of 'backroom decision making' paradoxically does not support a defensive attitude against tourism growth. On the contrary, while key entrepreneurs with tourism interests often publicly complain about not being acknowledged, they in fact easily find their way to local political representatives to further their interests. And the proposed *Tourism Platform* will sanction this. An opposing attitude is found among local islanders who do *not* take part in the tourism production and among *Othersiders* who have pro-environmental attitudes. They are suspicious about the commodification of space and are considered 'progressive'. For them, the more traditional political system not only supports the growing domination of tourism, but tourism development is also associated with inadequate and uncontrollable policy-making.

A comparison of 13 policy documents, dating from 1989 until 2000, shows that only four of them pay some attention to liveability. In the Recreation Blueprint (*Recreatiebasisplan*) of 1989, liveability is an abstract and rather unspecified subject. The planning document aims at recreational zoning and on saving vulnerable nature areas. Recreational developments may not have negative effects on liveability, as the document states. It is unclaer what criteria should be used to assess negative impacts. Other recreation planning documents (Gemeente Texel 1998a, 1999a) pay attention to the consequences of growth in tourism, but they analyse the developments that are taking place rather than provide a strong policy perspective. They raise the issue of liveability incidentally without specifying it as a policy target. In the development plan for the municipal country-side (Gemeente Texel 1996, 1998b), issues of liveability do not appear. In three documents on safety and liveability (Gemeente Texel 1991, 1999b; Grontmij 2000), liveability is defined according to specific problems such as noise and other hindrances around cafes and discos, criminality, employment, provisions for the elderly, and day nurseries.

In Texel liveability as a *feeling*, which is often hardly specified, is very much related to a feeling of loss of control over a changing situation. These feelings have much to do with lack of citizen involvement in decision-making. Nevertheless, seven more recent documents have been produced with the involvement of local participants (Lengkeek and Van der Velden 2000:23-27). This involvement can be understood as an aspect of liveability, but involvement is limited to organisations rather than individuals. In their research Lengkeek and Van der Velden (2000:35-36) demonstrate a gap between issues dealt with in policy documents and issues raised in interviews with locals. The policy documents present spatial issues such as multiple land-use, housing, the quality and diversity of the landscape, as well as economic and social-cultural measures such as improvements of agrarian nature management, subsidies for historical landscape elements, and the improvement of the quality of tourist products and services (hotels, restaurants, museums, and infrastructure). In the interviews with local people, many more aspects emerge. Respondents raise issues which have to do with the identity of the villages, the one-sidedness of the tourist population (predominantly luxury tourists), a growing scepticism towards local products, the importance of the local newspaper and local traditions, and the influence of citizens and their commitment to local politics and policies. Although the 2003 *Policy Document on Tourism and Recreation* (Gemeente Texel 2003) acknowledges liveability aspects, these aspects give no direction to the policy document or course of action for the next ten years. They are bypassed in favour of village development plans, which have to be prepared by village development committees as, according to the municipality: 'liveability is only a picture at a given moment of time of which only citizens are able to acquire knowledge' (Gemeente Texel 2003:35, authors' translation). Active participation of villagers and village development committees has become one of the main issues of local policies (Gemeente Texel 2002). This is a significant change in the approach of local policy. However, the biggest village on the island, Den Burg, surprisingly does not have a village development committee. The democratic role of village committees is also discussed. Moreover, recent research showed that despite the small size of the villages, members of these committees are not well known and most people were ignorant of or were not enthusiastic about the functioning of these committees (Instituut voor Publiek en Politiek 2001).

In sum, feelings of discontent are not, or at least are not *perceived*, as adequately represented in terms of policy and planning. To overcome the distrust in local politics by certain groups, the most recent policy document once again stresses the importance of promoting participation and the strengthening of a social infrastructure (Gemeente Texel 2003). Also important is the way Texel is conceptualised by people and institutions on the *Other Side*, the mainland, which creates commotion and confusion. Texel is impinged upon by governmental policies at the provincial, national, and European levels, by certain principles of nature conservationists and by the practices of tourism entrepreneurs, which are not rooted in Texel. The rather strict national planning system with its particular focus on the protection of the Wadden Sea area, the implementation of guidelines for the conservation of birds and habitats, and the possible inclusion of the Wadden Sea in the list of world heritage sites of UNESCO are just a few of the developments Texel is facing. The local newspaper, *Texelse Courant*, also elaborates on the drawbacks or advantages of the building of new restaurants and a discotheque in De Koog, the construction of bungalows by companies from the mainland, and on the *rumours* about the *possibility* of competition or even takeover by companies from the mainland of the TESO company (the Texel ferry company, owned largely by shareholders living on the island).

Therefore, a good understanding of the grounds for discontent is the first step to solve problems, even if it reflects the frustration of a few. As Lengkeek and Van der Velden (2000:15) state, part of the solution is the *recognition* of the problems and the creation of *trust* in the process to resolve the problems. It is exactly because trust in local politics has been lacking on Texel, that local actors sometimes take over roles of the municipality, as in the case of the 1999/2000 exercise in scenario-building for assessing the future, called Texel 2030. The *Texel 2030* process, instigated by the Texel Tourism Board (VVV), formally aimed at making a contribution to the public debate and decision-making on a new Tourism Master Plan for the island.

However, it also served to increase the power of the tourism sector in local policies (Philipsen *et al.* 2003). The process was intended to develop scenarios for the future of Texel. It included a *search conference* in 2000 to discuss possible future developments for Texel. In this discussion tourism played a key role. The conference brought together different experts both from the mainland and the island (environmental planners, nature conservationists, tourism experts, farmers, and people from cultural institutions). The conference resulted in four different scenarios for the future. These scenarios were presented to and discussed with the local community of Texel during a *choice conference* (also in 2000), at the end of which the local community was asked to give their preferences. Texel 2030 aimed at an integrated portrayal of the future of Texel. The result of the process was turned into a new, fifth scenario called *Texel Unique Island*, which pictures an *ideal* situation on which new policies and decisions were supposed to be based. It was supposed to give more direction to short-term planning and policies.

The project seemed very promising in terms of participatory planning. It definitely had merits in terms of creating an understanding of the future of Texel and of joint learning and innovation. This is well illustrated by the fact that the scenarios, as well as nine representations of individual opinions on the character and future of Texel, are now permanently on exibition in Ecomare, the most visited attraction on the island with over 300,000 visitors in 2002. However, in other respects the *Texel 2030* project was not as successful as presumed (Philipsen *et al.* 2003). Although people from the island, especially from the tourism sector, initiated the project, experts from the *Other Side* dominated. Political, scientific, and technocratic discourses prevailed. For many people from Texel, the issues at stake were too abstract, scenarios too extreme, and the time frame (2000-2030) too long (Van der Duim *et al.* 2001; Philipsen *et al.* 2003). Although a considerable number of people from Texel were involved in the process, including students from secondary schools, it was not perceived by everyone as a process 'owned' by the islanders. This was also confirmed by the results of research by Van der Duim *et al.* (2001). Even though the local newspaper and television announced the *Texel 2030* events for weeks, only half of the people interviewed were aware and informed of this process. Only 17 percent answered the question about whether their voice was heard. Two-thirds of this group felt that their opinion was not taken into account. An additional problem in the process was the inability of participants to disconnect the overall development perspectives from their direct interests: some of them felt strongly threatened by certain or even all of the perspectives.

Furthermore, the municipality, as anticipated, was ambivalent and did not take a leading role, as it was accustomed to a more ambiguous political process. According to Philipsen *et al.* (2003), on the one hand, the municipality facilitated the process by its membership of the Board of VVV Texel and seemingly supported the need for a balanced and integrated vision on the future of the island. On the other hand, it re-adopted the existing policy of *divide and rule* the moment resistance from farmers and (to a lesser extent) *Ten for Texel* emerged. Both separately submitted a report to the municipality in which the results of *Texel 2030* were questioned. *Ten for Texel* particularly voiced the issue of liveability. As a result, the municipality eventually took the reports of the Texel 2030 process seriously, as well as the reports of the farmers and *Ten for Texel,* and contracted a consultant from the mainland to make a new vision for the island. This vision was published in 2002, once more after an extensive process of consultation, meetings, and discussion (Gemeente Texel 2003). By doing so, they again framed the issues in terms of *represented space.*

Conclusions

Coastal tourism development, particularly on islands, is closely intertwined with cultural, social, economic, and political practices, which are related to fields other than tourism. Tourism product development in Texel is gradually dominating spatial practices on the island. As it is now all pervasive, Texel and tourism have a love-hate relationship. Tourism is blessed for its economic impacts and reassertion of some local practices. However, relatively small tourism-related problems and conflicts illustrate a more general mistrust about the role of the local government and associated interest groups. Distrust not only concerns the closed networks on the island itself, but also the governmental institutions and advisory agencies from the mainland, the *Other Side*. Apprehension is shared between original islanders and *Othersiders* living on the island. The combination of closed policy networks and local interest groups that distrust the policy-making practices blocks both adequate future planning and innovative approaches to the issues of tourism growth on an island with limited space and resources.

A possible solution to this stalemate is the acceptance of the viewpoint that the reality of tourism on the island is multi-layered. First, the clarification of the *spatial practices* in unequivocal facts and figures is needed. As long as the phenomenon of coastal and island tourism is undocumented, the definition of the situation will be strongly influenced by the *imagined space*. Second, ignoring the imagined space directly leads to distrustful relationships, exclusion of groups and their interests, and often long-lasting opposition to some changes or any change at all. It must be understood, thirdly, that groups who are excluded from the policy networks can interpret the official representations of space as brutal and offensive. Although Texel's civil society is gaining more influence, as the *Texel 2030* process and more recent policy documents illustrate, not all interests, let alone liveability aspects, are sufficiently represented in these debates.

These liveability aspects are not directly related to the unequivocal impacts of tourism, but to *perceived* impacts and the way these perceptions are dealt with in the context of politics, policies, and planning. A part of the problem is the fact that liveability is a fuzzy concept. Although the concept of liveability appears more often in recent policy documents, it is not always clear what that means in terms of practices. In most cases, liveability is used to describe situations where qualities and the vitality of social entities are threatened. Therefore, it has a strategic and defensive connotation. The more contested the situation, the more contested the meaning of the concept. When, on the contrary, liveability is conceived in a more positive, *pro-active* way, spatial practices and the imagined space of various social groups and interests can be taken into account. This produces a richer representational tourist space, which enhances local identities and furthers place attachment and trust in policy institutions.

Note

1. Othersiders are in Dutch: *Overkanters*, literally: 'those from the other side', referring to people from the mainland. Depending on the context, it can also refer to people living on Texel, but not born there; or even to people not stemming from a *genuine* Texel family, with roots going back several generations.

References

Barnard, W. and J. Rommets
1998   *Welkom op Texel, 100 jaar gastvrij eiland.* Den Burg: Stichting VVV Texel Promotie.

Boomars, L. and M.C. Hidding
1997   *Leefbaarheidseffectrapportage, Leefbaarheid niet langer een blinde vlek in de besluitvorming.* Wageningen: Wageningen University.

Briguglio, L., B. Archer, J. Jafari, and G. Wall
1996   *Sustainable Tourism in Islands and Small States: Issues and Policies.* London and New York: Pinter.

Conlin, M.V. and T. Baum
1995   *Island Tourism: Management Principles and Practice.* Sussex: Wiley.

Doody, P. [o.a.]
1997   Dunes of Europe – Recreational Impacts and Nature Conservation. In: J.M. Dees (Ed.), *Coastal Dunes. Recreation and Planning.* Leiden: EUCC.

EIM
2001   *Monitor Texelbezoek. Jaarrapport 2000.* Zoetermeer: Economisch Instituut voor het Midden en Kleinbedrijf.

Gemeente Texel
1974   *Recreatiebasisplan.* Den Burg: Gemeente Texel.
1989   *Recreatiebasisplan.* Den Burg: Gemeente Texel.
1991   *Leefbaarheid op Texel.* Herziene versie. Den Burg: Gemeente Texel.
1996   *Bestemmingsplan buitengebied Texel.* Den Burg: Gemeente Texel.
1998a   *Discussienota over recreatie op Texel. Discussienota Recreatiebasisplan.* Sector Ruimte en Wonen. Den Burg: Gemeente Texel.
1998b   *Herziening bestemmingsplan buitengebied Texel.* Den Burg: Gemeente Texel.
1999a   *Documenten recreatiebasisplan.* Den Burg: Gemeente Texel.
1999b   *Convenant veiligheid en leefbaarheidsafspraken Texel.* Den Burg: Gemeente Texel.
2002   *De toekomst van Texel. Structuurvisie 2020.* Den Burg: Gemeente Texel.
2003   *Concept beleidsnota Toerisme en recreatie op Texel. Kwaliteit en Ontwikkeling.* Den Burg: Gemeente Texel.

Gómez, M.J.M. and F.V. Rebollo
1995   Coastal Areas: Processes, Typologies and Prospects. In: A. Montanari and A.M. Williams (Eds.), *European Tourism, Regions, Spaces and Restructuring.* Chichester: John Wiley and sons. Pp. 111-126.

Grontmij
2000   *ISV-notitie Texel.* Alkmaar: Grontmij.

Grontmij / Buck Consultants International (BCI)
1994   *Sociaal-economisch structuuronderzoek Texel.* Eindrapport. Zeist/Nijmegen: Grontmij/BCI.

Hpart
1990   *Gemeente Texel. Recreatiebasisplan 'basisgegevens'.* Assen: Hpart.

Instituut voor Publiek en Politiek
2001   *Volksraadpleging over het functioneren van raadsleden en politieke partijen.*
Amsterdam: Instituut voor Publiek en Politiek.

Lengkeek, J. and K. van der Velden
2000   *Eiland in evenwicht. Een verkenning van leefbaarheidsaspecten in relatie met toeristische ontwikkeling op Texel.* Publicatienummer 173. Wageningen: Wetenschapswinkel Wageningen Universiteit.

Lengkeek, J.
2002   *De wereld in lagen. Sociaal-ruimtelijke analyse nader verklaard.* Wageningen: Wageningen University.

Lefebvre, H.
1991   *The Production of Space.* Oxford: Blackwell Publishers.

Meethan, K.
2001   *Tourism in Global Society. Place, culture, consumption.* New York: Palgrave.

Opperman, M. and S. McKinley
1997   Sexual Imagery in the Marketing of Pacific Tourism Destinations. In: M. Oppperman (Ed.), *Pacific Rim Tourism.* Wallingsford: CAB International. Pp. 117-128.

Philipsen, J., V.R. Van der Duim, and R. Sidaway
2003   *Texel 2030.* Unpublished paper. Wageningen: Wageningen University.

Priestley, G.K., J.A. Edwards, and H. Cocossis (Eds.)
1996   *Sustainable Tourism? European Experiences.* Wallingsford: CAB International.

Schutz, A.
1975   *Collected Papers III.* Studies in the Phenomenological Philosophy. The Hague: Martinus Nijhoff.
1990   *Collected Papers I The Problem of Social Reality.* (Orig. 1962). Dordrecht: Kluwer Academic Publishers.

Short, J.R.
2001   *Global Dimensions: Space, Place and the Contemporary World.* London: Reaktion Books Ltd.

Spyksma, J.
1996   *Op weg naar een theorie voor de praktijk van leefbaarheid.* Op-bouw Cahier 4. Den Haag: Dr. Gradus Hendriks Stichting.

Texelse Courant
2003   *Verbreding toeristisch seizoen stagneert.* Den Burg: Texelse Courant 3 januari 2003:5.

Van der Duim, V.R., J. Caalders, A. Cordero, L. van Duynen Montijn, and N. Ritsma
2001   *Developing Sustainable Tourism: The Case of Manuel Antonio and Texel.* Wageningen/San Jose/Utrecht: Wageningen University/Flacso/Buiten Consultancy.

Van der Duim, V.R. and J. Caalders
2002   *The Margins of Texel.* Paper presented at the ATLAS-conference 2002, Estoril, Portugal.

Van Ginkel, R.
1995   *Groen-Zwart, Texels in het hart. Beschouwingen over een eilandcultuur.* Amsterdam: Het Spinhuis.

Waters, M.
2001   *Globalization,* 2nd Edition. London: Routledge.

WLTO/KAVB
2000   *Met het oog op ... morgen. De Texelse land- en tuinbouw.* Den Burg: WLTO/ KAVB.

Zarkia, C.
1996   Philoxenia: Receiving Tourists – but not Guests – on a Greek Island. In: J. Boissevain, *Coping with tourists: European reactions to mass tourism.* Oxford: Berghahn Books.

12

Izola's Fishermen between Yacht Clubs, Beaches, and State Borders: Connections between Fishing and Tourism[1]

Nataša Rogelja

Introduction

I remember how several years ago I watched some slides with my friends back home from my summer vacations on the Adriatic coast. The photographs that captured my friends' and, above all, my attention as the photographer were undoubtedly those that portrayed colourful wooden boats in the port, silhouettes of the fishing vessels with the setting sun in the background, tanned and weather-beaten faces of fishermen, and bits of coastal villages that I had managed to cut out from the neon advertisement signs. At the time when I joined a research project at the Institutum Studiorum Humanitatis (ISH) and started my fieldwork in the Upper Adriatic region, I also started to look through the tourist brochures and postcards of this region. I found that many of the photographs in the tourist brochures and postcards were very much the same as mine. Several questions piqued my curiosity. For instance, where did the interest for certain images stem from, and which mechanisms were involved to produce the aesthetic and emotional response in the viewer? What, if any, are the consequences of these ritualised images in everyday life, in the concrete dimensions of space and time? These questions were pertinent to me throughout my research on fishing and tourism in Izola.

Interestingly enough, in the final stage of writing this paper, I came across an advertisement published in the nautical review VAL [wave], which triggered another association (Fig.12.1). The photograph in the advertisement was taken in the port of Piran. It showed a young woman in a white miniskirt sitting on a fishing net full of fish, sunbathing and reading the very same review she was advertising. Behind her, there was an elderly man cleaning the net, peering at the same time over the woman's shoulder. On the one hand, then, he was interested in the review, and on the other, one could say he was making a pass at the woman. Two main stereotypes in the advertisement are thus represented: that of a fisherman and that of a tourist. One possible interpretation is that the fisherman corresponds with the old, archaic, passive principle, whereas the tourist corresponds with the modern, perhaps more aggressive principle (she assumes the right to sit on his net while the fisherman is cleaning it). Furthermore, the fisherman is here to stay, whereas the tourist comes and goes. The fisherman works, the tourist relaxes. The tourist is flirting with the landscape surrounding her, while the fisherman is part of this landscape. The fisherman is flirting with the young woman, and at the same time, he is flirting with the nautical world: the tourist forms a part of his scope of flirting. Although the two figures could be seen as very different in many ways (for example female – male, archaic – modern), they appear to interact harmoniously with each other. The advertisement, though, stresses both harmony and tension between the two stereotypes; it demonstrates the coming together of the two (different) worlds, which are affectionate yet incompatible. It can be observed that in the review the advertiser intends to state that they are capable of overcoming this incompatibility. The review is only the channel, or the medium; but on the level of content, one could talk about the broader field attached to imagery and the sea.

I will discuss the connection between fishing and tourism in Izola on two levels. The first level reveals *fishermen as tourist workers* and is based primarily on my ethnographic evidence. It brings in the fishermen's perspective: their view of tourism and tourists.[2] The other level highlights *fishing as a part of the tourist landscape*. I will present an analysis of the selected tourist brochures and postcards printed over the last ten years and comment upon the image of fishing they present. In the ensuing discussion, I will attempt to place these two views in dialogue with each other. There will also be some references from an interview about visitors'/tourists' reflection on the subject discussed. One of my aims is thus to identify the major ways in which different actors involved in the research make sense of the connection between fishing and tourism through metaphorical and/or concrete-action dimensions.

Fig. 12.1. The Fishermen and the Tourist (from nautical review VAL [wave]. Ljubljana: June 2001).

The idea of bringing together the analysis of fishermen's perspectives with an analysis of tourist brochures and postcards is based on the presupposition that '[t]he ethnography of local tourism and of localities bidding for tourist attention shows the role of larger processes that define economic and cultural realities' (Pálsson and Durrenberger 1996:7). The dialogue between the two levels seems reasonable because it broadens the scope from the local to the national and transnational scale. These latter two scales also contribute to a proper outline of the concrete dimensions of people in action. My second presupposition is that through tourist brochures, the local and broader scales can be observed. In my opinion, tourist representations are, on the one hand, contextualised with actual tourist imagery while, on the other, they allude to national discourses. In this paper, I will pay attention to local details and their attachment to the broader context, where the scales of discourse will be local and national. In doing so, I will base my arguments upon the writings of Ulf Hannerz, emphasising the redefinition of the anthropological project in the sense of the following:

> One necessary ingredient in making anthropology contribute realistically to an understanding of the contemporary world [...] might be not to look just in front of us, first, at whatever we take to be another

culture, and then over the shoulder, at the audience at home, but also sideways, at the various other people also situated at the interfaces between cultures and engaged in making the global ecumene. There are journalists and filmmakers there, tourists and tour guides, social workers, jurists, business consultants (Hannerz 1993:48 cited in Pálsson and Durrenberger 1996:6).

I also base my arguments upon the theoretical starting points of various contributions in an anthology entitled *Images of Contemporary Iceland: Everyday Lives and Global Contexts* (Pálsson and Durrenberger 1996). Its authors talk about local communities as communities situated in the space — time continuum. In doing so, they stress the chaotic flow of images and identities in their broader contexts and the plurality of voices in the process of imagining. Some authors (MacCannell, Hewison, and Greenwood) regard connections between local and broader contexts as an alienating reconstruction of the local as a process in which, as MacCannell suggests, the local is subsumed to the global (MacCannell 1992; MacDonald 1997:157). Although, for example, tourist heritage representations certainly involve some of the processes of 'inauthentication' of culture, I am inclined to agree on this point with MacDonald. She talks of the representations of Aros, a tourist centre in Scotland, as those that involve a good deal of translating the local into categories with a more global semantic scope. At the same time she stresses that the creators of tourist representations are very concerned with presenting a sense of local distinctiveness (MacDonald 1997:156,157).

Orientation: Geographic and Political Context of Fieldwork Area

The region of my fieldwork is the maritime zone of the Upper Adriatic, in the coastal towns of Piran, Portoroz, Izola and Koper. These small towns[3] lie in the northeastern region of the Upper Adriatic near the Gulf of Trieste and are part of the state of Slovenia. This coastal region is geographically part of the so-called Istrian Peninsula. The Istrian Peninsula is at present politically divided among three countries: Italy, Croatia, and Slovenia.

Before the end of WWII, the predominantly Italian speaking population prevailed. The statistics for Koper, for example, demonstrate that in 1910, the population was 78.2 percent Italian, 18.5 percent Slovenian, 1.3 percent Croatian, and 9.5 percent of the inhabitants had other ethnic self-ascriptions. In 1991, in contrast, the population was 2.2 percent Italian, 82.2 percent Slovenian, and 15.4 percent Croatian (Bufon 1999:170). The formerly predominant Italian speaking inhabitants have also withdrawn from various others of the above-mentioned coastal towns. After WWII, the northern stretch of the border between Italy and Yugoslavia was set along the line of the old border between the Republic of Venice and the Hapsburg Monarchy. A provisional solution was found for the southern stretch by means of establishing the so-called Free Territory of Trieste, which was divided into two zones: zone A and zone B. When the Peace Treaty of London came into force on the 5th of October 1954, zone B and its towns of Piran, Portoroz, Izola, and Koper were transferred to Yugoslavia. This transfer resulted in a massive exodus of Italian-speaking inhabitants. In the case of Piran, the percentage of the Italian speaking population decreased from 90 percent to a mere 15 percent and, in the case of Koper, from 78.2 percent to 2.2 percent (Pletikosič 1995:21; Bufon 1999:170). The new government of Yugoslavia sought to replace the old populace with immigrants. After 1954, people immigrated to these coastal towns from various places of origin, mostly from coastal hinterlands, places in Slovenia and Yugoslavia.

Due to the vast emigration of Italian speaking inhabitants, several traditional economic trades from the pre-1954 period started to disappear. These were mining, fishing, working at Piran's salt works, and other maritime professions. The reasons for the departure of the Italian speaking inhabitants varied, but were mostly political. The new government invested considerable effort into reviving some of the traditional trades that had disappeared from these towns. In 1951, for example, a school for maritime studies and fishing was established in Portoroz. Some of today's fishermen learnt about the sea and the fish not from their families, but in this school. The number of fishermen increased again (from 1951 to 1962, 212 persons finished the program of fishing and maritime studies). In the case of Piran in 1953, the RIBIČ [Fisherman] Company was established. It went bankrupt in 1959, and its property was transferred to the RIBA [Fish] Company from the neighbouring town of Izola. On top of this, the program of maritime studies and fishing was cancelled, and fishing again plunged into stagnation. In the 1980s, however, the number of fishermen increased, and the statistics for 1996 demonstrate that there were, for example, 40 fishermen in Piran, whose only source of income was fishing, and 39 persons who engaged in fishing as their secondary activity. In the post-1991 period, new problems arose for the fishermen. With the establishment of the new state border between Slovenia and Croatia, the situation changed. Fishermen from Slovenia lost some resources in the now Croatian waters, where they used to fish, and had to adapt their strategies in various ways. One of these, which I am particularly interested in, is the strategy of connecting fishing with tourism.

Only recently, in 2002, new problems arose due to the harmonisation with EU legislation, on the one hand, and conflicts between Croatia and Slovenia about the sea border, on the other. According to the EU regulations, there should be a security belt of 3 nautical miles in which dragnets are prohibited. The majority of the Slovenian territorial seawaters is within the security belt, which is in most areas less than 3 nautical miles and 4.5 nautical miles at the widest. That means that fishing boats with dragnets will be forced to cross the state border between Slovenia and Croatia on a daily basis.[4] The recent conflict between Slovenia and Croatia about the sea border only complicates this problem for fishermen. The unsolved political problem between the two states makes it difficult for the fishermen to do their daily work while the media discourse uses the fishermen in the sense of assigning them the role of 'front men' in the conflict. The titles, such as 'Fishermen – fighters for the Slovenian southern border' or 'Croatia – Slovenia fishing conflicts', appearing in the Slovenian media actually try to involve the fishermen in the political conflict and use them for purely nationalistic interests. To what extent the fishermen are becoming involved personally in this conflict is a subject for further research.

Fishermen[5] as Tourist Workers

In this part, I will try to describe the phenomena of the connection between fishing and tourism through exploring answers to the following questions: which are the concrete forms of this connection? How is it represented from the fisherman's perspective? And how is the connection possible in the first place? This latter question puts into the foreground the opinions of fishermen – tourist workers on tourists' expectations and wishes.

Fig. 12.2. Map of the Area (from Discover Slovenia 1996. Ljubljana: CZ).

Connection between Tourism and Fishing in Numbers

According to the data of Občina Koper – sekretariat za finance in gospodarstvo [Municipality of Koper – public sector for finance and economy] dated April 23, 1997, there were 74 fishermen involved in fishing as their primary occupation and 107 fishermen involved in fishing as their secondary occupation on the coastal strip between Piran and Ankaran (Fig.12.2). The decision to limit my ethnographic evidence to the coastal area that is now part of the state of Slovenia is not based on the presupposition that people involved in fishing and tourism in the selected area share a different cultural repertoire from the people involved in the same work outside the state border. Rather, it is based on the fact that one of the changes that fishermen in Slovenia find most influential to their situation is the establishment of the new State. The new State border caused losses of the previous fishing territory along what is nowadays the Croatian coast. The closure of fishing territory and the prohibition of fishing with dragnets during the late spring and summer periods meant a dead season for fishermen using this kind of fishing technology. Additionally, in the period of the dead season, the state of Slovenia does not now support fishermen in paying their health insurance, and from 1991, laws relating to fishing are the responsibility of the Ministry for Agriculture, Forestry and Food in Ljubljana.

Fishermen, who in the summer period combine fishing and tourism, also engage in passenger transportation. In the area between Ankaran and Piran, there are 16 such boats that combine fishing and tourism, while in Izola, there are 8 such boats.[6] The individual fishermen, as well as the company RIBA, are involved in this combined business.

About Different Ways of Fishing – Tourists or Visitors?

The analysis of my ethnographic evidence highlights three predominant forms of tourist fishing boat excursions, and for the purposes of this paper I will use them as descriptors. They are: panoramic tours, picnics and other forms of excursions with restaurant-type service, recreational fishing for visitors and the demonstration of fishing. In this last case, we can talk of two sub-forms: firstly, the work on fishing boats is adapted to the visitors (it takes less time, for example). Secondly, visitors do not disturb the ordinary working routine on the boat but are just additional crew members. I will call the latter *participation*. Officially, participation is practised only in the company RIBA, whereas other fishermen sometimes take occasional visitors on board to fish with them or just observe them working, but as the fishermen say, they do not do so to earn money, but to please the visitors. The adapted demonstration of fishing mostly involves school groups, while in the case of the participatory fishing there are smaller groups of people (3-5 persons) who stay on board with fishermen the entire day. Fishing with a dragnet seems the most appropriate, if not the only appropriate way to enable such an experience for the visitors. Fishing with nets, for example, is unsuitable because there is a 12-hour period between setting and raising the nets. The catch of mullet, which is generally one of the big events in the area, is also unsuitable since the timing for catching them is unpredictable – it can often happen during the night. The most frequent excursions practised among fishermen from Izola between May and September are panoramic excursions and fish picnics (as they call excursions where seafood is offered). The average number of working days in the season varies between 70 and 100 days.[7]

CHAPTER TWELVE

The visitors who sign up for such excursions are mostly people living in Slovenia, which gives special character to this business. When fishermen talk about their visitors, they stress that they are not involved in business with tourists but deal mostly with organised groups. In saying that, the word *tourist* is attached to strangers, defined as those not living nearby and not speaking Slovene or Italian,[8] and the term *organised groups* is linked to school groups, work collectives, or other professional groups from various seminars and congresses, all coming from Slovenia. Other terms (rather than organised groups) with which the fishermen describe their guests are: *visitors, home guests, and the world of business.* As one of them said: 'We mostly work ... In this tourist business we do not engage at all, well, hardly ever ... because we work hardly ever with the agencies, and we have very few strangers. Mostly we have Slovenians, various companies, clubs and groups from all parts of Slovenia' (Izola, 2001).

Different forms of excursions offered on fishing boats, as the fishermen stressed, also differ considerably in terms of their content. If the panoramic excursions, fish picnics, and recreational fishing are connected with amusement and relaxation, demonstration fishing can be seen as an educational experience, and participatory fishing as a kind of 'special' event that includes emotional and physical engagement. The differences in terms of content can be partly linked up with different forms of tourist gaze: collective tourist gaze, educational tourist gaze, and romantic tourist gaze. The typology of tourist gazes made by Urry (1990) reflects the differences in the nature of tourist experiences, expectations, and wishes but as a model cannot always be applied to ethnographic data. To a certain degree it can be argued that in the case of panoramic excursions, the focus of interest is not so much on 'authenticity' as on amusement and relaxation. However, in the case of participatory fishing, the connection is rendered more obvious; it is precisely to do with immersing oneself in the supposed authenticity, trying to become, as one of fisherman stated, 'a fisherman for one day'. In the latter, the working routine is the object of the tourist gaze, moreover the form and the content of a certain image becomes the subject that one should live through as much as possible. In a certain sense, one could talk about the 'exoticising' of fishing practice.

The Construction of the Connection: Between State Borders and Beaches

The establishment of the state border that caused losses of the previous fishing territory along what is nowadays Croatian coast is the most frequent explanation for combining fishing with tourism. Some of the fishermen stressed that they were practising similar excursions even before the founding of the state of Slovenia, but these actions were, as one of them said: 'unorganised, lacking in seriousness and forced'.[9]

> As I said ... 15 years ago we began ... I could say ... we were forced to do this because of the inquiry of guests and so on ... and we were doing this by the way, during the summer ... we did it on Friday, Saturday, Sunday. When we saw that there was a lot of interest, we began to take it a little bit more seriously, and then the prices were also set, you understand (Izola, February 2001).

Along with the arguments about the establishing of the new state border that caused the combined activity, other explanations were also cited. These included: 'the demand and interest on behalf of clients; a new service on the market; lack of territory for the existing number of fishermen along the present Slovenian coast; and the overfished Slovenian sea'. These explanations are justified with the following statements: 'everybody thinks fishing is a harmful technology; it is said that our sea is very small, and we have to protect it; fishing must be reduced'. Such explanations are given on TV, in newspapers, in the statements of public figures.[10] With such statements, the fishermen's explanations highlight the positive aspects of combining fishing with tourism, and it is often stressed that the state agencies should support such activities.

The fishermen also stress the interest of their customers as an important factor in establishing such an activity. Above all, this is mentioned in cases when fishermen speak about the demonstration fishing or the participatory fishing. Consequently, the attractiveness of their product is mentioned in a way that it brings something new to the existing market by connecting the fishing world with the tourist market and at the same time allowing them the opportunity to maintain their close relationship with the sea.

I started this in 1993, after the break-up of Yugoslavia, I made my living just from fishing ... Me and my entire family. And you have to maintain such a big boat, and you have to maintain three families. And obviously ... I mean, what can we do ... but to reorganise ourselves and change our work into something completely different, or try and live with the sea again. And then we tried tourism, and 4 to 5 months we only engaged in fishing. This way the whole year is covered: a little bit of fishing and a little bit of tourism. If it is not so, you cannot live properly. Tourist workers ... yes you could say that we are, but we are still with sea and so on ... With the same boat we catch fish and tourists. This is it ... (Izola, May 2001).

Although it seems that the only or primary reason for fishermen involved in the tourist business was the new political situation after 1991, the fishermen also identified other meaningful reasons. The explanations for fishermen's involvement in tourism can be related to ecological, political, and tourist discourses. For the purposes of this paper, I will divide them into three categories: those talking about fishermen's own interests, those talking about visitors' interests, and those based on ecological reasons. In the first case, the primary stress is given to higher income, diversified work during the summer and winter periods, livelier work in general, and finally also to the fact that you can remain connected to the sea. The visitors' interests involve, above all, relaxation, entertainment, healthy food and air, the possibility of fishing with fishermen, education, the sea, and authentic experiences. Finally, the ecological reasons given by fishermen for being involved in the tourist business were that the sea is too small, polluted, and overfished for the overly large number of fishermen of the region. Although these factors are interconnected, I can speculate that the visitors' interests are closely related to the tourist discourse, while the economic and ecological reasons are closely related to the political and environmental-protection discourses.

Visitors and Their Wishes

One of the explanations for why this connection comes about in the first place is the aforementioned interest of visitors. In this context, we could ask: what questions and expectations belonging to society are the fishermen confronted with; to what degree do the fishermen enter into this 'debate', and finally, what attempts do they make in answering them? Although this paper also takes partly into consideration the visitors' perspective that will be discussed in the following sections, the opinions of fishermen will be mostly discussed in this section. In connection with panoramic excursions, the most highlighted aspect – meant to be crucial in attracting visitors – was amusement and relaxation. In the opinion of some of my interviewees, the 'amusement on the boat' was different and much better than the 'amusement on the land'. The fishermen described visitors' reactions as follows: 'they become very talkative, they lighten up, they relax, they sing, they take off the tie, sometimes there is a bit of adrenaline because of a wave and afterwards even greater enjoyment, they enjoy the sea and nature'. Apart from the ambience, the other attractive aspects emphasised include: the fact that they are with 'real' fishermen; that a lot of the fishing equipment stays on the boat also during the summer and is shown to people; and that very fresh fish that is considered a healthy food is on offer. Often, fishermen stress that they are trying to get the fish that swam in the sea only several hours ago. It is assumed that visitors could not get hold of such fresh fish. The positive side to recreational sport fishing is primarily that many people can fish together and compete with each other, proving themselves as fishermen. On the other hand, fishermen can show the visitors the fishing territories.

> These visitors come for their own pleasure, because they want to fish. That is why I took them to the fishing spots, where there is fish. And fishing ... as we know ... you can catch something or you might not ... In the meantime they get hungry, thirsty and become a bit moody. Some were successful and the other were not ... If they are successful in fishing, they are pleased; if they are not, they get angry. So you must be able to adapt to situation and satisfy visitors. If they did not catch anything, you offer them some fish snack for comfort (Izola, April 2001).

Participatory fishing is stressed as something very distinctive among all other forms of tourist products. Often, this product is not meant to be profitable as a job, but as an activity, which in the first place came from visitors' interests. It aims to please the visitors, and after all, as one of the fisherman said, visitors are 'living with fishermen for a day, which is something special; they become one of them for a day'. Fishermen also stressed that visitors are interested in the state border between Slovenia and Croatia. As one of them explained:

CHAPTER TWELVE

Some attractions are shown, let's say, if there are special wishes we take them there ... Usually, they want to see our state border on the sea ... interestingly we do not know exactly where it is ... some of them imagine that there is a wire on the sea. And then ... you say we are out, we are in (Slovenia)... (Izola, March 2001).

Fishing as a Part of the Tourist Landscape

A specific form of the relationship between fishing and tourism can be noticed in the tourist discourse. In selected tourist brochures and postcards, we can also find motifs presenting fishing and fishing-related activities, objects and people, among other things (Figs. 12.3, 12.4, 12.5, and 12.6).[11] They can be seen together with images of sailing boats, surf, tanned bodies, and architecturally interesting towns, to mention some of the most frequent ones. They form part of the tourist landscape, fitting into the specific range of social admiration, claims, and expectations.[12]

Tourist images are understood through various topics, each of them contributing to the effect of a specific image. Shedding light on certain representations and their contexts can, in part, answer the question of why specific motifs are popular and to what their messages are bound. Tourist representations reveal a net of social rela-

Fig. 12.3. *Postcard Piran* (photo: S. Simič).

Fig. 12.4. *Postcard Izola* (photo: Jugovič and Nevečny).

tions, attitudes towards nature, wishes, expectations, and the formation of new identities. We can look upon concrete tourist representations as the reifications of the popular current issues. John
Urry's objects of the tourist gaze are, for example, placed in a complex and changing hierarchy. As he argues:

> An array of tourist professionals develops attempting to reproduce
> ever-new objects of the tourist gaze. These objects are located in a
> complex and changing hierarchy. This depends upon the interplay
> between competition between interests involved in the prevision of
> such objects on the one hand, and changing class, gender, and gener-
> ational distinctions of the taste within the potential population of vis-
> itors, on the other (Urry 1990:3-4).

There has been much overgeneralised theorising within the studies
of tourism about genealogies and classifications of the relationship
between tourists and their motifs. Critiques of such approaches
challenge these theories with more ethnographic approaches (Edensor 1998; Boissevain 1996). Tim Edensor stresses that tourism consists of a range of practices and epistemologies, which emerge from
particular locations (Edensor 1998:3). The particularity of domestic
tourism, for example, raises new questions about the relationship
between the centre and periphery, hosts and guests, et cetera.[13]

CHAPTER TWELVE

Some studies (Boissevain 1996) have already shown how the notion of domination (economic, cultural, etc.) of peripheries over centres may be oversimplified. In the presented case of local tourism that takes place on fishing boats, one cannot talk just about the relationship between the centre and periphery, but in most cases about the relationship between the periphery and periphery. Even though it is difficult or even impossible to fix the centre and periphery, bearing in mind that the latter, as Tom Selwyn writes, may have regional, class, and ethnic dimensions and also that neither centres nor peripheries are immutably fixed in a geographical or historical sense (Selwyn 1996:9-14), we can trace certain peculiarities in the presented case that can be schematised as a periphery – periphery relationship. Fishermen as well as visitors both locate the 'centre' within the region of Ljubljana valley (Ljubljana being the capital city of Slovenia), their class identity is perceived as close, and even the work of the fishermen within tourism is compared to agro – tourism. Visitors such as peasant women and miners have stressed, for example, the equality between their work and fishermen's work. The topic of difficult, hard physical work that supposedly characterises these professions has appeared many times in conversations with visitors. As some visitors stressed, they were enjoying beautiful surroundings (the sea, fresh air, seagulls, and fishing boats were mentioned several times in connection with beautiful surroundings). They were relaxing, having fun, enjoying seafood, and observing interesting things, such as fishing equipment and the state border on the sea. Thus, the interest of visitors is focused around two central points, the first and most important being mental and physical relaxation due to the sea environment and the second being about 'getting to know our culture, people, and land', which can be related to the nationalist discourse. The peculiarity of the case presented is that one cannot talk about the relationship between urban tourists and rural landscapes.[14] In his 'Atmosphic Notes from the Fields: Reflections on Myth-collecting Tours', Tom Selwyn explores several features of walking tours in the Israeli countryside. He finds lessons for the understanding of the relationship between nationalism and tourism in Israel from the British case. He argues that, for an urban tourist, rural manor houses appear as representative of the authentic and powerful heart of the national heritage and are attractive because the symbolism surrounding them offers answers to fundamental questions about 'where we come from, where we are and where we are going' (Selwyn 1996:148). In the case of the periphery – periphery relationship, however, it more likely seems as if the first question about 'where we come from' is left out. Hosts and guests are from this perspective somehow more related and equal.

Thus, the representations of fishing that are meant for local and broader consumption must also be understood within the framework of the case presented here. In the following, I will comment upon the photographs depicting fishing themes, as well as texts referring to fishing (both accompanying the photographs and those found in various guides).

The Construction of the Image of Fishermen between the Mediterranean, the Good Old Times, and the Unpredictable Sea

The representations of fishing in the selected tourist brochures and postcards take up approximately 10 percent of all the presented (visual and textual) information. Even though this text does not examine in detail the motifs and perspectives of producers of the tourist material, there are a few facts that should be highlighted before moving further. When dealing with tourist brochures and other materials aimed at tourists, one must bear in mind that much can depend on *who* produces the information. The producers of tourist brochures and postcards that I am referring to in the following analysis are independent authors (photographers, text writers, and designers), government tourist departments, or private publishing houses and institutes. The selected material is not directly related to the commercial advertising material (this being so in the case of travel organisation and hotel advertisements) but must be seen either as a wish to present truly 'informative information' or as an independent author's work. The other interesting thing that should be stressed is the fact that almost all of the producers involved work and live in Slovenia, and many of them are locals from the region that is being examined. The situation presented here is thus the following: native producers who produce their publications (mostly, but not exclusively) for local consumption. One important frame of reference is thus home-centred and can be linked for the most part with local and national discourses.

In general, the visualisation of fishing focuses on three main fields: the representation of boats required for fishing, the representation of fishing equipment, and the representation of people (mostly men) involved in fishing or activities connected with it (for

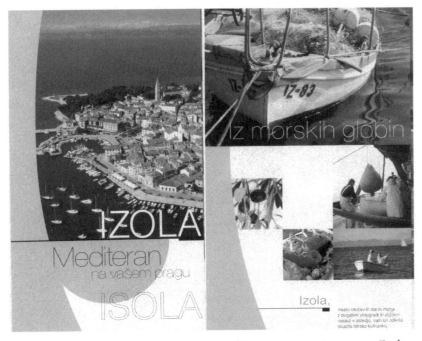

Fig. 12.5. From Tourist Brochure Izola – Mediterranean na vašem pragu [Izola –
Mediterranean on your doorstep] (Izola: Turistično informativni center Izola. 1998).

example cleaning nets). In the set of the selected material, we find 13
photographs that show fishing boats, 10 of which show older
wooden boats equipped for fishing with ordinary nets, and only 3 of
which show boats equipped with dragnets. Among the fishing
equipment shown, there are mostly nets, but we see also ropes and
barrels for salted sardines. The nets are either shown as the main
motifs and are set in the foreground, as a decoration, or set in the
context of their use (cleaning or fishing). The third type of visual representations of fishing shows men involved in different ways in the
fishing economy. Most of them show men in the centre of the photograph, their work is placed at the centre of attention, and interestingly, more than half of these photographs show elderly men.
Smaller wooden boats, fishing nets, and elderly persons leave an impression of times gone by, an impression which, in my opinion, also
carries a nostalgic flavour (e.g. sepia-coloured photographs, the sil-
houette of a fishing boat at sunset). The common denominator of
these images can be understood through the concept of good old
times, which in its turn contains ideas of rurality, honesty, and origi-
nality. The same can be said for most textual parts of tourist brochures referring to fishing. It is described as a part of the economic

E ach story has its beginning.
Once upon a time Izola was an
island. Its Italian name still bears
evidence of this past. Somehow
these few letters in their own way
marked the origins of what is one of the smallest
Slovenian towns for ever.

As time passed the island was united to the
mainland, but nevertheless Izola maintained its
close relation to the sea and still lives closely
related to it - through the fishing, with its mild
winters and hot summers, inviting to spend the
holidays just here, on the seaside... One of the
many hotels, tourist-camps and private rooms is
waiting for you and the beaches, remarkably
well kept and offering plenty of opportunities for
entertainment, are certainly worth a visit. And
so are also the many restaurants offering sea
food and national cuisine.

Take a stroll through the narrow streets of the
town, passing palaces and churches, along
shops and cafés and go farther until reaching the
remains of the Roman port Haliaetum. Maybe
take the road to the village of Korte or deeper
into the heart of Istria and then return back to
the marina and to the light-house, with the sea
always at your side.

In Izola, where the music of your vacation has
the sound of the sea.

Fig. 12.6. From Tourist Brochure: Izola – Isola (Izola: Turistično gospodarsko zdruzenje. 1999).

history of coastal towns. On the one hand, it is seen as a part of an unbroken coastal tradition, virtually a museum piece that has been preserved and is still being used today. On the other hand, the importance of fishing for the establishment of the coastal towns is accentuated. Fishing is portrayed as a primal peculiarity of day-to-day history that runs alongside 'mainstream' political and cultural history, and while the political history changes rapidly, fishing has a more constant role. In some parts, fishing is presented as being indigenous to the area, and this being the case, it is used in the introductory part of the tourist materials. Alongside personal characteristics (kind, pleasant, charming), national (Slovenian), and geographic adjectives (coastal), the adjective fishing is also used, representing one of the most outstanding characteristics of Izola. For example: 'Izola, Slovenian coastal tourist town with a smile and a fishing tradition'. The frequent use of the adjective fishing seems to be of special interest because in the introductory sections, the author wishes to present, in just a few words, the main characteristics of specific towns in the most attractive way. The strong positive connotation of the adjective fishing can be noticed in such cases. On the basis of interviews with the producers of tourist brochures, I would argue that the adjective fishing (town) hints at the following information: Izola has not turned its back on the good old times and is still an honest and pleasant town. A special effect is added by the use of the diminutive form of the word town [mestece instead of mesto]. The implication that small is honest is often used in tourist mottos that promote Slovenia as a small and honest country. Moreover, fishing and fishermen are mentioned in connection with fishing holidays and with the characteristic cuisine of Izola that offers supposedly healthy seafood.

The texts accompanying the photos serve to highlight further the other contexts as well. Two of them in particular, in my opinion, deserve special attention: *the sea* and *the Mediterranean*. Descriptions of the sea are highly romanticised, and the connection between the inhabitants of the coastal towns and the sea presented in tourist brochures carries a transcendental note. One of the tourist brochures, ubiquitous in the year 2000, stressed the close relation between the inhabitants of Izola and the sea, a relationship which the tourist is also invited to experience. The text also emphasised the importance of fishing in keeping this connection alive.

> Each story has its beginning. Once upon a time Izola was an island ... As time passed the island was united with the mainland, but nevertheless Izola maintained its close relationship to the sea through fishing. Izola's mild winters and hot summers invite you to spend the holidays just here, on the seaside in Izola, where the music of your vacation has the sound of the sea (*Izola – Isola* 1999. Izola: TGZ).

A recommendation for seaside tourists generally follows this, advising them to appreciate the connection with the sea and its 'healing and spiritual powers'. Much more than just a sea in which we could swim and have fun, we are introduced to the sea that is the object of admiration, through which we come into contact with nature, wilderness, and the eternal. The poem by Jorge Luis Borges, which is included in one of the tourist brochures, emphasises the fact that the sea is also an inspiring object; the experience of the sea, as presented here, is (first and foremost) spiritual. The poem begins with the following words: 'Long before the time condensed to days, the eternal sea already washed the shores...' (cited in *Izola – Isola* 1999. Izola: TGZ).

If the context of the sea can be described in words of romanticised wilderness and healing effects, we need to understand the context of the Mediterranean also within a wider political and cultural framework. The titles of the brochures such as 'Mediterranean in Slovenia' and 'Izola – Mediterranean' on your doorstep tend to display the 'Mediterranean-ness' of the region. Not only in the titles, the adjective Mediterranean is used over and over again in the text: Mediterranean food, Mediterranean climate ... It is possible to understand the emphasis on the 'Mediterranean-ness' of the region in several ways: as flirtation with the imaginary concept(s) of the Mediterranean; the Mediterranean as an important cultural-historical area; a place where the so-called western civilisation originates; and the Mediterranean representing a previously established tourist region.

The emphasis on the Mediterranean can partly be understood through the process of increasing popularity of the Mediterranean as a tourist region, which could be, observed in several phases as Orvar Löfgren stresses. The starting point, as Orvar Löfgren puts it, could be traced to the 17th and 18th centuries when the first Mediterranean tourists were members of the English upper class drawn by their wish to learn about classic culture through the towns of Italy and France. Löfgren connects the second phase with the new means of transport that extended the frontiers of the tourist Mediterranean. Education was no longer the focus of travelling; the institutionalisation of free time occurred, the important components of travel became relaxation and fun, and the summer holidays came into being. Löfgren suggests that a third phase is characterised by a stepping away from the four 'S's (sun, sand, sex, sea). The tourist experience is in the third phase marked by the great R that unites romance, special experience, and the re-establishing of the connection between man and nature (Löfgren 1991:157-168).

I would argue that the tourist material examined in this study reflects elements from these various phases, but that, on the whole, the representations of fishing correspond mostly to the last phase.

Fishing: Between Ethnography and Tourist Imagery

Confronting tourist brochures and postcards from the area in question with ethnography derives from the presupposition that the fields in question (tourist imagery and concrete social action) are connected, that they inform each other, and that the understanding of local actions demands a closer look at the broader discourses as well. What I suggest in this paper is that tourist representations are highly contextualized – firstly, within the wish to present local distinctiveness and, secondly, within the popular tourist imagery – while at the same time, they show the tendency for the 'correct' national presentation. Images from within the tourist landscape are actually concrete forms, covering the needs of *invented traditions of imagined communities* as well as adapting to other current trends. Tourist representations are neither unchangeable nor are they unidirectional. Although they radiate the illusion of stability and closeness, they are in fact, as far as their external appearance is concerned, very adaptable and readily dynamic. Tourist representations are formed from the beginning through the processes of gazing on the one hand and showing on the other. This formation is a vivid process in which the imagery and the concrete action are not only intertwined, but they also mutually form, shape, and react. In the same way that tourist representations require appreciation of their context, the identity of an individual or group also does not rely only on the observed activities within the locale. Instead, it is formed on the crossroads of influences that stem from beyond its immediate surroundings. E. George Marcus stresses that: 'It is the various elements of this process of dispersed identity construction – mobile, related representations in many different places of many different characters – that must be grasped as social fact' (Marcus 1996:46).

If I make an excursus to my ethnographic evidence; when I asked some people involved in the fishing business about their opinion of the tourist representations that involved fishing motifs, two interesting points arose out from these conversations. With regard to romanticised tourist motifs, such as fishing boats with the sunset in the background, they stressed the 'fakeness' of the images in question and explained them as motifs that must be such, for in the first place they are meant to be attractive for tourists. In contrast, 'realistic' ethnographic images such as photos of fishing equipment were evaluated positively as interesting. In connection with this latter opinion, I observed how fishermen involved in the tourist business are showing people fishing equipment and their personal photos of the most successful catches of the year. A very similar ap- proach, in the sense of what is/could be interesting for people visiting the coastal area, can also be observed in the local maritime museum, where fishing equipment and 'realistic' ethnographic images are meant to be the central objects of the tourist gaze. On the other hand, some of the photographers and text writers of the selected tourist brochures and postcards also actively cooperate with certain ethnologists from Piran's Maritime museum. They are both interested in the 'realistic' ethnographic representation of local culture and find themselves often in the position of 'teachers' of the local culture. The point I want to make here is that one can observe how discourses and perspectives are informing each other and are being intertwined at several points.

Thus, as viewed from the perspective of the people who make a living from combining these two activities, the connections between fishing and tourism can be divided into three groups on the level of content: educational excursions for primary and secondary schools, panoramic excursions for pleasure, and participation in fishing as a special experience. It is between these last two that a stark contrast is evident. The first has an air of easy, carefree fun and even reckless-ness about it, while the other is connected to a more 'profound' expe-rience. The profundity of this experience is characterised mostly by the notion of bonding with the sea and the fishing. The sea, as under-stood here, takes on the role of representing the concept of wilder-ness, a notion that one should not treat as a defined physical area, but as a state of mind. Fishing adds to this experience a link to the primal and the rural, since it represents an activity that every day inevitably includes a confrontation between man and nature. Maritime anthro-pologists often stress that 'being with nature' is also one of the posi-tive attributes of being a small-scale fisher. According to anthropo-logical data, fishing is often perceived as a 'natural way of life', in contrast with the 'city way of life' that is supposedly characterised by criminality, alienation, consumerism, violence, and so on (Einarsson 1996:49; Acheson 1981:296).

One could say that, when considering participatory fishing, the desired tourist experience is not limited to the surroundings; it ex-tends to the fishermen and their working day, which in turn become the objects of the tourist gaze. The nature of the participation in fish-ing can mostly be linked to the representations of fishing in tourist brochures and postcards, while the content of panoramic excursions corresponds with a field that is not close to the fishing motifs in various tourist representations. Rather, it is much closer to the concept of the holiday as a time of leisurely fun. Despite the emphasis on the positive connotations of participation in fishing, the fishermen/tourist workers emphasise the appeal of all three forms on offer, in the sense of connecting *the world of fishing with the tourist product*. The world of fishing in this statement is to be understood in an abstract sense and is thus closely related to romanticised tourist (re)presentations of fishing. Not dissimilar to that seen in *the world of fishing*, the term *tourist* also takes on an abstract role. When generalising, fishermen/tourist workers talk about tourists, but when describing individual instances (such as describing specific trips and activities), they tend to use more precise terms, talking about women from the countryside, miners, high school students, or other such groups. Since the adjective tourist tends to have a negative connotation (for example: 'the fishing holiday is not what it used to be, it's become a tourist show...'), the position of not being involved in tourism is a most convenient one.[15] It makes an excuse either for the visitors who allegedly are not tourists, or the hosts who allegedly are not tourist workers but actually fishermen.

Although certain assertions in the tourist representations and in my ethnographic evidence are compatible, discrepancies between the two can be found. One of the reasons for combining fishing with tourist activities, as stressed by fishermen, is the image of fishing as a harmful economic practice, whose replacement with tourist activities is in the 'interest of nature'. Fishing, as portrayed in tourist brochures and postcards, does not mention this aspect. There, the characteristics of fishing describe it as a benign, naive, and simple activity (the photographs of nets, smaller wooden boats). Although fishing is actually mentioned frequently as a harmful activity in the media discourse (with the notable exception of instances dealing with 'national pride'), fishing in the tourist discourse is presented in a completely different light: as a romanticised activity. Along these lines, the invitation to participate in an excursion on a fishing boat, as mentioned in the tourist guides, is portrayed using photographs of older wooden boats. In practice, the excursions take place on larger boats with dragnets. The implicit mention of boats with dragnets cannot be explained only through the prism of aesthetics (the smaller boats supposedly being deemed as being more attractive). It can also be understood in connection with dragnets being seen as a harmful technology, a topic of many discussions among people involved in fishing, as well as being mentioned in newspaper articles.[16]

Hence, in conclusion, I suggest that the contexts of representations of fishing in the selected study material serve as the focal points through which the ethnographic evidence and the tourist discourse can be brought into a dialogue. They can be divided into three clear contexts: a) the Mediterranean context, b) the context of the sea, and c) the context of good old times. Let us now summarize some points we have made so far. To travel through an imaginary Mediterranean landscape by delving into tourist brochures and bringing them to life within our mental preconceptions could be to distance ourselves from the civilised world, to come into contact with the rural and the 'natural'. Going to the seaside could mean or connote swimming, sunbathing, tanned skin, 'authentic' contact with the outdoors and the sea, freedom and health. Or seeking to embrace a 'simple' life-style could suggest coming into contact with what are seen as the 'good old days', with a more traditional and therefore 'just' society. Even if the contact alone is an abstraction, the motifs of tanned fishermen, fishing boats at sunset, and the cleaning of colourful nets on a white pier are actually the condensed forms of such demands, admiration, wishes, and experiences. These not only concern the tourist, but also reveal a wider social space. Motifs appear in interaction, so looking upon them as if they were unidirectional is, in my opinion, of limited use. When speaking about the ethnography of local tourism on the basis of the connection between fishing and tourism, one must bear in mind the various correlated representations of fishing that bring one to the understanding of local particularities. These representations are *de facto* living in the same *habitus* as the actors involved in the research. Tourist representations are only one of many fields of reference. This is not to say that one should see people as the passive recipients of external influences. On the basis of my ethnography and analysis of tourist representations, I suggest that people are not only aware of the external images that are based on them, but that people are also trying to cooperate actively with the images and make them part of their daily activities.

As Tim Edensor has stressed, at symbolic sites as well as around certain tourist motifs, there tend to be several interpretations of what are considered 'authentic' attributes (1998:3). As far as my ethnographic evidence is concerned, the interpretation of the three contexts (the Mediterranean context, the context of the sea, and the context of good old times) that encompass fishing motifs can mostly be understood in two ways: on the one hand, through nationalistic discourse in the sense of 'getting to know our traditional culture' (one can talk about discovering 'authentic we'), while on the other hand, through the tendency of linking the sea with healing powers (in connection with physical and mental health), fun, and relaxation. If the first corresponds with the context of good old times and the context of the sea is perceived through fun and health experience, the context of the Mediterranean, as far as my ethnographic evidence is concerned, is somehow left out in the case of the selected example of domestic tourism. It looks like the context of the Mediterranean has other political-ideological connotations that are/could be more evident or more important in other situations. If I were to speculate, one of these could be the tendency to distance Slovenia from the Balkans and move it closer towards the Mediterranean and so-called Western Europe.

It is possible that a given image will survive a variety of vacation landscapes. Its content, possibly only its metaphorical meanings, will have changed, but the form will seemingly stay the same. In tourist brochures and postcards, fishing representations map out only a section of the vacation landscape; it appears that the part of the demand spectrum they cover is exactly the one concerning nature, the rudimentary, and the times gone by.

Notes

1. I am very grateful to Taja Kramberger, Braco Rotar, Alenka Janko Spreizer, Irena Šumi, Julie Wilson and Ana Jelnikar for they have contributed to this article by offering extremely helpful comments and suggestions on earlier drafts of the text.
2. The concept of the actor's perspective is being used in the sense of structural organization of the observation (researcher's observation) that defines the observed.
3. Portoroz has approximately 4,000 inhabitants and Koper approximately 24,000.
4. This depends on Croatia allowing Slovenia across its maritime border to the open sea.
5. Talking about fishermen as a unified field of reference demands certain reflections. To mention just some of them: the field of self-attribution; the analysis of the ethnographic evidence of the area researched; the popular uses of the word fisherman; the lexicographic uses of the word fisherman; the analysis of the use in the media discourse; and the analysis of the use of the word fisherman in Slovene ethnological production. The paper presented does not discuss these reflections in detail. The word fisherman is used here for the people who are officially involved in fishing as their primary or additional occupation. Detailed references will be included in the introductory parts of my doctoral dissertation.

6. Numbers refer to my ethnographic evidence.
7. Numbers refer to my ethnographic evidence.
8. Izola lies in the bilingual coastal area, where both Italian and Slovene are considered to be official languages.
9. The word *forced*, as I understood it, was meant in a way that the interest of visitors had always existed but, prior to Slovenia's independence, fishermen were neither prepared for the tourist business nor were they interested in it.
10. Although the statements of my informants do not draw on concrete articles, one could easily trace such information in the Slovene media (compare: Hlaj, N. 2001. Ribiči se še vedno kregajo. In: *Primorske novice* 19.1.(6):5; Podbevšek, A. 2001. Kam so šle vse ribe? In: *Jana* 21.8.(34):27-28 ; Šoštarič, M. 1994. Ribičev je le preveč. In: *Delo* 22.7.(168):3; Šuligoj, B. 1994. V zalivu ni reda, zato ribje jate še kar bezijo. In: *Delo* 28.1.(23):8; 1995. Boj za ribolovne koncesije. In: *Delo* 20.1.; 1999. Sramota za drzavo. In: *Delo* 7. 4.).
11. Selected tourist brochures and postcards:
    tourist brochures: *Izola-fotovodnik* 1995. Inštitut za komunikacije in informatiko. Ljubljana; *Koper-fotovodnik* 1995. Inštitut za komunikacije in informatiko. Ljubljana; *Piran-fotovodnik* 1994. Inštitut za komunikacije in informatiko. Ljubljana; Simčič Sime 1996. *Piran*. Ljubljana: Inštitut za komunikacije in informatiko; Simčič Sime 1996. *Izola*. Ljubljana: Inštitut za komunikacije in informatiko; Simčič Sime 1996. *Koper*. Ljubljana: Inštitut za komunikacije in informatiko; *Mediteran na vašem pragu-Izola* 1998. Izola: Turistično informativni center; *Mediteranska Slovenija* 1999. Ljubljana: Slovenska turistična zveza; *Izola – Isola* 1999. Izola: Turistično gospodarsko zdruzenje.
    Postcards: *Slovenska riviera na 14 razglednicah*. http://www.si21.com/sisart/razglednice.html (May 1, 2001); *Razglednice slovenske obale* published by Sidarta and selected postcards of publishing houses Sisart, Confidia, Jugovič&Nevečny.
12. The term landscape is understood here as a mental category, within a specific time and space dimension. In his article *L'ethnologie et le paysage*, Gerard Lenclud stresses that landscape refers to two levels of reality: subjective and objective; to take this twin subjective-objective as a whole is, in his opinion, a precondition for analysis. The word landscape refers to a specific fragment of the world, as seen through a mental lens; the landscape as a mental category must therefore be understood as historically and culturally preconditioned. The conceptual scheme of the tourist discourse, which landscapes the coast between Ankaran and Piran is, in regard to what has just been said, just one of the many possible interpretations. In the article above, Gerard Lenclud mostly discusses the topic of the landscape as an object of research in ethnology. He concludes that the mental reconfiguration of a place or object into a specific landscape cannot be observed but just deduced (Lenclud 1995). Following his argument, it seems reasonable to talk about the reconfiguration of a place or an object into a specific landscape in the case of finished landscape representations and its creators. Here surely belong photographers, writers, and designers of tourist informative material and postcards. I will limit my analysis to finished representations and for the time being leave out the research carried out among the makers of tourist representations and leave out their relationship to the local as well as the broader context.

13. On the basis of my ethnography, I determine domestic tourism as a set of leisure activities within the borders of a national imagined community, practised by the people who are citizens of the selected political unit of the national state or belong in any other respect to the selected imagined community.
14. See endnote 11.
15. Negative connotation of the word tourist refers to my ethnographic data.
16. See Podbevšek, A. 2001. Kam so šle vse ribe? In: *Jana* 21.8.(34):27-28.

References

Acheson, J. M.
1981   Anthropology of Fishing. *Ann. Rev. of Anthropology* 10:275-316.

Boissevain, J.
1996   *Coping with Tourists: European Reactions to Mass Tourism.* Oxford: Berghahn.

Bufon, M.
1999   Slovene Istria and Neighborhood: Problems of Shaping of Social and Cultural Spaces. In: Z. Šmitek and R. Mušič (Eds.), *Mediterranean Ethnological Summer School* 3. Ljubljana: Filozofska Fakulteta. Oddelek za etnologijo in kulturno antropologijo. Pp. 159-176.

Edensor, T.
1998   *Tourists at the Taj: Performance and Meaning at the Symbolic Site.* London and New York: Routledge.

Einarsson, N.
1996   A Sea of Images: Fishers, Whalers, and Environmentalists. In: G. Pálsson and E. P. Durrenberger (Eds.), *Images of Contemporary Iceland.* Iowa City: University of Iowa Press. Pp. 46-59.

Greenwood, D.
1989   Culture by the Pound: an Anthropological Perspective on Tourism as Cultural Commoditization. In: V. Smith (Ed.), *Hosts and Guests.* Philadelphia: University of Pennsylvania Press.

Hewison, R.
1987   *Heritage Industry,* London: Methuen.

Hlaj, N.
2001   Ribiči se še vedno kregajo. *Primorske novice* 19.1.(6):5.

Lenclud, G.
1995   L'ethnologie et le paysage. In: *Paysage au pluriel. Pour une approche ethnologique des paysages.* Collection Ethnologie de la France, cahier 9. Paris: Editions de la Maison des sciences de l'homme. Pp. 7-18.

Löfgren, O.
1991   *On Holiday: A History of Vacationing.* Berkeley: University of California Press.

MacDonald, S.
1997   A People's Story; Heritage, Identity and Authenticity. In: C. Rojek and
       J. Urry (Eds.), *Touring Cultures*. London: Routledge. Pp. 155-175.

Marcus, E. G.
1994   After the Critique of Ethnography: Faith, Hope and Charity, But the
       Greatest of These is Charity. In: R. Borofsky (Ed.), *Assessing Cultural
       Anthropology*. New York: McGraw-Hill. Pp. 40-54.

Pálsson, G. and E. P. Durrenberger (Eds.)
1996   *Images of Contemporary Iceland. Everyday Lives and Global Context*. Iowa
       City: University of Iowa Press.

Pletikosič, I.
1995   *Prostorski učinki migracij v Piranu*. Ljubljana: Univerza v Ljubljani, FF,
       Oddelek za geografijo.

Podbevšek, A.
2001   Kam so šle vse ribe. *Jana* 21.8. (34):27-28.

Rojek, C. and J. Urry (Eds.)
1997   *Touring Cultures: Transformations of Travel and Theory*. London: Rout-
       ledge.

Selwyn, T.
1996   Atmospheric Notes from the Fields: Reflections on Myth – collecting
       Tours. In T. Selwyn (Ed.), *The Tourist Image. Myths and Myth Making in
       Tourism*. Chichester: John Wiley and Sons. Pp. 147-162.

Simčič Sime
1996a *Piran*. Ljubljana: Inštitut za komunikacije in informatiko.
1996b *Izola*. Ljubljana: Inštitut za komunikacije in informatiko.
1996c *Koper*. Ljubljana: Inštitut za komunikacije in informatiko.

Šoštarič, M.
1994   Ribičev je le preveč. *Delo* 22.7.(168):3.

Šuligoj, B.
1994   V zalivu ni reda, zato ribje jate še bezijo. *Delo* 28.1.(23):8.
1995   Boj za ribolovne koncesije. *Delo* 20.9.
1999   Sramota za drzavo. *Delo* 7.4.

Urry, J.
1990   *The Tourist Gaze*. London: Sage Publication.

Index

women
  as agricultural laborers 87,
    89, 116
  as entrepeneurs 118, 148
  as fish sellers 71, 116
  as housekeepers 23, 75, 101,
    118, 120
  as intermediaries and media-
    tors 116, 118, 132, 148
  burden of domestic labour
    on 101
  carrying water 121

change in position of 36,
  113, 118, 124
employment in ware-
  houses 89
in restaurants 62, 78
increasing social mobility
  of 100
tourism and 28, 45, 102,
  113, 118-119

yachts 42, 101, 189-190, 238,
  281

List of Contributors

Frédérique Alban is a lecturer in economics at the University of Western Brittany (Brest, France). She is member of the Center for the Law and Economics of the Sea (CEDEM). Specialized in fisheries economics and coastal zone management, she studies interactions between fishing, aquaculture and tourism, in marine protected areas.
  frederique.alban@univ-brest.fr

Jeremy Boissevain is Emeritus Professor of Social Anthropology, University of Amsterdam. He has published extensively on local politics, ethnic relations, small entrepreneurs, ritual change, tourism and civil society. His most recent works include *Revitalizing European Rituals* (London: Routledge 1992) and *Coping with Tourists: European Reactions to Mass Tourism* (Oxford: Berghahn Books 1995).
  boissevain@pscw.uva.nl

Raoul V. Bianchi is a Senior Research Fellow in the International Institute for Culture, Tourism, and Development based at London Metropolitan University. His research focuses on the sociology of tourism development, the politics of tourism and heritage, and the relationship between tourism, migration and citizenship. He has a particular interest in southern Europe and the Canary Islands.
  r.bianchi@unl.ac.uk

Jean Boncoeur is Professor of Economics at the University of Western Brittany (Brest, France) and director of CEDEM, a research unit specialised in marine law and economics. He has been working for the last ten years on the economics of marine renewable resources and the marine environment, and is involved in several European and French research projects dealing with these topics.
  jean. boncoeur@univ-brest.fr

Julian Clifton completed a Ph.D. at Liverpool University and has been a lecturer in Geography at Portsmouth University since 1997. His teaching activities focus upon environmental management, protected area management and ecotourism, with particular reference to developing countries. His research interests focus on the management of tourism and the sustainable usage of resources in marine and terrestrial protected areas in Indonesia and Malaysia.

julian.clifton@port.ac.uk

René van der Duim studied tourism at the Institute for Tourism and Transport Studies in Breda and sociology at Tilburg University. He was a lecturer in leisure and tourism studies at the Institute for Tourism and Transport Studies in Breda and worked as a member of staff at the Foundation for Outdoor Recreation in The Hague. Since 1991 he has lectured and executed research projects at the Department of Socio-spatial Analysis of Wageningen University. His research focuses on the relation between tourism and sustainable development, specifically in the Netherlands, Costa Rica and Kenya.

Rene.vanderDuim@wur.nl

Katia Frangoudes has a Ph.D. in Political Sciences from the University of Paris VIII. She started her research activities in the field of social history of Thai women. Then she worked in the area of fisheries management and coastal zone management in Europe as the coordinator of EU-funded research programmes under the 4th and 5th RDT framework programmes. She is now at the Center for the Law and Economics of the Sea (CEDEM) at the University of Western Brittany (Brest, France), where she coordinates a thematic network on 'women in fisheries and aquaculture in Europe'.

Katia.Frangoudes@univ-brest.fr

Michael J. Ireland is a social anthropologist with a research interest in the impacts of tourism on indigenous peoples. His fieldwork experience spans 20 years in locations as diverse as Cornwall, Scandinavia, and Western Siberia. Current research interest include Scandinavian tourism, accent change in Cornwall, and second homes as an unspoken crisis in West Cornwall. He is course leader and senior lecturer at the College of St Mark & St John, Plymouth, Great Britain.

MIrel52686@aol.com

Maria Kousis is Professor of Sociology at the University of Crete and Resource Editor of *Annals of Tourism Research*. She has recently edited a special issue of *Theory and Society* on Contentious politics and *The Economic Opportunity Structure* (with Charles Tilly) (2004); and a volume on *Environmental Politics in Southern Europe: Actors, Institutions and Discourses in a Europeanizing Society* (Kluwer 2001) (with Klaus Eder). She has published 'Tourism and the Environment: A Social Movements Perspective,' (*Annals of Tourism Research* 2000), and other articles in *Mobilization, Environmental Politics, Annals of Tourism Research, Humanity and Society,* and *Sociologia Ruralis.*

kousis@social.soc.uoc.gr

Jaap Lengkeek is Chair of the Department of Socio-spatial Analysis of Wageningen University. He studied cultural anthropology and sociology at the University of Amsterdam. He was successively employed at the Faculty of Planning of the Free University of Amsterdam, the Institute for Preventive Medicine (TNO) in Leiden and the Foundation for Outdoor Recreation in The Hague. Since 1986 he has worked at Wageningen University. His field of expertise is sociology, environmental psychology, theoretical aspects of leisure, tourism, sustainable development and quality of life, planning and policy, cultural history and social club life.

Jaap.Lengkeek@wur.nl

José J. Pascual is Titular Professor of Social Anthropology at the University of La Laguna since 1993. Before that, he was the Curator of Ethnography in the Archaeological and Ethnographical Museum in Tenerife from 1987 to 1991. He was awarded his Ph.D. in 1989 for a thesis about the artisanal fisheries in the Canary Islands. His research has been focused since the 1980s on fisheries and natural resource management, especially in the archipelago. He has published several books and articles about this subject, and joined different research projects and teams.

jjpascualf@terra.es

Nataša Rogelja studied at the Faculty of Arts, University of Ljubljana, and received her B.A. degree in ethnology and cultural anthropology and sociology of culture in 1988. She is a junior researcher and doctoral candidate at ISH – Ljubljana Graduate School of the Humanities (Centre for Mediterranean Studies). Since 2000 she has been a teaching assistant for social anthropology at ISH. Her principal research interests are in maritime anthropology (epistemology of maritime anthropology, aqua tourism, inshore waters and multi-use conflicts, fishing communities of the Upper Adriatic) and anthropology of tourism (tourist imagery, tourism and nationalism).

natasa.rogelja@guest.arnes.si

Agustín Santana Talavera is Professor of Anthropology at the University of La Laguna, Tenerife, with a special interest in tourism and heritage. He has published extensively on his research on tourism in Spain and is the editor of the on-line journal, PASOS, Journal of Tourism and Cutural Heritage.

atalavera@ull.es

Tom Selwyn is Professor of Anthropology at London Metropolitan University. He presently directs two EC TEMPUS projects concerned with tourism, pilgrimage, and the cultural industries: one in Bosnia-Herzegovina and the other in Palestine. Additionally he co-directs the EC's MED-VOICES project in the Mediterranean region. His research interests include tourism (a recent work being *The Tourist Image: Myths And Myth Making in Tourism*, Chichester, John Wiley, 1996), the symbolism of landscape, nationalism, and political anthropology. His main geographical focus is the Mediterranean, in particular Israel/Palestine. He is also Honorary Librarian of the Royal Anthropological Institute.

t.selwyn@londonmet.ac.uk